HUMAN SECURITY IN SOUTH ASIA

This book delves into the theory and praxis of human security in South Asia. Home to almost a quarter of the world's population and fast emerging markets, South Asia holds social, geopolitical and economic significance in the current global context.

The chapters in the volume:

- examine the challenges to human security through an exploration of environmental issues including water availability, electric waste, environmental governance and climate change;
- explore key themes such as development, displacement and migration, the role of civil society, sustainable development and poverty; and
- discuss developmental issues in South Asia and provide a holistic picture of non-military security issues.

Bringing together scholars from varied disciplines, this comprehensive volume will be useful for researchers, teachers and students of international relations, human rights, political science, development studies, human geography and demography, defense and strategic studies, migration and diaspora studies, and South Asian studies.

Adluri Subramanyam Raju is Professor and former Head of UNESCO Madanjeet Singh Institute of South Asia Regional Cooperation (UMISARC) and Centre for South Asian Studies, and Coordinator of the UGC Centre for Maritime Studies, Pondicherry University, India. He is the recipient of the Mahbub Ul Haq Award (Regional Centre for Strategic Studies (RCSS), Colombo, 2003); Scholar of Peace Award (WISCOMP, New Delhi, 2002) and Kodikara Award (RCSS, Colombo, 1998). He was Salzburg Seminar Fellow (2006). He received the National Best Teacher Award (C.V.S. Krishnamurthy Theja Charities, Tirupati, 2017) and Best Teacher Award twice (Pondicherry University, 2013 & 2018). He was a visiting fellow at the Bandaranaike Centre for International Studies, Colombo, May 2012. He is on the editorial board of five journals.

HUMAN SECURITY IN SOUTH ASIA

Concept, Environment and Development

Edited by Adluri Subramanyam Raju

LONDON AND NEW YORK

First published 2020
by Routledge
2 Park Square, Milton Park, Abingdon, Oxon OX14 4RN

and by Routledge
52 Vanderbilt Avenue, New York, NY 10017

Routledge is an imprint of the Taylor & Francis Group, an informa business

© 2020 selection and editorial matter, Adluri Subramanyam Raju;
individual chapters, the contributors

The right of Adluri Subramanyam Raju to be identified as the author of
the editorial material, and of the authors for their individual chapters, has
been asserted in accordance with sections 77 and 78 of the Copyright,
Designs and Patents Act 1988.

All rights reserved. No part of this book may be reprinted or reproduced or
utilised in any form or by any electronic, mechanical, or other means, now
known or hereafter invented, including photocopying and recording, or in
any information storage or retrieval system, without permission in writing
from the publishers.

Trademark notice: Product or corporate names may be trademarks or
registered trademarks, and are used only for identification and explanation
without intent to infringe.

British Library Cataloguing-in-Publication Data
A catalogue record for this book is available from the British Library

Library of Congress Cataloging-in-Publication Data
A catalog record for this book has been requested

ISBN: 978-1-138-55668-3 (hbk)
ISBN: 978-0-367-35512-8 (pbk)
ISBN: 978-0-429-33187-9 (ebk)

Typeset in Bembo
by Apex CoVantage, LLC

Dedicated to
UNESCO Goodwill Ambassador (Late) Dr. Madanjeet Singh
Philosopher, Diplomat, Philanthropist, Writer, Artist
Founder: South Asia Foundation, New Delhi

CONTENTS

List of illustrations	*x*
Notes on contributors	*xi*
Acknowledgements	*xiii*

Introduction   1
Adluri Subramanyam Raju

PART I
Human security in South Asia: conceptual issues   **11**

1 Human security: a conceptual framework   13
Adluri Subramanyam Raju

2 Measurements of human security: a conceptual analysis   24
Swaran Singh and Archana R.

3 Human security and beyond   35
Santishree D. Pandit

4 Human security in South Asia: the locus of a cooperative
context   48
I. P. Khosla

viii Contents

5 Is the region ready? Can the state deliver? Essay from India 60
   D. Suba Chandran

6 Is the region ready? Can the state deliver? Essay
   from Pakistan 69
   Salma Malik

PART II
Environmental issues and human security **81**

7 Water insecurity in South Asia: challenges of human
   development 83
   Vandana Asthana

8 Climate change and human security: a case study
   of the Maldives 104
   Rabindra Sen

9 Dangers of electronic waste in India: a concern
   for human security 114
   Gopalji Malviya

PART III
State, development and displacement in South Asia **119**

10 Correcting anomalies of a dysfunctional state through
    civil society: initiatives to complement global
    attempts for human security 121
    C.K. Lal

11 Human development vis-à-vis Gross National Happiness
    in Bhutan: challenges and achievements 132
    Maitreyee Choudhury

12 Linkages between migration and poverty in Nepal 151
    Amrita Limbu

13 Sustainable development model: experience from India 161
    Rashmi Bhure

Contents **ix**

14 Reintegrating India's Maoists: surrender and rehabilitation 171
P. V. Ramana

15 Development-induced displacement: case studies from India 186
Apoorva R. Heroor and Praveen Tiwari

Index *195*

ILLUSTRATIONS

Figure

12.1	Poverty rates and number of households receiving remittances	156

Tables

14.1	Monetary incentive for surrender of weapons and ammunition by Naxalites	174
14.2	State-wise all-India Naxalite surrenders: 2006–2009	175
14.3	State-wise all-India Naxalite surrenders: 2010–2016	175
14.4	Chhattisgarh: Naxalite surrenders: 2001–2010	176
14.5	Andhra Pradesh surrenders of Naxalites: 1998–2012	179
14.6	Cash rewards on underground cadre	180

CONTRIBUTORS

Vandana Asthana, Department of Political Science & International Affairs, Eastern Washington University, US.

Rashmi Bhure, Head and Associate Professor, Department of Politics, SIES College, Mumbai, India.

D. Suba Chandran, Professor and Dean, National Institute of Advanced Studies, Indian Institute of Science, Bangalore, India.

Maitreyee Choudhury, Director, Centre for Himalayan Studies, North Bengal University, West Bengal, India.

Apoorva R. Heroor, former Post-Graduate Student, Centre for South Asian Studies, Pondicherry University, India.

I. P. Khosla, former Secretary, Ministry of External Affairs, Government of India, New Delhi, India.

C. K. Lal, Senior Journalist and Political Columnist, Kathmandu, Nepal.

Amrita Limbu, PhD Scholar, Western Sydney University, Australia.

Salma Malik, Assistant Professor, Department of Defence & Strategic Studies, Quaid-i-Azam University, Islamabad, Pakistan.

Gopalji Malviya, former Head, Department of Defence & Strategic Studies, University of Madras, Chennai, India.

xii Contributors

Santishree D. Pandit, Professor, Department of Politics & Public Administration, Savitri Phule Pune University, Pune, India.

Archana R., Ph.D. Scholar, Centre for International Politics, Organisation and Disarmament, Jawaharlal Nehru University, New Delhi, India.

P.V. Ramana, Research Fellow, Institute for Defence Studies & Analyses, New Delhi, India.

Rabindra Sen, Retired Professor, Department of International Relations, Jadavpur University, Kolkata, India.

Swaran Singh, Professor, Centre for International Politics, Organisation and Disarmament, Jawaharlal Nehru University, New Delhi, India.

Praveen Tiwari, former Post-Graduate Student, Centre for South Asian Studies, Pondicherry University, India.

ACKNOWLEDGEMENTS

We express our gratitude to the South Asia Foundation, New Delhi, for financial support to carryout academic activities at the UNESCO Madanjeet Singh Institute for South Asia Regional Cooperation (UMISARC) and the Centre for South Asian Studies, Pondicherry University. We express our gratitude to Prof. Anisa Basheer Khan, former vice chancellor (officiating), Pondicherry University, for her support in organizing the seminar. We also express our gratitude to Prof. Gurmeet Singh, vice chancellor, Pondicherry University, for his constant encouragement and support to carryout academic activities at the Institute and the Centre. We would take this opportunity to thank all the authors sincerely for contributing their valuable articles to this volume. It is impossible to produce a volume of this nature without editorial and administrative support and so we thank all, particularly Dr. S.I. Humayun and group captain R. Srinivasan, for supporting us in this regard.

INTRODUCTION

Adluri Subramanyam Raju

During the Cold War period, the military security acquired special attention, and thereby the states allocated more budget for defence-related activities. In the post–Cold War period, there were rapid changes on many fronts – economic, social, political, environmental and human. These changes provided not only opportunities but also challenges to the security of people. The non-military threats are gaining importance, posing a far more serious and immediate challenge to the security of human beings than the military threats. As a result, the focus has been extended from the protection of borders to the security of people.

Human security is concerned with people – how they live, how they exercise their choices and whether they live in conflict or in peace. Mahbub ulHaq in the United Nations Development Programme's (UNDP's) Human Development Report of 1994 observed that

> [h]uman security is a child who did not die, a disease that did not spread, a job that was not cut, an ethnic tension that did not explode in violence, a dissident who was not silenced. Human security is not a concern with weapons – it is a concern with human life and dignity. . . . It is concerned with how people live and breathe in a society, how freely they exercise their many choices, how much access they have to market and social opportunities – and whether they live in conflict or in peace.[1]

Hence, there is a pressing need to focus on the humanistic aspect of the security debate.

It is the state's obligation, apart from protecting people from external conflicts, to ensure that its people enjoy their rights to life with a sense of dignity without any fear. Thus, the state has to reorient its policies to address the problems of human beings. The threats to human security are far more numerous and complex than the threats to state security.

There are two approaches to human security, that is UNDP and Canadian. Both approaches oppose traditional instruments of security – force, deterrence and balance of power.[2] The UNDP has called for "a transition from the narrow concept of national security to the 'all-encompassing concept of human security'".[3] Its emphasis is on economic development, whereas the Canadian approach's focus is on political development.[4] The UNDP approach is that freedom from want is essential, whereas the Canadian approach argues for freedom from fear. Both are equally important for ensuring the security of human beings. Freedom from fear would be meaningful only when freedom from want is ensured, and freedom from want is possible only when freedom from fear is achieved.[5]

In 2000, 189 nations pledged to free people from extreme poverty and multiple deprivations. This pledge became the eight Millennium Development Goals to be achieved by 2015. Furthermore, the world recommitted itself to accelerate progress towards these goals in September 2010. The policies are not only human-centric; they also try to empower those who are most at risk or most insecure.

South Asia

South Asia is one of the very few regions in the world with quite a few significant commonalities among its countries. They are not only geographically close to each other but also linguistically and culturally homogenous. On the other hand, the region is afflicted by a number of problems – social, political and economic. Disputes, mutual distrust, misunderstanding and suspicion still prevail in the region. Conflicts and disputes have pushed the region backwards.

Since the boundaries are the manifestations of national identity in the region, the states are rigid in their stand and disputes continue to remain between India and its neighbours. The political differences and disputes have stalled the prospects of cooperation in the region. The states are giving greater importance to military security. They are constantly increasing their military capabilities, thus creating mistrust and insecurity among the neighbours. They have focused more on defence-related issues than on human-related issues. A majority of people are not in a position to afford food, resulting in hunger and starvation, and have inadequate access to water and primary health care. The deprivation of basic needs has resulted in increasing poverty levels, unemployment and violation of human rights by individuals, organizations and state. The governments of respective states in South Asia are unable to address these issues adequately.

Witnessing conflicts, particularly between India and Pakistan, South Asian countries must realize the fact that war is no longer an option. It is to be noted that in the history of humankind no single problem was solved through conflicts. Furthermore, the region is affected by many non-traditional security threats which have a transnational dimension; no individual country would be able to address them.

There is a sharp increase in environmental degradation, unemployment, poverty, epidemics, terrorism, ethnic or religious animosities, civil wars, drug trafficking, the massive spread of AIDS and so on. All these issues pose a far more serious and immediate challenge to the security of human beings. Hence, there is a need to focus on the humanistic aspect of the security debate. The main objective of the South Asian Association for Regional Cooperation (SAARC), which envisages promoting the welfare of the people of South Asia and to improve their quality of life, is largely unfulfilled by the governments of South Asian countries. A new South Asia is to be built, with the states and people working with greater understanding and cooperation to have a conflict-free and well-developed region. The people's security and well-being lie not in conflicts but in peace, cooperation and development. A future South Asia can be seen only when the states work towards human development.

Poverty is one of the foremost concerns for the entire region, despite the continued efforts taken by their respective governments. Although there are numerous initiatives that have been implemented to eradicate poverty, unfortunately they are not reaching the poor. As a result, the poor become poorer. The states are not able to implement laws effectively, resulting in ineffective governance and pervasive corruption. Unless there is understanding and cooperation among the countries, it would be difficult to eradicate poverty in the region. It is noteworthy to mention that the Social Charter (2004) of SAARC envisages removing poverty, controlling population growth, empowering women, promoting human rights and developing human resources.

In view of this, the UNESCO Madanjeet Singh Institute of South Asia Regional Cooperation & Centre for South Asian Studies, Pondicherry University, Pondicherry, organized the international workshop on Human Security in South Asia: Emerging Trends and Challenges during 16–18 March 2016. The workshop made an attempt to construct a new South Asia by finding ways and means to have a better future for the citizens of South Asia. It focused on moving from state-centric to the people-centric perspective by addressing issues that directly influence their lives and day-to-day activities. This volume certainly enhances the quality of literature on the subject and helps not only scholars but also policy planners/makers to understand the nuances of various issues related to human security in South Asia.

Structure of the volume: The volume consists of three parts and fifteen chapters.

Part I: Human security in South Asia: conceptual issues

Part I of this volume contains six chapters. Because human security is a complex subject, it is necessary to define it as a concept and set its parameters. Unless the conceptual base is clear, developing the idea of human security, particularly in the context of South Asia, constructing the arguments and opinions would be difficult. It is also necessary to appreciate that human security, as a concern over its individual dimensions, has existed for millennia. We may even argue that the Canadian approach to human security of freedom from fear has its philosophical foundations in what President Franklin D. Roosevelt called the Four Freedoms[6] – freedom of speech and expression, the freedom to worship God in his own way, freedom from want and freedom from fear. It is pertinent to note that freedom from fear was

4 Adluri Subramanyam Raju

considered relevant since 1941, when, as the world silently stood watching, Hitler's war machine steamrolled across Europe, consuming in its wake the lives of millions of Jews. The horrors of the Holocaust were too shocking to be ignored by universal human conscience. It was also a period when ideological differences moved the political machinery across the globe. The foremost concerns in the years after World War II, therefore, were aggression and armed conflicts. The UN Charter of 1948, universally adopted by most of the free countries of that time, concerned itself with the prevention of conflict and promotion of peace – in other words, freedom from fear.

It is not till the collapse of the USSR in 1991 that the importance of addressing issues that construct human security as a necessity came to be cognized. Taking this aspect further, Part I begins with laying down a conceptual framework. It further explores certain parameters with which human security could be measured. Unless a measurable dimension is added, human security would obviously remain a mere idea, and therefore this concern is addressed adequately. It further explores the one aspect of global governance matrix that possibly hinders a universalized approach to human security – the state-centric approach in the international political order. It argues for the individual human to be placed at the centre of a state's approach to security.

Looking a step further, Part I appraises India as a test case for addressing issues concerning human security. An important observation is made about the role of civil society in promoting human security as against the conventional 'state to provide' approach. The last two chapters in this part are test cases of India and Pakistan. The part includes two authoritative deliberations on whether South Asia's biggest role players, India and Pakistan, are ready with an environment that promotes human security. The pitfalls in the countries' approach to human security and its relevance and impact on the whole of South Asia are discussed in these two chapters.

Adluri Subramanyam Raju, in his chapter titled "Human security: a conceptual framework", argues that the discourse on human security gained importance after the disintegration of the Soviet Union. The chapter tries to make a theoretical analysis of the concept of human security by discussing various perspectives on human security made by institutions, scholars and diplomats.

Swaran Singh and Archana R., in their chapter on "Measurements of human security: a conceptual analysis", maintain that the notion of human security is based on the realization that security has wider connotations, which transcend physical security or national security. The pioneering studies on the concepts of freedom from 'fear' and freedom from 'want' and the measures taken to positively enhance the sense of well-being of humans have been done by Amartya Sen and Mahbubul Haque. Experts from India like Kanti Bajpai and Satish Kumar have made pioneering efforts evolving both human security and a national security index. Various indices to audit and understand human security helps the policy makers by pinpointing the areas related to human security that need to be worked on.

In her chapter on "Human security and beyond", Santishree D. Pandit maintains that the concept of human security fractured the dominance of the state-centric

Introduction **5**

approach of international order. The chapter generates discussions on who is to implement human security initiatives and whether the individuals can be given such a high stake in the security paradigm. It analyses the human-security scenario in South Asia and discusses the initiatives to be taken to resolve the issues faced by the region in the human security arena.

I.P. Khosla's chapter, "Human security in South Asia: the locus of a cooperative context", explains that the concept of human security has evolved through different stages since its origin. The chapter examines the stages of evolution of the concept and the relevance of the concept to the South Asian region. It also analyses the human security situation in South Asia and proposes different means to improve the situation in the region through increased cooperation among the member countries of South Asia.

D. Subha Chandran's chapter on "Is the region ready? Can the state deliver? Essay from India" maintains that the study of human security started in South Asia during the 1990s as a part of the expansion of the concept of security both at the global and regional levels. Almost three decades after the introduction of the concept, the status of human security studies in South Asia requires serious introspection. The question of the efficiency of state institutions in addressing the issues of human security is an important aspect of this chapter. The performance of the state as the sole provider of security raises doubts on the capability of the state to deliver, given the problems of governance. The role of civil society in enhancing human security in South Asia provides another dimension to the issue. With the recent advances in communication and social media, the state has to confront both the positive and negative influences of these developments on human security initiatives and perform accordingly.

In her chapter titled "Is the region ready? Can the state deliver? Essay from Pakistan", Salma Malik argues that a holistic and comprehensive manifestation of security involves the incorporation of economic, social and political factors, and it should be viewed through the traditional as well as non-traditional lens. The progress made by Pakistan in the areas of human security, including the capacity of the state to adapt and the measures taken by the state to augment human security initiatives, provides an interesting aspect in the study of human security. The capacity of the state to cater to the demands of human security and the factors affecting its progress are important considering the states' involvement in the conventional conflicts in the region.

Part II: Environmental issues and human security

Part II contains three chapters that address the relationship between humans and the environment and the challenges appended to the question of sustainable development. Scientists, academics and policy makers have come together to evaluate and address the issues concerning human impact on the environment and the resultant degradation. Climate change and environmental impact are at the heart of everything concerning agriculture to industrialization. Governments have come to recognize that it is time to act not merely on the challenge of climate change but also, more importantly, on climate management.

South Asian countries particularly have huge issues connected to the environment. As a matter of fact, elsewhere, the UN and the Organization for Security and Co-operation in Europe used 'Green Diplomacy' to resolve the disputes between Armenia and Azerbaijan, since their border issues essentially revolved around sharing of natural resources. Similar contingencies attend the disputes between South Asian neighbours. A careful consideration of regional dynamics reveals that behind the precipitous relationship between India and Pakistan, amongst a host of other issues, are the Indus Water Treaty and, in its aftermath, issues of projects like Kishanganga. Similarly, Bangladesh, Nepal and Bhutan have many-sided interests affecting their economies on account of major projects undertaken by India on its rivers and forests adjoining these countries. The Teesta River project, for example, is a major concern in the relations between India and Bangladesh since the Teesta flood plains cover nearly 14 per cent of the cropped area in Bangladesh and therefore affect the livelihoods of nearly 9.1 million people. Excessive trawling remains a major concern between India and Sri Lanka, and the resultant confiscation of boats and arrest of fishermen from Tamil Nadu remains a delicate issue in the national politics of both the countries.

It is but necessary in a climate that is teeming with environmental issues that we look at environmental governance issues which may help in promoting better governance and cooperation between South Asian neighbours. It is also evident that water is at the heart of the environmental issues besetting this region. Growing population, increasing demand for water and human development are keenly debated in this part, with an emphasis on making potable water accessible to all for human development.

While all the countries of the region are affected by climate change, the Maldives faces a critical future. Melting glaciers in the Antarctic and other climatological factors have placed the country at the peril of 'sinking'. Scores of islands in this country face the danger of submersion with sea rise. It is expected that it will vanish under the sea in about eighty years.[7] The climate threat to the Maldives, therefore, is discussed in detail not only with the view to detail the concerns of a nation but also as a lesson for other countries similarly 'endangered' to take note and avoid colossal human devastation.

Amongst the many risks to the environment that humans have created, electronic waste has come to occupy prime concern. Increasing levels of electronic use and the pace at which technology outpaces itself are concerns that are threateningly real. For India specifically, having grown into an information technology giant of its own standing, this challenge needs to be cognized first and addresses before it is too late. This part ends with a chapter that concerns this dimension.

Vandana Asthana in her chapter titled "Water insecurity in South Asia: challenges of human development", maintains that South Asia faces serious issues in the use of water resources for human development and sustainable use. For South Asia, being a region of rapid population growth, the demand for water is increasing substantially, and countries in the region are beginning to experience moderate to severe water shortages. The chapter maintains that availability and accessibility of clean, freshwater in the region is an issue of paramount importance from a human development perspective.

Rabindra Sen, in his chapter "Climate change and human security: a case study of the Maldives", argues that climate change is an issue of great importance to the Maldives that the very survival of the country is at stake due to the risks posed by the rise of sea level. The chapter analyses the nature and gravity of the problems of climate change and sea-level rise faced by the Maldives. It also focuses on the efforts of the Maldives through the UN and other organizations to shape and influence the international debate on the issue of climate change.

Gopalji Malviya's chapter "Dangers of electronic waste in India: a concern for human security", focuses on the handling of electronic waste in India, which is a serious issue concerning the environment and human security. The need for appropriate technical and legal mechanisms to address the emerging challenge of electronic waste disposal is detailed in the chapter.

Part III: State, development and displacement in South Asia

The six chapters in this part address four major conceptual issues surrounding human security in South Asia viz. governance, internal security and migration as a result of development and poverty. Across millennia, today the world lives in an atmosphere where development has to be both designed and brought about by the state. The question of state-assisted development depends on the quality of governance, and the first chapter in this part addresses precisely the issue of governance in a region where serious challenges exist to the physical security of its citizens. Rooted as they are in their historical origins, the challenges to the physical security in this region have resulted in colossal military expenditure and serious setbacks to economic development by the four wars that have occurred in a span of two decades. Arguing that peace is a precondition for development, the opening article calls on civil society to take initiatives to resolve physical security through coordination with governments.

While pundits of social, economic and political sciences talk of development in many tongues, Bhutan in South Asia adopted a differing yardstick towards development which it has called Gross National Happiness (GNH). The moderate success achieved by Bhutan in this dimension has generated keen interest in its experiment both at the UN and in many other developing nations. The story of GNH therefore is of relevance to human security and development.

Poverty is the most compelling challenge that South Asia faces. Home to over one sixth of humanity, crippling levels of poverty in this region is not merely a regional concern but also has global implications. Aside from its own burden, poverty has also been the main reason for another feature of South Asia that has both regional and international ramification – migration. Any talk of human security in this region will be meaningful only when these two aspects of regional life are suitably addressed. Two successive chapters in this part deal with both these aspects, taking the case of Nepal and India.

An unfortunate part of development initiatives in South Asia is the forced migration as a result of development activities of the government. The issue of sustainable development and rehabilitation come to centre stage while deliberating this issue. Interestingly, the question of rehabilitation also pertains to insurgents and anti-national elements that abound this region. The two chapters at the end of this part address the Maoist surrenders and displacement due to nuclear power plants as a case study to evolve strategies to tackle the challenges of rehabilitation.

C.K. Lal's chapter, titled "Correcting anomalies of a dysfunctional state through civil society: initiatives to complement global attempts for human security", maintains that the capacity of a state to ensure good governance is a necessary condition for human security. The record of governance in South Asia indicates that intolerance is on the rise throughout the region. The chapter explains that countries are unable to ensure even internal physical security let alone human security, and this poses a serious threat to the human development scenario in South Asia. This issue can be addressed through civil society initiatives, and it could prevent a failing state from failing completely.

Maitreyee Choudhury's chapter "Human development vis-à-vis Gross National Happiness in Bhutan: challenges and achievements", explains instead of measuring development in terms of gross domestic product or even the Human Development Index (HDI), countries like Bhutan opted for their own way of measuring human development. Even before the United Nations introduced the HDI, Bhutan brought forth the idea of GNH, which is the guiding philosophy for its development. By adopting the concept of GNH, Bhutan tries to achieve positive results in the context of the environment, socio-economic development, traditional culture and good governance. The country has achieved moderate success in implementing the idea into practice, and the UN and many countries across the world have considered this as an alternative model of development in terms of human well-being.

Amrita Limbu, in her chapter "Linkages between migration and poverty in Nepal", explores the interrelation between poverty and migration in Nepal, mainly focusing on poverty as an influencing factor for migration. The role of external remittances in poverty reduction, as well as the subsequent consequences, including the lessening dependence on agriculture and the question of long-term livelihood, is discussed in detail in the chapter.

Rashmi Bhure, in her chapter titled "Sustainable development model: experience from India", maintains that the South Asian region is a large market in the global economy with an increasingly young working population. At the same time, the region has a high poverty rate and a large number of undernourished population, which makes it a region of contradictions. The chapter explains various non-traditional security issues such as poverty, health and sanitation have an impact on the lives of people in the region. To address these challenges, the author argues that the region needs to promote an inclusive development strategy that will lead to sustainable development. Thus, a 'bottom-up' approach to development can be materialized with the participation of people in an integrated model of development.

P.V. Ramana's chapter, "Reintegrating India's Maoists: surrender and rehabilitation", explains that the implementation of surrender and rehabilitation policy is important in Maoist-affected states in India as it helps the surrendered rebels to join the mainstream and to not return to the path of violence. The chapter focuses on the need for a robust surrender and rehabilitation policy at the national level and the importance of effective monitoring of policy implementations.

In the chapter titled "Development-induced displacement: case studies from India", Apoorva R. Heroor and Praveen Tiwari argue that developmental projects which benefit society create large-scale displacement, both voluntary and involuntary, of the population. The protection provided by the existing laws and the compensations provided by the government and private companies are not sufficient to re-establish the lives of these displaced people. The chapter discusses economic, sociological and psychological impacts which surround involuntary displacements using case studies of Kudankulam nuclear power plant and Thervoy Kandigai-Kannankottai reservoir project.

Notes

1 Human Development Report, 1994, New York: Oxford University Press, 1994, p. 22.
2 I.P. Khosla, "Evolving a Theoretical Perspective on Human Security", in P.R. Chari and Sonika Gupta (eds.), Human Security in South Asia, New Delhi: Social Science Press, 2003, p. 24.
3 Human Development Report, no. 1, p. 24.
4 Kanti Bajpai, "Human Security: Concept and Measurement", Kroc Institute Occasional Paper, No. 19, August 2000, p. 35.
5 A.K.M. Abdus Sabur, "Evolving a Theoretical Perspective in Human Security: The South Asian Context", in Chari & Gupta, no. 2, p. 44.
6 Franklin D. Roosevelt speaks of Four Freedoms, A&E Television Networks, www.history.com/this-day-in-history/franklin-d-roosevelt-speaks-of-four-freedoms, history.com, 16 November 2009, accessed 9 May 2019.
7 See www.express.co.uk/travel/articles/879410/maldives-holiday-pacific-islands-sinking-disappear-climate-change, accessed 3 April 2019.

PART I

Human security in South Asia

Conceptual issues

1

HUMAN SECURITY

A conceptual framework

Adluri Subramanyam Raju

Introduction

Human security: a conceptual understanding

Human security is concerned with people, and hence, there is a pressing need to focus on the humanistic aspect of the security debate. According to Haq,

> the defining difference between the economic growth and the human development schools is that the first focuses exclusively on the expansion of only one choice – income – while the second embraces the enlargement of all human choices – whether economic, social, cultural, or political.[1]

The concept of security is extended from the military to the political, the economic, the environment or human security. In other words, human security does not mean that issues related to the military can be ignored. They are equally important in protecting people from violence and restoring democracy. For instance, the state has to protect its people from terrorist activities. The fight against terrorism will reinforce a focus on state security and defence of borders, and thus, one cannot ignore military preparedness against non-state belligerents. The state is expected to maintain the security of its borders as well as the security of the individuals. It is the state's obligation, apart from protecting people from external conflicts, to ensure that its people enjoy their rights and live with a sense of dignity without any fear. The state has to re-orient its policies to address the problems of human beings. Thus, the absence of a bipolar world order and the quest for a new international system initiated a debate on an alternative approach to security, that is, comprehensive security, combining traditional and non-traditional dimensions. Human and

14 Adluri Subramanyam Raju

state security should be treated on par since both are equally important. Both are interlinked and cannot be separated.

United Nations Development Programme (UNDP) and Canadian approaches to human security

In the past seven decades, the scholars and policy-making community in South Asia constructed and debated the issue of security from a military point of view. South Asian states have focused more on defence related issues than on human-related issues. As a result, majority of people are not able to afford to have food resulting in hunger and starvation, in access to clean water, primary health care, deprivation of basic needs, increasing poverty, unemployment, violation of human rights by the individuals, organizations and state. The governments of respective states in South Asia are concerned less with these issues, and they are unable to address them adequately.

Human security is a vast and complicated concept. One of the greatest tasks that researchers and policy makers often have is trying to define the concept. This is primarily because "human security is not a coherent concept or school of thought. Rather, there are different, and sometimes competing, conceptions of human security that may reflect different sociological/ cultural and geostrategic orientations".[2] It must be remembered that human security has been defined by scholars trying to give it more shape and conceptual meaning instead of a vast all-encompassing concept as otherwise portrayed, hence argued to be meaningless.[3] Largely, however, we may come to accept two leading inclinations towards the definition of human security.

The UNDP Human Development Report, 1993, indicated for the first time in an official document that the individual must be placed at the centre of international affairs. The report expressly states that "the concept of security must change from and exclusive emphasis on national security to a much greater stress on people's security, from security through armaments to security from human development, from territorial security to food, employment and environmental security".[4]

In the 1994 UNDP Report, human security is referred to as

> first safety from such chronic threats as hunger, disease and repression. And second, it means protection from sudden and hurtful disruptions in the patterns of daily life – whether in homes, in jobs or in communities. Such threats can exist at all levels of national income and development.[5]

Furthermore, it maintains that

> The world can never be at peace unless people have security in their daily lives. Future conflicts may often be within nations rather than between them-with their origins buried deep in growing socio-economic deprivation and disparities. The search for security in such a milieu lies in development, not in arms.[6]

According to the UNDP,

> Human security is a universal concern. It is relevant to people everywhere, in rich nations and poor. . . . The components of human security as interdependent. When the security of people is endangered anywhere in the world, all nations are likely to get involved. . . . Human security is easier to ensure through early prevention than later intervention . . . is people-centered . . . concerned with how people live and breathe in a society, how freely they exercise their many choices, how much access they have to market and social opportunities – and whether they live in conflict or in peace.[7]

The core concept of human security strives to ensure for the individual "safety from chronic threats as hunger, disease and repression. And second, it means protection from sudden and hurtful disruptions in the patterns of daily life – whether in homes, in jobs or in communities".[8]

In 2005 Kofi Annan stated that the UN's three key goals were security, development and human rights. He structured this report around three pillars of an emerging human security concept: freedom from want (a shared vision of development), freedom from fear (a vision of collective security) and freedom to live in dignity (under the rule of law, human rights and democracy).[9]

The Canadian approach was, however, a bit different and was summed by then Canadian foreign minister Lloyd Axworthy as "[h]uman security includes security against economic privation, an acceptable quality of life, and a guarantee of fundamental human rights".[10] And while the UNDP focused on freedom from want, freedom from fear and freedom to live in dignity, the Canadian model highlighted primarily the freedom from fear.[11]

It can be noted that both these approaches are, however, emancipatory in nature. However, fundamentally, in the UNDP approach,

> global society itself must be restructured to bring about a condition in which both direct and indirect threats will disappear. That restructuring should basically be a developmental one. Thus, the UNDP urges that a new human development paradigm must be evolved with an accent on equity, sustainability, and participation.[12]

For this "global governance should be democratized, with the developing world better represented in international institutions".[13]

The Canadian approach, however, "cautions that human security is not directly translatable into policy imperatives. It is more "a shift in perspective or orientation . . . an alternative way of seeing the world".[14] Canada's real concern is over the *policy implications* of the almost revolutionary agenda offered by the UNDP: "The very breadth of the UNDP approach . . . made it unwieldy *as a policy instrument*"[15] and emphasizes on "improving democratic governance" and "strengthening the capacity of international organizations".[16]

16 Adluri Subramanyam Raju

In this light, one may go on to understand poverty as a threat to human security, in both the Canadian and the UNDP approach. This is because poverty not only reduces the possibilities of individuals' access to security in other components that encompass human security, it also removes those choices from them. Hence, poverty-stricken people would not only live with want; they would also live with fear and in all probability live without dignity. The UNDP approach calls for an overhaul of how global governance is undertaken and emphasizing on the cooperation of countries to ensure that citizens are able to live with security.

The Canadian approach says that "poverty and insecurity . . . are interlinked in a vicious cycle" and "[b]reaking the cycle requires measures to promote human development, through access to reliable employment, education and social services".[17] Human development and human security are "mutually reinforcing" and "development assistance" can complement "political, legal, and military initiatives in enhancing human security".[18]

Caroline Thomas[19] looks into the role of how global governance and economic policies have not helped in removing the human insecurity even with the hope of the 'peace dividend' and questions the interests that govern global governance institutions and results that they have yielded. It might be said that she clearly agrees in the requiring of an overhaul of global governance and insists on 'redistribution'[20] as the strategy that should be at their core. That being the case, it might be said that poverty and governance as closely interlinked in an inversely proportional way. Good governance leading to less poverty, if governance is influenced by similar economic policies that look at redistribution of wealth from the north to the south.

Understanding the differences between Canadian and UNDP approaches, Bajpai proposes a definition for human security so as to assist in further research and global policy analysis and creation. His proposed definition is

> Human security relates to the protection of the individual's personal safety and freedom from direct and indirect threats of violence. The promotion of human development and good governance, and, when necessary, the collective use of sanctions and force are central to managing human security. States, international organizations, nongovernmental organizations, and other groups in civil society in combination are vital to the prospects of human security.[21]

He further goes on to suggest the creation of a Human Security Audit to create the Human Security Index.[22] He also elaborates on what it should have and how it may be used. Besides him, there are other scholars who suggest a mechanism to measure human security.

Gary King and Christopher J.L. Murray developed a formulation to calculate human security and proposed several concepts that would assist in this task. Their basic premise started from the understanding of security as being based on the risk of severe deprivation and depending on the concept of poverty.[23] Understanding that poverty was being influenced by more than just income, they were also able to suggest the concept of generalized poverty. "Building on the concept of generalized poverty and the forward looking nature of our (their) conception of security"[24] was then used to define Years of Individual Human Security as the expected number of years of life spent outside the state of generalized poverty.[25] They also went on to develop methods to measure the Population Human Security and Domain-Specific measures.

Kofi Annan describes human security as follows:

> Human Security in its broadest sense embraces far more than the absence of violent conflict. It encompasses human rights, good governance, access to education and health care and ensuring that each individual has opportunities and choices to fulfil his or her own potential. Every step in this direction is also a step towards reducing poverty, achieving economic growth and preventing conflict. Freedom from want, freedom from fear and the freedom of future generations to inherit a healthy natural environment-these are the interrelated building blocks of human and therefore national security.[26]

Amartya Sen and Sadako Ogare define it as follows:

> Human Security means protecting fundamental freedoms-freedoms that are the essence of life. It means protecting people from critical (severe) and pervasive (widespread) threats and situations. It means using processes that build on people's strengths and aspirations. It means creating political, social, environmental, economic, military, and cultural systems that together give people the building blocks of survival, livelihood, and dignity.

The vital core of life is a set of elementary rights and freedoms people enjoy. What people consider to be 'vital' – what they consider to be 'of the essence of life' and 'crucially important' – varies across individuals and societies. That is why any concept of human security must be dynamic. And that is why we refrain from proposing an itemized list of what makes up human rights.[27]

According to Tadjbakhsh,

> to be secure in this sense entails, to be free from both fear (of physical, sexual or psychological abuse, violence, persecution, or death) and from want (of gainful employment, food, and health). Human security therefore deals with the capacity to identify threats, to avoid them when possible, and to mitigate their effects when they do occur. It means helping victims cope with the consequences of the widespread insecurity resulting from armed conflict, human rights violations and massive underdevelopment. This broadened use of the word "security" encompasses two ideas: one is the notion of "safety" that goes beyond the concept of mere physical security in the traditional sense, and the other the idea that people's livelihoods should be guaranteed through "social security" against sudden disruptions.[28]

18 Adluri Subramanyam Raju

Newman argues that

> [c]omponents of human security are interdependent, severe threats to human security are not confined to single communities, and human security is easier to ensure through early prevention. The emphasis in the human needs model is upon safety and freedom, especially in critical situations, rather than upon the broader concept of human *development*, which is concerned with widening people's choices. (emphasis as in original)[29]

The following is a definition of human security as opined by the UNDP. The UNDP's approach to human security is purely developmental, and we can see this approach being reflected in how it refers to human security. It is

> first, safety from such chronic threats as hunger, disease and repression. And second, it means protection from sudden and hurtful disruptions in the patterns of daily life – whether in homes, in jobs or in communities. Such threats can exist at all levels of national income and development.[30]

However, this is arbitrary in nature, and understanding this, it was required to understand what constitutes human security. As mentioned by the UNDP, there have always been two components of human security: freedom from fear and freedom from want.[31] This needs to be dealt with by taking action against the threats that affect human security. Such a list is "long, but can be considered under seven main categories: economic security; food security; health security; environmental security; personal security; community security; political security".[32]

These seven categories are elaborated by the UNDP as follows:

1   *Economic Security:* Economic security "requires an assured basic income –usually from productive and remunerative work or in the last resort from some publicly financed safety net".[33] This means that policies should be able to adhere to providing people with either jobs that allow them to get an income from work or have a conducive atmosphere where entrepreneurs are able to achieve remunerative work or, in the last instance as mentioned earlier, there should be social safety nets that would bring in to the fold the unemployed and provide for them an income that gives them access to a basic standard of living.

2   *Food Security:* Food security means that all people at all times have both physical and economic access to basic food. This requires not just enough food to go round. It requires that people have ready access to food – that they have an 'entitlement' to food, by growing it for themselves, by buying it or by taking advantage of a public food distribution system. The availability of food is thus a necessary condition of security – but not a sufficient one. People can still starve even when enough food is available.

3   *Health Security:* One of the major reasons for insecurity in developing countries is the lack of good health facilities or mechanisms to ensure good health

of citizens. This results in high mortality rates and lower life expectancies. To address this problem, the UNDP highlighted the need for health security as part of the threat to human security.

4   *Environmental Security:* Human beings depend on a healthy physical environment. However, the environment is under severe strain from stresses caused due to the population and massive industrialization. These effects have caused degradation of land, reduction of water for irrigation and drinking water, pollution of the air causing respiratory problems and so on. This shows not only the requirements of a clean, sustainable format for development, allowing for human beings to exist in a secure environment; it also shows the interconnectedness between the environment and the health of human beings and its importance as elicited earlier.

5   *Personal Security:* One of the important aspects of human security for people is their security from physical violence. Human life is increasingly threatened by sudden, unpredictable violence in developing countries. The threats take several forms: "threats from the state (physical torture); threats from other states (war); threats from other groups of people (ethnic tension); threats from individuals or gangs against other individuals or gangs (crime, street violence); threats directed against women (rape, domestic violence); threats directed at children based on their vulnerability and dependence (child abuse); and threats to self (suicide, drug use)".[34]

   This not only shows the varied and all-encompassing nature of personal security but also shows the extent to which human security as a concept is meant to cover. This highlights how policy should be re-oriented so that security is not planned to protect the abstract notion of what the state is but to protect and secure the individual human that sustains and constitutes the state.

6   *Community Security:* Many people "derive security from their membership in a group – a family, a community, an organization, a racial or ethnic group that can provide a cultural identity and a reassuring set of values".[35] Globalization, with mass media and the accompanying cultural amalgamation, threatens vibrant communities across the globe, creating in its wake a singular, global community rooted from its traditions and geography. Such harmful effects must be kept in check, if not stopped. Even though this security must be reinforced, it must be done so carefully as community radicalism, communalism and other extremist forces also use the securitization of this to create insecurity in other communities.

7   *Political Security:* One of the most important aspects of human security is that people should be able to live in a society that honours their basic human rights. Apart from the representation of people in the decision-making process, this also seeks to ensure that governments do not oppress their own people. Civilian unrest resulting in military intervention is one aspect that seeks to protect from. But apart from this, police brutality and the control over ideas and information should be removed. "One of the most useful indicators of political insecurity in a country is the priority the government accords military strength since governments sometimes use armies to repress their own people".[36]

There are links and overlaps among these seven elements of human security. "A threat to one element of human security is likely to travel-like an angry typhoon to all forms of human security".[37]

With this understanding of human security according to the UNDP, it is possible to move on to the understanding of human security as espoused by Canada, with reference to Axworthy, who not only was instrumental in defining human security as understood by Canada but also developed its official stance with regard to the development of the concept, theoretically, as well as policy.

When trying to define human security, Axworthy explains, "In essence, human security means safety for people from both violent and non-violent threats. It is a condition or state of being characterized by freedom from pervasive threats to people's rights, their safety, or even their lives".[38] It shows that the shift in focus is moved away from what was entirely a development-oriented approach by the UNDP to a humanitarian perspective that calls on the need for protecting people so as to ensure their basic rights. And so, while acknowledging the need for the UNDP developmental approach, he sums up that "[t]ogether, human security and human development address the twin objectives of freedom from fear and freedom from want".[39]

Unlike UNDP's approach stating that human security provides for human development, he states that "[h]uman security provides an enabling environment for human development", while also that "[h]uman security is enhanced by reducing people's vulnerability and by preventing the conditions which make them vulnerable in the first place".[40] He brings about this change in the approach to human security, because it was felt that human security as defined by the UNDP was "unwieldy as a policy instrument".[41] And hence, what should be done is to use the concept of human security as "a template to assess policy and practice for their effects on the safety of people".[42]

This demonstrates a sea change from the UNDP's approach and calls for interventionist methods to be adopted to ensure human security. The policy implications as highlighted by Axworthy are that

> [f]irst, when conditions warrant, vigorous action in defence of human security objectives will be necessary. At the same time, the human costs of strategies for promoting state and international security must be explicitly assessed. Third, security policies must be integrated much more closely with strategies for promoting human rights, democracy, and development. Fourth, due to the complexity of contemporary challenges to the security of people, effective interventions involve a diverse range of actors including states, multilateral organizations, and civil society groups. Fifth, effective responses will depend on greater operational coordination. Sixth, civil society organizations are seeking greater opportunity and greater responsibility in promoting human security.[43]

This nature of human security being used as a means to measure policy could be seen in how the Millennium Development Goals (MDGs) were defined.

MDGs

In 2000, 189 nations "made a promise to free people from extreme poverty and multiple deprivations. This pledge became the eight Millennium Development Goals to be achieved by 2015. In September 2010, the world recommitted itself to accelerate progress towards these goals".[44] This pledge was the outcome of the UN Millennium Declaration, which showed that the world had "a collective responsibility to uphold the principles of human dignity, equality and equity at the global level".[45]

The eight goals are to eradicate extreme hunger and poverty; achieve universal primary education; promote gender equality and empower women; reduce child mortality; improve maternal health; combat HIV/AIDS, malaria and other diseases; ensure environmental sustainability; and develop a global partnership for development. As can be seen from these eight goals, it can be understood how these policies are not only human-centric, but they also try to empower those who are most at risk or most insecure.

The need for development and governance, to eradicate/reduce poverty was highlighted in the Millennium Declaration. And it was understood that "success in meeting these objectives depends, *inter alia*, on good governance within each country".[46] The declaration emphasizes the global understanding of the relationship between good governance and poverty eradication:

> The internationally agreed framework of eight goals and eighteen targets was complemented by forty eight technical indicators to measure progress towards the Millennium Development Goals. These indicators have since been adopted by a consensus of experts from the United Nations, IMF, OECD and the World Bank.[47]

It is understood that poverty is focused as part of the MDGs. Although, this is not the sole focus of the MDG, it may be said that holistic development as envisioned through the holistic approach to security from the theoretical framework of human security definitely does play a role in ensuring that development not only means the increase in the gross domestic product (GDP) but also growth on the ground in ensuring people to feel free from want and free from fear.

Also, poverty, as understood by these organizations, is on economic grounds. That is, poverty is understood in terms of living on less than $1 a day and all steps to deal with to elevate people to better standards of living and to enable them to get access to resources that remove them from a state of poverty.

In September 2000, the UN General Assembly, in adopting the Millennium Declaration, identified poverty eradication as the central plank of its vision for a new global order.[48] The first target of the UN MDGs is the reduction of poverty and hunger.[49]

It is noteworthy to mention here what the UN Human Settlements Programme in its preamble to the UN Habitat Agenda says:

> We recognize the imperative need to improve the quality of human settlements, which profoundly affects the daily lives and well-being of our peoples.

There is a sense of great opportunity and hope that a new world can be built, in which economic development, social development and environmental protection as interdependent and mutuality reinforcing components of sustainable development can be realized through solidarity and cooperation within and between countries and through effective partnerships at all levels. International cooperation and universal solidarity, guided by the purposes and principles of the Charter of the United Nations and in a spirit of partnership, are crucial to improving the quality of life of the peoples of the world.

Sustainable human settlements development requires the active engagement of civil society organizations, as well as the broad-based participation of all people. It equally requires responsive, transparent and accountable government at the local level. Civic engagement and responsible government both necessitate the establishment and strengthening of participatory mechanisms, including access to justice and community-based action planning, which will ensure that all voices are heard in identifying problems and priorities, setting goals, exercising legal rights, determining service standards, mobilizing resources and implementing policies, programmes and projects.[50]

Conclusion

The chapter has made an attempt to theorize the concept of human security. It discusses various definitions made by different institutions, scholars and diplomats on human security. In contemporary times, every state has to look at the human security dimensions while formulating the policies either at a national or an international front. The human security dimension brought a paradigm shift in understanding the security concept.

Notes

1 Aasha Kapur Mehta, Andrew Shepherd, Shashanka Bhide, Amita Shah and Ananda Kumar, Chronic Poverty Report: Towards Solutions and New Compacts in a Dynamic Context, New Delhi: Indian Institute of Public Administration, 2011, p. 24.
2 E. Newman, "Human Security and Constructivism", International Studies Perspectives, no. 2, 2001, p. 240.
3 Kanti Bajpai, "Human Security: Concept and Measurement", Kroc Institute Occasional Paper, No. 19, August 2000, p. 2.
4 C. Sommaruga, "The Global Challenge of Human Security", Foresight, vol. 6, no. 4, 2004, p. 210.
5 UNDP, United Nations Development Program, 1994, http://hdr.undp.org/en/media/hdr_1994_en_chap2.pdf, p. 23, accessed 10 April 2019.
6 Ibid., p. 1.
7 Ibid., p. 22.
8 Ibid., p. 23.
9 H.G. Brauch, "Conceptualising the Environmental Dimension of Human Security in the UN", International Social Science Journal, vol. 59, no. 1, 2008, p. 19.
10 C. Thomas, "Global Governance, Development and Human Security: Exploring the Links", Third World Quarterly, vol. 22, no. 2, 2001, p. 161.
11 Bajpai, no. 3, p. 18.

Human security **23**

12 *Ibid.*, p. 31.
13 *Ibid.*, p. 32.
14 *Ibid.*
15 *Ibid.*
16 *Ibid.*, p. 33.
17 *Ibid.*, p. 35.
18 *Ibid.*
19 Thomas, no. 10, pp. 159–175.
20 *Ibid.*, p. 174.
21 Bajpai, no. 3, p. 48.
22 *Ibid.*, p. 53.
23 G. King and C.J.L. Murray, "Rethinking Human Security", Political Science Quarterly, vol. 116, no. 4, 2001, p. 593.
24 *Ibid.*, p. 595.
25 *Ibid.*
26 Cited in Ademola Abass, Protecting Human Security in Africa, London: Oxford University Press, 2010, p. 168.
27 Cited in Sabina Alkire, "Concepts of Human Security", in Lincoln Chen, Sakiko Fukuda-Parr and Ellen Seidensticker (eds.), Human Insecurity in a Global World, New Delhi: Viva Books Pvt. Ltd., 2005, p. 32.
28 For a discussion on problems conceptualizing human security, S. Tadjbakhsh, "Human Security: The Seven Challenges of Operationalizing the Concept", UN, Human Security: 60 Minutes to Convince, New York: UNESCO, 2005.
29 Newman, no. 2, p. 243.
30 UNDP, no. 5, p. 23.
31 *Ibid.*, p. 24.
32 *Ibid.*, pp. 24–25.
33 *Ibid.*, p. 25.
34 *Ibid.*, p. 30.
35 *Ibid.*, p. 31.
36 *Ibid.*, p. 33.
37 *Ibid.*
38 L. Axworthy, Human Security: Safety for People in a Changing World, Center for Peace and Development Studies, 1999, www.summit-americas.org/Canada/HumanSecurity-english.htm, accessed 10 April 2019.
39 *Ibid.*
40 *Ibid.*
41 *Ibid.*
42 *Ibid.*
43 *Ibid.*
44 UN, Milennium Development Goals, UNDP (n.d), www.undp.org/content/undp/en/home/mdgoverview.html, accessed 10 April 2019.
45 UN, Millenium Declaration, 18 September 2000, www.un.org/millennium/declaration/ares552e.pdf, p. 1, accessed 10 April 2019.
46 *Ibid.*, p. 4.
47 UN, UN Millennium Project: Goals, Targets, & Indicators, 2006, www.odi.org/sites/odi.org.uk/files/odi-assets/publications-opinion-files/2181.pdf, accessed 10 April 2019.
48 United Nations General Assembly, 55th Session, 55/2, 18 February 2000.
49 UN Millennium Development Goals, www.un.org/millenniumgoals, accessed 10 April 2019.
50 United Nations Conference on Human Settlements (Habitat II), Istanbul, Turkey, 3–14 June 1996, pp. 9–16, https://books.google.co.in/books?id=7hiI4Myupv8C&printsec=frontcover&source=gbs_ge_summary_r&cad=0#v=onepage&q&f=false, accessed 10 April 2019.

2

MEASUREMENTS OF HUMAN SECURITY

A conceptual analysis

Swaran Singh and Archana R.

Introduction

Human security refers to the absence of threats to the well-being of individuals. It talks of freedom from 'fear' and freedom from 'want' and includes measures that are taken to positively enhance their sense of well-being to make life 'humane' and 'worth living'. Two scholars from South Asia, Amartya Sen and Mahbubul Haque, did pioneering work which was formalised by the UN Development Programme (UNDP) Reports. The notion of human security has evolved as part of the critique of traditional definitions of security that viewed it only in a limited space of physical security of territorial nation state which in practical terms often became regime security making masses expendable in name of national interest. Various existing indices that have since evolved to audit and understand Human Security include the Human Development Index, Humane Governance Index and Gross National Happiness Index. These have sought to enhance human security by pointing out the areas that need to be addressed, encouraging policy makers to take initiatives in that direction. Among others, experts like Kanti Bajpai and Satish Kumar from India have made pioneering efforts in this direction in evolving both the Human Security Index and the National Security Index. This chapter examines some of these extant debates, as well as the evolving contours of the human security concept, to assess how these indices can help direct various conceptual debates and policy options.

Human security has risen to be at the forefront of global debates on security. Thanks to the forces of the information revolution, communication and globalisation, the world is becoming increasingly aware of human suffering arising out of natural and man-made calamities. This has resulted in an increased focus from nation states to people. Accordingly, the traditional definitions of national security, limited to the preservation of territorial boundaries and sovereignty of state from external threats, make 'national' security an atavistic notion. The focus has since shifted to not just human security but human welfare making it the core element of state responsibilities, and this has resulted in a gradual shift in the perceptions of security that is cognisant of the larger requirements of human welfare. Attempts have been made since the time of Mahbubul Haque's Human Development Index (HDI) to develop various indices to measure human security. However, debates, as yet, remain inconclusive as to which set of these indices best brings out the essence of human security. Then South Asia has its added complications that make this debate not only especially complex but also worth exploring by regional experts.

This chapter does not intend to indulge in a technical assessment of human security indices inasmuch as conceptually trying to engage them. The chapter argues that at this stage it is the definitional unwieldiness of the concept that renders ineffective attempts at identifying which of various indices best reflects the concept of human security. Meanwhile, the greater the choice of indices, the greater is the ability to bring out various aspects that have been overlooked so far in developing a holistic understanding of the human security concept. The chapter also grapples with South Asian discourses to bring out the relevance of human security in the South Asian context considering the deprivations and turmoil that the region, as a whole, has been experiencing all this time. South Asia, this chapter argues, perhaps presents an ideal launch pad for a paradigm shift in the security discourse from one that highlights the traditional notions of state survival to one that seeks to make human beings as the focal point and the end of security policies and practices.

Definition of *human security*

'Freedom from fear', 'freedom from want' and 'freedom to live in dignity' are the words that best bring out the essence of human security discourse. But what are the situations that have to be avoided or positively ushered in to secure human beings from a state of fear, want or ignominy? The answer to the preceding question leads to the obvious conclusion that human security is one of the most expansive concepts ever encompassing security and development studies and more. The identification of definitional boundaries of a concept and parsimony in the numbers of variables while attempting to measure a concept remain necessary preconditions for building a consensus on the phenomena being studied and to ensure ease of understanding causation, respectively. But it is also true that the more accommodative the rubric of human security becomes, the richer and more relevant the discourse transforms, owing to the wider issue areas being studied that, in turn, enhance the pursuit of human well-being.

Enormous mind power has gone into defining human security. Of all the existing definitions, the most evocative one has been given by Amartya Sen and Sadako Ogare. They define human security as

> [the protection of] the vital core of all human lives in ways that enhance human freedoms and human fulfillment. Human security means protecting

fundamental freedoms – freedoms that are the essence of life. It means protecting people from critical (severe) and pervasive (widespread) threats and situations. It means using processes that build on people's strengths and aspirations. It means creating political, social, environmental, economic, military and cultural systems that together give people the building blocks of survival, livelihood and dignity.[1]

Having conceded, at this stage, the nebulous nature of contours of human security, it is pertinent to point to the convenience and pragmatism of formulating working definitions of human security to suit the research endeavour in hand rather than identifying a single universally accepted definition of human security. In doing that, it perhaps remains most apt to examine the evolution of the human security concept and to explore discourses that have moulded the ongoing debate on this as-yet-contested concept. It will also be useful to explore how the evolution of practices has influenced the formulation of the human security concept and vice versa.

Evolution of the concept of human security

Theoretically speaking, the evolution of human security can be viewed from 'universalist' perspectives of having been the fundamental concern of humans since ancient times, although it evolved as part of discourses within various kingdoms, religions, ethnicities, communities or clans. It can also be examined from 'contractarian' perspectives that explain the origins of the nation-state.[2] But, not to go too far back in its evolution, the post-Cold War years have witnessed debates on development and security overlapping and gradually shifting security debates from nuclear armageddon to existential threats from extant development models leading to irreversible climate change, migration and pandemics, with their disastrous consequences for all. This made high levels of defence expenditure by major powers come under question as well as various extant models of rapid industrialization with a view of attaining prosperity and lifting the population out of poverty. This has resulted in multiple debates on new sectors like environmental security, the blue economy and sustainable development and so on. Traditional security and development frameworks were no longer seen as enough to address the host of new challenges that the world has increasingly been facing, namely environment degradation, pandemics, migration, human rights violations and so on.

In this rising sandstorm of multiple challenges that know no national boundaries, the concept of human security arose when the discourse on development and security were unable to address those challenges and ensure overall wellbeing of human beings.[3] It is beyond dispute that the UN Development Programme (UNDP) was the first to comprehensively enunciate the concept of human security through the *United Nations Development Report* of 1994. Security studies had also undergone a paradigm shift with the conceptualisation of human security, and there has been increasing accommodation of this new concept in the traditional notions of security. Various other schools of thought like neo-Marxists, feminists, constructivists and critical theory proponents have also contributed to this evolution, where the traditional concept of security has evolved to making 'individual' as the reference object of security, although most of them continue to still consider the state as the major security provider. Neo-liberals have also emphasised the increasing role of market and marketisation of security apparatus from private security companies to increasing public–private partnership in defence production.

Caution, however, needs to be exercised while outlining the merger of the notions of human and national security. To go into depths to compartmentalise the two is an unproductive exercise. The human security debate does not see the state as expendable, as objectives of human security cannot be achieved without the institutional support and resourcefulness of the state. The best efforts of non-governmental organisations (NGOs), both domestic and transnational, to further human security will not bear fruit but for the patronage of the state. Also, human security can only be ensured if the state is secure, although it would require a far more positive action to shift focus from safety to the well-being of its people. Thus, state security and human security are not necessarily mutually exclusive. So human security only seeks to bring the paradigm up to speed with the brave new world where both the stakeholders and the target of security have metamorphosed, yet it does not question the state being the primary provider and facilitator.

Measurement of human security

In the traditional understanding of security (basically national security), the focus had been on protecting state territoriality from external and physical threats and absence of war was considered as a sufficient measure of security. Also, military preparedness was seen as its major precondition that may include arms race stability based on mutually assured destruction as its most potent strategy. Measurement of human security, on the other hand, involves a lot more affirmative action for creating conditions favourable for realising one's full potential making life worth living. Measurement of its efficacy therefore becomes a far more complicated exercise. It plays an especially critical role in policy formulations and comparison that it would facilitate across the countries of the world like measuring human security amongst South Asian countries. The objectives of measuring human security were very succinctly brought out by Kanti Bajpai as follows:

1 Developing a social early warning system.
2 Focusing attention on problem areas.
3 Redefining national and international policy priorities.
4 Setting national and international standards.
5 Generating new social scientific knowledge.[4]

The preceding list by Kanti Bajpai clearly outlines the desirability of measuring human security in concrete terms. Such measurement would essentially involve operationalisation of the concept of human security. Parsimony is desirable for the effective and efficient operationalising of variables. But the ideals of parsimony coupled with the expansive nature of the concept of human security have frustrated many an attempt at forging a comprehensive index that measures human security. Second, when there is no consensus on what comprises human security, to begin with, how can the intellectual community arrive at an understanding of how best to measure human security? But perhaps reverse is equally true that such efforts at listing indices generate debates that can further sharpen conceptualisation of human security. Then there would also be contextual variations of how we operationalise it or even how it is defined precisely.

The debates on separating the 'freedom from fear' and 'freedom from want' approach is perhaps relevant here. It is argued that many accomplishments in the realm of human security were attained as a result of the adoption of freedom from fear or, in the Canadian approach of human security, which concentrates on violent threats, for the survival of the individual from multivariate conflicts.[5] The achievements include legislation made to reduce violence against human populations. The recent conventions include the arrangement to ban landmines and cluster munitions, regulation of small arms and addressing challenges of recruitment of child soldiers. This, however, does not undermine the fact that programmes like the Millennium Development Goals (MDGs), constructed with an idea of human security that stresses on 'freedom from want', have also contributed greatly in bringing to the forefront of government policy decisions that focus on the security of billions of disadvantaged people. Sustainable Development Goals (SDG) that requires efforts towards the social, economic and political upliftment of people must be done in a way as to not hamper the ability of the future generations in meeting their own needs, and this has been a much-appreciated upgrade over the MDGs.

Then there is this repertoire of 'development' indices with their myriad indicators that can be classified broadly into two categories based on the coverage of variables. Issue-specific indices that seek to measure specific components of human security including food security, gender inequality, environmental sustainability, corruption, transparency, peace and literacy, among others. The efficacy of these indices is limited to the components they measure and cannot be conflated to comment on the general well-being of the populace. Then comprehensive indicators that, on the other hand, try to paint a broader picture of the state of human well-being using tools including the HDI, the Gross National Happiness (GNH) index, the Happy Planet Index, the World Database of Happiness, the Human Insecurity Index and so on. Some of the latter also make use of multiple other indices to arrive at a broader picture of human security in terms of human well-being.

While attempting to measure human security, the following needs to be kept in mind. There cannot be a single index, however comprehensive it claims to be, to practically cover all issues of concern to human well-being or a lack thereof and the judgment as to what contributes or erodes human well-being is essentially subjective and, to an extent, culture-specific. There have been considerable debates on the Western civilisation's influence on concepts such as human rights, human freedom and human security and their emphasis on individuality, agency and liberty to the detriment of some values cherished by various Asian communities that talk of Asian values, including the primacy of the community and its distinct value systems. The travails of disregarding these civilisational differences can be avoided by allowing the flourishing of concepts that suit the states in question. A combination of indices could also be used to make an understanding of a situation more appropriate or comprehensive. For instance, the HDI is a very popular yet limited index to measure human security. HDI can be used in combination with other indices including the GNH index and the Gender Development Index (GDI) to make it more accurate as also more effective. But the need for comparison across states in order to understand relative positions of states vis-à-vis the others will always encourage the development and usage of various specific/comprehensive indicators of human security with limited variables for the sake of simplicity and measurability.

States have often innovated when it comes to identifying indices for measuring security. Such indices take into account components of the state's values and think fit to include in the computation of its security and that of its people. Sometimes states also make a distinction among its citizens, residents and aliens. One such index is the National Security Index developed by the Foundation for National Security Research in India. It is a unique index as it shortlists countries whose values on parameters including population (above US$50 million), GDP (above US$500 billion) and defence expenditure (above US$5 billion) is beyond the threshold identified. The shortlisted countries then are assessed on six parameters, namely economic, military, population, technological, energy and foreign affairs capabilities with the respective weights of 2.5: 2.5:1.5:1.5:1:1.

Successful attempts have also been made to bring out indicators to measure human security in a comprehensive manner. The HDI was one of the first such indicators and a popular one at that. The updated HDI, for instance, is a composite measure of life expectancy at birth (health), mean years of schooling and expected years of schooling (education) and Gross National Income (GNI) per capita (PPP US$; standard of living). The inequality-adjusted Human Development Index (IHDI) attempts to make the HDI more relevant in an increasingly unequal world by accounting for the disparities in the distribution of the measures among the population. The IHDI is a geometric mean of the indices that compose the HDI which have been adjusted for inequalities using the Atkinson inequality measure.[6]

Amartya Sen had set into motion a paradigm shift in the perception of the well-being of individuals by his 'capabilities' approach. This approach assesses well-being by measuring what human beings are capable of achieving rather than the amount of resources they possess or utility derived from them. This approach treats people as ends in themselves. The ability of people to use resources to satisfy their needs is not the same. This approach, however, accounts for this fact as well. It takes into consideration the agency of individuals and choices available to individuals to attain their life goals.

A sample of five indices are selected and presented to showcase the repertoire of variables involved in measuring various aspects of human security. They are the

Global Peace Index, the GNH index, the Happy Planet Index, the GDI and the Prototype Human Security Index. First, the Global Peace Index was formulated with the objective of identifying the relative peacefulness of countries in the world which, in turn, has a bearing on human security.[7] The three domains that compose the index are the level of safety and security in society, the extent of domestic and international conflict and the degree of militarisation.[8] The strength of this index lies in the quantitative nature of the indicators that measure the level of violence in society. As opposed to the highly objective and quantitative nature of the Global Peace Index, the GNH index consists of indicators whose ascertainment is apparently very complex and subjective.[9] For instance, community vitality, one of the indicators of the GNH is measured by taking into account social support, community relationship, family relationships and perceived safety which can only be judged qualitatively.[10] The subjective nature of the indicator by no means dismisses its novelty and the farsightedness. Variables especially the ones like happiness and well-being are highly subjective and the indicators that are chosen to measure the same differs greatly. The Happy Planet Index,[11] for instance, helps in identifying how well nations perform while supporting their inhabitants to live good lives while ensuring their ability to do so in the future.[12] The GDI is a composite measure intended to identify disparity in human development between women and men across three dimensions, namely health, education and living standards.[13] It is computed as a ratio of female-to-male HDI values.[14]

The prototype Human Security Index of David Hastings is one of the most comprehensive indices to facilitate measurement of human security. It is a composite of the Basic HDI and the Social Fabric Index.[15] The Social Fabric Index is, in turn, made up of the Gender Equality Index, the Peace Index, the Environment Index, the Corruption Control Index and the Information Empowerment Index.

Although the chapter began with the objective of identifying the best indicator among the existing ones, the chapter concludes that no significant gains accrue from the same exercise. This research endeavour, however, has facilitated an understanding of the richness and diversity of human security indices and afforded a multidimensional perspective of the phenomenon of human security. It can also be concluded that while the measurement of human security requires parsimony, the need for maintaining the rubric of human security as wide as possible should also be factored in. An ideal balance would be to identify various components of human security and formulate suitable indices for each region or select a group of them based on contextual analysis. Whether or not to provide any hierarchy amongst these variables all remains inconclusive and could widely transform both the outcomes and the analysis of any operational policies. Maybe area or regional studies could also contribute to better understanding.

South Asia and human security

At the most cursory level, it is nuclearisation of South Asia, terrorism, ethnic conflicts, religious turmoil, the violation of human rights and the growing number of refugees, increased poverty, more disparity between rich and poor and no apparent end to environmental degradation are a few problems that make this region noticeable.[16] But at a much deeper level, this region is also one of the unique places in the world where states have overlapping communities which, in many cases, share far less cultural traditions rituals and rites with other communities of their own nation state compared to their cross border community. But given colonial and Cold War legacies of disputed boundaries especially in face of the obsession of these newly independent states with territorial sovereignty most of these have been cut off from their cross-border kith and kin, leaving longings and creating situations in which these minorities feel marginalised or states are suspicion of their links with neighbouring countries. But the reverse can also be true. South Asia also remains a special example where these cross-border linkages can serve as bridges rather than as barriers or buffers for these common cross-border communities.

The fact that most South Asian states are multi-ethnic, multicultural and multilingual buttresses the fact of these intrinsic cultural and historical inter-societal linkages where states are seen a villain of peace reinforcing divisions instead of appreciating connectivity. Large swathes of what is now South Asia and beyond were ruled over by kings from late medieval India till the Europeans arrived to take advantages of deteriorating and falling empires and principalities. Finally, the British ruled much of South Asia for several centuries. However, in spite of their exploitative motives and enormous leverages, their rule also created connectivity and enhanced old ideas as well as germinated new shared identities. But colonial experiences are generally seen as negative, and the level and models of flawed economic development that British imposed on these colonies and challenges of poverty and underdevelopment that South Asia faces today are seen today as most formidable challenge to their human security discourse that seeks to transform their mechanics and missions in order to ensure security as potentially full of promise.

Some of these regional initiates have also succeeded. South Asian Association for Regional Cooperation (SAARC) has served as the platform for South Asian countries to deliberate on various issues concerning their region including on issues of human development and human security. The charter of SAARC that was made public in 2004 apparently gives a lot of weight to human security without actually naming it. The charter begins by reaffirming

> that the principal goal of SAARC is to promote the welfare of the peoples of South Asia, to improve their quality of life, to accelerate economic growth, social progress and cultural development and to provide all individuals the opportunity to live in dignity and to realize their full potential.[17]

The emphasis on human dignity shows the right direction in which the social charter is aimed at. It is one of the most eloquent agreements that acknowledges the primacy of the human being and seeks to address various issues to enhance human well-being. Article 2 (1) of the charter states as its objective the following: "Place

32 Swaran Singh and Archana R.

people at the centre of development and direct their economies to meet human needs more effectively".[18]

At least theoretically speaking, SAARC has done stellar work in the field of human wellbeing including the Convention on Combating and Prevention of Trafficking in Women and Children for Prostitution, Convention on Promotion of Welfare of Children, SAARC Convention on Narcotics Drugs, SAARC Regional Convention on Suppression of Terrorism and Additional Protocol on Terrorism. With its more than a quarter of century of working together, SAARC as a regional organisation is surely capable of providing the most effective platform for countries in the region to engage, showcase and share best practices, especially in the realm of social development. A case in point would be the issue of open defecation that undermines the basic need for human dignity. It is interesting to note that, in South Asia, Bangladesh's progress in combating open defecation and having been declared an open defecation–free country in South Asia. South Asia, specifically India, Pakistan and Nepal, has the highest incidence of open defecation in the world, second to no other region, including Africa. Bangladesh's enormous success in battling open defecation despite its budgetary constraints should be studied by the others in South Asia to together achieve the United Nations International Children's Emergency Fund's goal of achieving an open defecation free world in 2025.

On the optimistic side, experts have noticed a transition in South Asia from traditional security to human security in which the concept of security has increasingly come under scrutiny from scholars and practitioners alike. Indeed, classical formulations on security are seen today as "too universalistic in its emphasis on force" which remains too dangerous for the nuclearised South Asian region where "interdependence is knitting nations together willy-nilly", forcing them to evolve a "much more expanded notion of security" that brings them closer to engaging human security discourse.[19] Especially with the increasing engagement of younger South Asian scholars with the globalised world, their access to and participation in ongoing global discourses have reduced the lag time of South Asian security debates which are increasingly staying in tandem with global trends as well as contributing to global trends. Works of some of the South Asian scholars therefore have become integral to these debates on evolving indices of measuring and examining human security analysis and policies as also in further sharpening the conceptual contours of human security as a concept. South Asia therefore seems increasingly ordained to become part of the global discourse on human security and to benefit from ongoing global discourses and policy practices as well.

Conclusion

To conclude, therefore, although that conceptually human Security paradigm which remains contested and a work in progress yet, there is a considerable body of knowledge that reflects evolving consensus on the need to increase the focus on human security in the security praxis or in building security apparatus by the states. Second, there is also an increasing body of knowledge devoting academic resources

Measurements of human security **33**

and attention to the evolving complex indices of measuring human security and using these as yardsticks for evaluating analysis and policy practices. Third, in spite of a deeply felt need for adopting human security framework for South Asian nations, these countries remain mired in traditional security crisis around territorial sovereignty and have done precious little to capitalise on the sentiment or this opportunity to engage human security debates and to enhance their shared positive linkages and efforts. Four, given continuing complexities of the South Asian region, instead of eking out incremental changes, these countries must decide to leapfrog to the human security paradigm from their extant traditional frameworks of security.

The SAARC as a regional organisation has made substantial progress in cooperating on public health, gender issues and the welfare of children in the social front issues that remain at the core of human security discourse. These initiatives can be extended further to sharing best practices on humane governance, transparent and accountable institutions. The eight nations can identify and address human security indices that best suit their context and evolved shared ways of capitalising on the enormous human capital of the region which is relatively young and can greatly benefit from exponentially growing physical and virtual connective and access to global markets and resources. Issues of the mobility of the peoples to facilitate employment and afford a better standard of living, therefore, can be encouraged on priori basis besides addressing specific hurdles like streamlining the existing visa exemptions for many categories of people, especially intellectuals and entrepreneurs.

Notes

1 Commission for Human Security Report, 2003, New York: UN, 2003, p. 4, www.un.org/humansecurity/sites/www.un.org.humansecurity/files/chs_final_report_-_english.pdf, accessed 2 March 2016.
2 Saba Gul Khattak, Kiran Habin and Foqia Sadiq Khan, Women and Human Security in South Asia: The Cases of Bangladesh and Pakistan, Islamabad: Sustainable Development Policy Institute, 2008, p. 6.
3 Kanti Bajpai, "Human Security: Concept and Measurement", Kroc Institute Occasional Paper, 2000, p. 4.
4 *Ibid.*, pp. 55–56.
5 Taylor Owen, "Challenges and Opportunities for Defining and Measuring Human Security", Disarmament Forum, Human Rights, Human Security and Disarmament, three-2004.mercury.ethz.ch/.../04_defining+and+measuring+human+security.pdf, accessed 15 March 2016.
6 http://hdr.undp.org/en/faq-page/inequality-adjusted-human-development-index-ihdi#t293n106, accessed 11 April 2019.
7 Global Peace Index Report, 2015, New York: Institute for Economics and Peace, 2015, p. 4, http://economicsandpeace.org/wp-content/uploads/2015/06/Global-Peace-Index-Report-2015_0.pdf, accessed 4 March 2016.
8 There are 22 indicators under the three domains, namely number of external and internal conflicts fought; number of deaths from organised conflict (external); number of deaths from organised conflict (internal); level of organised conflict (internal); relations with neighbouring countries; level of perceived criminality in society; number of refugees and displaced persons as percentage of population; political instability; terrorist activity; political terror scale; number of homicides per 100,000 people; level of violent

crime; likelihood of violent demonstration; number of jailed persons per 100,000 people; number of internal security officers and police per 100,000 people; military expenditure as a percentage of GDP; number of armed-services personnel; volume of transfers of major conventional weapons as recipient (imports) per 100,000 people; volume of transfers of major conventional weapons as supplier (exports) per 100,000 people; financial contribution to UN peacekeeping missions; nuclear and heavy weapons capability; and ease of access to small arms and light weapons.

9   The nine indicators of the GNH are as follows: psychological well-being, health, time use, education, cultural diversity and resilience, good governance, community vitality, ecological diversity and resilience and, finally, the living standard.

10 Karma Ura et al., A Short Guide to Gross National Happiness Index, Thimphu, Bhutan: The Centre for Bhutan Studies, 2012, www.grossnationalhappiness.com/wp-content/uploads/2012/04/Short-GNH-Index-edited.pdf, accessed 15 March 2016.

11 Happy Planet Index ≈ (Experienced well-being × Life expectancy)/Ecological Footprint.

12 The Happy Planet Index: June 2012 Report, A Global Index of Sustainable Well-being, London: The New Economic Foundation, www.happyplanetindex.org/assets/happy-planet-index-report.pdf, accessed 4 March 2016.

13 Human Development Report, 2014, New York: United Nations Development Programme, p. 179, http://hdr.undp.org/sites/default/files/hdr14-report-en-1.pdf, accessed 13 March 2016.

14 The HDI is a composite of life expectancy, education levels and per capita income.

15 David A. Hastings, "From Human Development to Human Security: A Prototype Human Security Index", UNESCAP Working Paper, October 2009, www.unescap.org/resources/unescap-working-paper-human-development-human-security-prototype-human-security-index, accessed 19 March 2016.

16 Syed Hussain Shaheed Soherwordi, "Human Security in South Asia: Military Expenditure Dimension of India and Pakistan", Pakistan Horizon, vol. 58, no. 1, January 2005, p. 35.

17 Social Charter of the South Asian Association for Regional Cooperation (SAARC), 2004, www.jus.uio.no/english/services/library/treaties/02/2-03/saarc-social-charter.xml, accessed 21 April 2019.

18 Ibid.

19 Bajpai, no. 3, p. 3.

3

HUMAN SECURITY AND BEYOND

Santishree D. Pandit

Introduction

> *Where the mind is without fear and the head is held high, Where knowledge is free . . .*
> *Rabindranath Tagore[1]*

The concept of security has for too long been interpreted narrowly: as security of territory from external aggression, or as protection of national interests in foreign policy or as global security from the threat of a nuclear holocaust. It has been related more to nation-states than to people. The superpowers were locked in an ideological struggle-fighting a cold war all over the world. The developing nations, having won their independence only recently, were sensitive to any real or perceived threats to their fragile national identities. Forgotten were the legitimate concerns of ordinary people who sought security in their daily lives. For many of them, security symbolized protection from the threat of disease, hunger, unemployment, crime, social conflict, political repression and environmental hazards. With the dark shadows of the cold war receding, one can now see that many conflicts are within nations rather than between nations.

> *NDP, HDR, 1994[2]*

The components of human security are *interdependent*. When the security of people is endangered anywhere in the world, all nations are likely to get involved. Famine, disease, pollution, drug trafficking, terrorism, ethnic disputes and social disintegration are no longer isolated events, confined within national borders. Their consequences travel the globe.

> *UNDP, HDR, 1994[3]*

36 Santishree D. Pandit

Academic arguments and pursuits regarding human security accelerated with the United Nations Development Programme's (UNDP's) emphasis on the individuals against the state. It indeed triggered the contest between the state and the individual, dominating the international relations to date. Human security, thus, fractured the dominant state-centric approach to international order. Having said so, it is also an admitted fact that state is still the stark realistic organ to look after the welfare of the individuals without the rise of any other viable alternative to it. It also forces to open the debate between who is to implement the human security, whether security debate can be extended to such a broad extent and whether individuals can be given such a high stake in the security paradigm.

Having said so, it is also pertinent to note that individuals are a core part of international order, the placement of them, as envisaged through the latest Human Development Index (HDI) is of importance, since the scale of insecurity among individuals is giving rise to several related sub-issues, like mass refugee creation and migration, affecting the international order, per se.

Traditional approaches to security study: human security perceived

> "Security is taken to be about the pursuit of freedom from threat and the ability of states and societies to main of change, which they see as hostile. The bottom line of security is survival, but it also reasonably includes a substantial range of concerns about the conditions of existence. Quite where this range of concerns ceases to merit the urgency of the "security" label (which identifies threats as significant enough to warrant emergency action and exceptional measures including the use of force) and becomes part of everyday uncertainties of life is one of the difficulties of the concept".[4]

Arguments regarding security have offered "securitization" concept, which is certainly the brainchild of the "Copenhagen school" of international relations.[5] The concept focuses, so its originators claim, on "societal security", as conceived within communities but not necessarily confined to state sovereignties".[6] Specifically, thus, the securitization thinkers concern themselves with the "how-possible" questions, namely, how, for example, does the notion of security come about or how is it politicized within a particular "objective" context. Securitization, therefore, makes us analyse why a particular issue is "securitized" as threats to the collective identity of whichever "referent object" is in question, including the state. Interestingly, this also means that security is necessarily a self-referential exercise in that it is through securitizing practices that a specific issue becomes a *security* issue. Going by this hypothesis, thus it can be argued that security is an issue-based subject and not an overall general subject. It is in fact objective, and not necessarily subjective in nature. In short, thus, a threat is a threat only because and only when it has been presented as such, not necessarily because there is an actual material or existential basis to it".[7]

For all the theoretical promise regarding "societal security", unanchored in the state, securitization remains very much a state-centred concept. However, "collective identity", inscribed as the endangered element within a securitized discourse, therefore becomes synonymous with national and state identity. From this hypothesis, it completely denounces the "imagined community" concept of Benedict Anderson.[8]

Construction and perception of threat, in such instances, thus, can easily fall prey to capture by a particular element of society and be used for its own purposes. It is not uncommon for states to go beyond contrasts with the "external world" in order to secure their identities, to the extent that this is possible, for others can justify as readily be found within state borders.[9] The arguments of "external threat", as the regular indictment of one's own citizenry through discourse and other practices, is part and parcel of the purchase of state or national identity. Thus, it is a practice of statecraft. In other subfields, scholars have argued heavily and highlighted the deployment of the rhetoric of "national security" by governments for perpetuating forms of "structural violence" against segments of their own citizenry.[10]

What this implies for human security is at best ambivalent. There is no substantial argument thus to defend the extension of security to the level of individual only. Arguing thus that "there are good reasons why the individuals and human race levels are difficult to construct as referent objects for security", Buzan, in an analysis of human security, has observed,

> States may not be a sufficient condition for individual security, and they may even be the main problem. . . . But they are almost certainly a necessary condition for individual security because without state it is not clear what other agency is to act on behalf of individuals. Because [the] state holds this position, they can claim their own right of survival over and above that of their individual citizens.[11]

Thus, bypassing the state is not a viable alternative to address human security issues.

Having said so, approach to the study of the subfield of 'human security' under security studies tends to have a three-level approach: individual, state and international systems.

Approaches to the security study also can be structured as traditional and non-traditional.

Non-traditional security (NTS) refers to security issues of the so-called low politics, including economic security, terrorism, environmental pollution, population explosion, drug trafficking, transnational crimes, AIDS and so on. These issues were often beyond the concerns of conventional security in the past.

A conception of security that is centred above all on the sanctity of the individual may be called human security. Thus, whether security can be extended to such a large extent? Or can be so all-encompassing? Is the main question first to be addressed?

Many non-traditional security threats are results of non-state actions rather than direct outcomes of actions of nation states. For instance, security problems concerning the environment, population, drug trafficking, AIDS and terrorism take place as a result of actions by many individuals and social groups. In most occasions, they are not necessarily products of state will but, instead, run counter to the orientation of policies and laws of states.

Unlike many traditional security issues, non-traditional security problems have their roots in the social, economic and cultural soil of different countries. Threats of NTS are rarely confined to certain single state or region. They instead often influence the living and development environment of the whole human beings. Once set in motion, they tend to show strong inertia, ineradicable in a short time and difficult to resolve by efforts of a few countries.

Human security and South Asia

In the specific region of South Asia, thus, the issue of human security will have to be addressed first from the state and then from the regional level. With territoriality as a stark reality of this region, where political boundaries mean life and death, where the states are at different levels of development and where most of the population of the world is concentrated, South Asia is indeed a challenge for the states, the region and the international order. South Asia is one of the most vulnerable regions in the world. NTS challenges loom large in this region, which includes severe food and water crises, a lack of health security, a high rate of poverty, climate refugees and so on, are creating severe impacts on human security as well as both domestic and regional stability in the region.

The nation states of this region are facing the crisis of intra-state rivalry as a result of which the intra-state conflict has taken the role of high politics. That has ushered in huge military spending by these states. In short, excessive military spending in South Asia has been one of the reasons for restricting expenditure on human security and NTS issues. For example, between 1998 and 2008, defence budgets increased by 41 percent. Developmental funds allocated thus for individuals of these countries have considerably reduced, which is causing problems for the citizens of these countries.

On a basic daily human requirement, in South Asia, the costs of food constitute the average household's largest expenditure. If food prices continue to rise without a matching increase in the incomes of people at the bottom of the economic ladder, it is estimated that approximately 100 million people could be pushed back into poverty.

Over the past twenty-five years, natural disasters and environmental degradation have killed nearly half a million people in South Asia and inflicted colossal damages estimated at US$59 billion. Thus, environmental disaster shall become a major threat to South Asian countries and particularly in recent years. The poorest people of the region are at most risk due to climate change. A large portion of the low-lying countries of South Asia can be submerged as a consequence of climate change and it may leave countless people as climate refugees.

The lack of long-term energy planning by South Asian countries has caused human suffering and significantly hindered the entire region's economic growth prospects.

While there is a growing recognition that both traditional security and NTS challenges require regional integration and regional solutions, a number of studies especially for the South Asia region have found that the main obstacle to such cooperation in countering NTS threats remains as mistrust and the absence of political will among the leaders.

Lack of water security in South Asia

Among several NTS issues prevalent in the South Asia region, which is incidentally one of the most populous subregions in Asia and the Pacific with relatively low agricultural, is water. As the most populous region of the world, this area is experiencing lower productivity due to low per capita water storage capacity and extremely high increase in groundwater usage and faster industrialization, as well as overexploitation and pollution, poor management and so on. It is found that about a billion people in this region do not use improved sanitation facilities while facing the daunting challenge to drinking water simultaneously. According to the latest report of the United Nations[12] on the lack of access to pure water, about "2.1 billion people lack access to safely managed drinking water services (WHO/UNICEF 2017)".[13] A detail list of the scarcity related to water is also provided in that report. The United Nations Environment Programme also cites that the poorest people in the region only have access to less than 5 percent of the planet's freshwater resources. A new Asia Society Leadership Group also warns that decreased access to a safe, stable water supply in Asia will have a profound impact on security throughout the region.

Lack of food security

According to the World Bank Report,[14] "[i]n South Asia, households who previously were living not far above the poverty line are likely to have fallen into poverty as the result of higher food prices".[15] The report states that "the World Bank is supporting Agriculture and Rural Development (ARD), with a project portfolio of $5.8 billion dollars to improve food production and security".[16] Again, according to the Food Price Watch,[17] global food prices increased 10 percent between June and July 2012, with staples such as wheat increasing 25 percent in the period. The crisis continues to have effects on food and nutrition security throughout South Asia. Bad weather, trade curbs, oil prices and biofuel diversions have all led to higher food prices, which destabilizes the incomes and food security of millions across the region. An alarming point of concern for taking preventive measures in this area.

Studies conducted in the South Asia region have confirmed that rises in the cost of food have led to a switch in consumption from nutrient-rich foods, such as vegetables, meats and other proteins to nutrient-poor staples, such as rice and wheat. There is also evidence of children's food intake being protected, typically at the

40 Santishree D. Pandit

cost of women's consumption.[18] The report also states that while the effects of the crisis are more severe, households may also sell productive assets, take children out of school and reduce expenses on health.[19] According to Kalpana Kochhar, chief economist of the South Asia region of the World Bank in the South Asia Economic Focus on Food Inflation, "[t]he poverty and nutritional impact of food price spikes on the poor is significant since they spend a larger fraction of their income on food than relatively better off individuals".[20] Another South Asia report, "Food Price Increases in South Asia: National Responses and Regional Dimensions",[21] found that households who previously were living not far above the poverty line are likely to have fallen into poverty as the result of higher food prices.

The report argued that while these are not preferred outcomes, they are sadly a reality for the many poor households that face rapidly fluctuating prices. Another similar type of report on South Asia, *Food Price Increases in South Asia: National Responses and Regional Dimensions*,[22] found that households who previously were living not far above the poverty line are likely to have fallen into poverty as the result of higher food prices.[23]

One of the most populous countries of South Asia, Bangladesh has remained a *chronically food-deficit country in the 1970s*.[24] The Food Security and Nutrition in Bangladesh report ends with this alarming observation:

> "Using a composite index of several dimensions of food insecurity, a recent study found that one-quarter of the population was food insecure in 2014, which amounts to 40 million people in absolute number. Among them, some 11 million people were found to suffer from acute hunger. Even larger numbers remain vulnerable to food insecurity in the face of periodic shocks. Furthermore, progress has been uneven across population groups – poorer groups have gained more slowly than richer groups, and women still bear the brunt when there is not enough food for the family. A further concern arises from recent slowdown in agricultural growth".[25]

In his research paper, "Status and Factors of Food Security in Pakistan", Abid Hussein[26] concluded that Pakistan is almost self-sufficient in food production even if only 30 percent of its production potential has been achieved. In spite of such a situation, the average food consumption of its people is still significantly below the standards set up for the national food security line. The study also established that the food gap in the country is 30 percent, while a 35 percent portion of available food is un-accessed due to various constraints spawned by physical, economic and sometimes natural factors. Out of the seven administrative units of Pakistan, Punjab and Sindh are the main food producing units while the Federally Administered Tribal Areas (FATA) are the most highly food deficit unit. Irrespective of the level of local food production, food gap still exists in all administrative units due to inefficient food procurement and distribution system, illegal movement of food commodities, poor monitoring of marketing systems, lower purchasing power and natural disasters.[27]

In terms of Sri Lanka, in the conclusion of the report of the National Strategic Review of Food Security and Zero Hunger, 2017,[28] it has been clearly stated that, ". . . clearly reveals that food and nutrition security in Sri Lanka, as targeted by SDG2, remains an unachieved social and economic goal in spite of numerous interventions by the government and development partners".[29]

In terms of India, ". . . has made rapid strides in improving rates of under- and malnutrition. Between 2006 and 2016, stunting in children below five years declined from 48% to 38%. Yet, India continues to have one of the world's highest child under nutrition rates, impacting the child's health and development, performance in school and productivity in adult life".[30]

Threat to health security

People in South Asia are at a higher risk of infectious diseases rather than from people in industrialized countries. The root causes are poverty, unhygienic living conditions, malnutrition, illiteracy, a lack of clean water, pollution, a lack of sanitary facilities and a lack of awareness about health security. For example, only in 2000, more than two-thirds of the estimated 3.7 million children died in South Asia due to infections such as pneumonia, diarrhoea and measles. The alarming health fact of South Asia is a reality. According to the World Bank Report of 2009, South Asia has both the highest percentage and the largest number of undernourished children in the world.

Malnutrition affects 43 to 46 percent of young children in India, Bangladesh and Nepal.

The number of malnourished people in the region as a whole rose from 283 million in 1990 to 314 million in 2005. Over 20 percent of children less than five years of age are underweight in most of the South Asian countries. Compared to 29 percent of the global population, about 74 percent of the South Asian population has no access to improved sanitation facilities. Another major challenge of health security in South Asia is HIV/AIDS.

According to the National AIDS Control Organization (NACO),[31] India HIV Estimation 2017 report, national adult (15–49 years) HIV prevalence in India is estimated at 0.22 percent (0.16–0.30 percent) in 2017.[32] In 2017, adult HIV prevalence is estimated at 0.25 percent (0.18–0.34 percent) among males and at 0.19 percent (0.14–0.25 percent) among females.[33] The adult HIV prevalence at the national level has continued its steady decline from an estimated peak of 0.38 percent between 2001 and 2003 to 0.34 percent in 2007, 0.28 percent in 2012, 0.26 percent in 2015 to 0.22 percent in 2017.[34]

In another world report it is estimated that 2.1 million people are living with HIV positive in India.[35]

On the other hand, although Pakistan's adult prevalence rate is 0.1 percent, the rate is increasing. Moreover, about 36 percent of the population of Sindh and Punjab was exposed to high arsenic levels in Pakistan.

The stark poverty and contrast of livelihood and earning make South Asia one of the poorest regions of the world. The region remains with large numbers of

42 Santishree D. Pandit

extreme poverty. Nearly 40 percent of the world's poor, who are earning less than a dollar a day, live in the region. South Asia is home to 22 percent of the world's population that generates only less than 2 percent of global income. South Asia is also the home of 23 percent of humanity, amongst whom 31.7 percent are living in abject poverty.

A report titled 'Food Price Increases in South Asia: National Responses and Regional Dimensions' states that due to high food prices, thousands of South Asians fall below the poverty line and remain at risk of starvation. If food prices continue to rise without a matching increase in incomes of people, it is estimated that approximately 100 million people could be pushed back into poverty.

Although economic growth has reduced poverty rate in South Asia, its total number of poor people has increased.

The number of poor people living on less than US$1.25 a day increased from 549 million in 1981 to 595 million in 2005. Only in India, the number of poor people increased from 420 million in 1981 to 455 million in 2005.

In addition, in India,44 percent of people live below the international one-dollar-per-day poverty line. Best estimates suggest that about one-third of the poor population in South Asia, between 135 and 190 million people, of whom 110 million to 160 million are Indians, is chronically poor. However, Bangladesh and Pakistan also have the majority of those remaining.

Environmental migration: a realistic threat to be addressed

One of the most severe threats of human security due to climate change is environmental migration in the region. The environmental scientists warn that by 2070, millions of people could become homeless in the Asia-Pacific region due to rising sea levels, whereas Bangladesh, India, Vietnam, China and Pacific islands are at most risk.[36] The Intergovernmental Panel on Climate Change Convention (IPCCC) has predicted that 1-metrerise in sea level may submerge about 17 to 20 percent of the total land mass of Bangladesh, creating 25 million to 30 million climate refugees.[37]

The Intergovernmental Panel on Climate Change (IPCC) also mentions that a rise in sea levels would have devastating consequences in low-lying areas of South, Southeast and East Asia, rendering millions of people homeless in Bangladesh, India and China. This will inevitably create environmental refugees. The 'Blue Alert, Climate Migrants in South Asia', a new Greenpeace report, warns that global temperature increase between 4°C and 5°C will drive mass migration in India, Pakistan and Bangladesh. It also estimates that more than 120 million people in India and Bangladesh will be homeless due to climate change. It is also a matter of concern that 22 million Bangladeshis could be displaced by 2050. The population of the island nation of the Maldives, off the west coast of India, is at high risk of becoming environmental refugees. The present scenario of human security in South Asia is raising alarming threats to regional security because no South Asian country, except Sri Lanka, ranks in the top hundred countries in the UNDP Human Development Index. The IPCC has identified South Asia as the most susceptible region in the world due to climate change. However, the international community also recognizes Bangladesh as most vulnerable due to hydro-geological and socio-economic factors, including flat, deltaic topography with low elevation; climate variability; high population density; poverty; and so on. The alarming human security scenario in South Asia, with special reference to India, is also quite alarming. India is one of the most disaster-prone countries in the world. About 1.2 billion people live in vulnerable areas to natural hazards such as floods, cyclones, droughts and earthquakes. About 76 percent of its coastline is prone to cyclones and tsunamis, while 59 percent of the country is vulnerable to earthquakes, 10 percent to floods and river erosion and 68 percent to droughts.

Conclusion

Probable approach to combat human security in South Asia

Preservation of water and global water partnership is urgency. Regional cooperation for enhanced water security in South Asia and trans-boundary water management are other viable approaches. Access to safe drinking water, joint watersheds and sustainable water management and equitable regional water sharing should be explored.

Nation states in this region should sit and think about intra-regional food trade, long-term planning for balanced food, SAARC Food Security Reserve, sustainable agriculture and a hunger-free South Asia; stable food prices and self-sufficiency in food and the creation of a regional food distribution system.

The elimination of contagious diseases, women's development activities; a reduction of the maternal mortality rate, a reduction of malnutrition, a clean and healthy South Asia, the professional exchange of doctors and trans-boundary health care services may also be explored.

What may be done for human security?

South Asian governments have not yet fully realized that military measures and domestic policies alone cannot overcome NTS challenges; rather, many of these challenges must be faced collectively and through regional cooperation.

A framework for managing regional disasters thus needs to be designed and executed effectively.

The framework should include a comprehensive strategy and action plan, cover institutional mechanisms, provide tools for mitigation measures and facilitate a legal framework and policy directions.

By comprehensive, plans should elaborate all-compassing actions, transcending state borders as necessary.

Special attention should be paid to strengthening networking among research institutions in the region working on NTS issues and encouraging them to provide inputs, ideas and strategies for joint action.

It is also equally important that this network of research institutions closely monitors and evaluates regional and subregional projects.

The Climate Action Plan (SAARC vision of 2025), the creation of the SAARC Food Security Reserve, a sustainable agriculture and a hunger-free South Asia, a regional food distribution system and inclusion of a regional food distribution system supported by regional transport system like 'Asian Highway Network' and 'Trans-Asian Railway' may constitute an important segment of SAARC's vision.

Thinking beyond nation-state boundary to combat human security

South Asian countries may launch an emergency food distribution system throughout the region. South Asian countries need to largely focus on reducing the threat of underlying causes of mortality risk, such as HIV and AIDS, malaria, tuberculosis and anaemia, among others. Launching the SAARC regional strategy with a particular focus on HIV/AIDS would substantiate SAARC's vision. South Asian governments may also develop different schemes like access to health service, insurance, housing schemes and social maternity benefits in order to reduce the rate of health risk.

Can there be a "South Asian Development Fund"

SAARC may consider raising a development fund and a poverty alleviation fund for the poor people in the region. South Asian countries may initiate concessional financing for the poorest member countries of the region. It may also design a poverty alleviation fund project for the eradication of poverty and the empowerment of rural and urban poor. SAARC could also launch an integrated approach to building institutions, providing micro-credit loans, granting small-scale infrastructure projects and so on. The purview of the poverty alleviation fund could also include rebuilding lives, fostering resilience and restoring assets for the poor.

Clash of interest

Barry Buzan argued that the state may not be a sufficient condition for individual security, and they may even be the main problem – the referent object. Buzan also argued that without the state, it is not clear what other agency is to act on behalf of individuals. Because states hold this position, they can claim their own right of survival over and above that of their individual citizens. Going by this hypothesis, in the context of South Asia, the most pressing question is, "Who should actually act on behalf of the individuals?" Is it the state? Is it a non-governmental organization? Is it a regional organization?

Collective effort to combat human security

> ". . . limited collectivities has proved the most amenable to securitization as durable referent objects. One explanation for this success is that such limited collectivities (states, nations, and, as anticipated by Huntington, civilizations) engage in self-reinforcing rivalries with other limited collectivities, and such interaction strengthens their 'we' feeling".[38]

Limited collectivities is, in fact, a reference to states; territoriality is a stark reality in Asia viz. South Asia; limited collective ability thus should be tested in this ground.

Holistic approach to human security in South Asia

The argument of whether 'freedom from fear' or 'freedom from want' is somehow overlapping:

The approach to resolve the human security situation should be holistic and all-encompassing in nature. Both 'freedom from fear' and 'freedom from want' are thus, more or less, two sides of the same coin, where both concepts seemingly overlapping. The requirement thus is to oversee the requirement of the individual or the groups affected through both of these overlapping concepts and thereafter move toward possible solutions.

Special positions of South Asia

South Asia by itself accounts for one-fifth of "We the peoples of the United Nations". Developments in South Asia must thus cut across the major fault line of the UN system with respect to the challenges of economic development, environmental protection, food and water security, democratic governance and human rights, nuclear war and peace, inter-state and internal conflicts and new security issues such as AIDS and international terrorism.

What happens in South Asia will surely shape the contours of the global community in the decades ahead. The scale of the problems faced in the region and the numbers of people involved are so huge that the success or failure of South Asia poses defining challenges to the core mandates of the UN as the global arena for problem-solving.

Resolute attitude to resolve the human security issue in South Asia

Can a "United Developmental Fund" be created? Can there be a "United Vigilance Group"? Can there be a "United Problem Resolving Group"? Can there be a "United Region Saving Group"?

Resolution of South Asia for human security

Intra-state conflict should not be allowed to come into force in resolving the human security issue. Cooperative security depends on mutual trust, transparency, attention to global norms and eschewing zero-sum approach to security. The nation states of South Asia require a broader look at the concept of national interest and cooperate accordingly to resolve the issues of human security. A comprehensive approach is thus an absolute requirement.

Resolution for combating human security

Dialogue, transparency, information sharing, capacity building, confidence-building measures and asymmetric reciprocity are at the heart of the cooperative approach to resolve the issues. Institution building is another important approach for the success of the cooperative initiative.

Institutional platforms are required at the national, regional and international levels. Broad participation of governmental, non-governmental and civil society stakeholders in these institutions are of utmost importance. Track II dialogues, thus, shall serve a useful purpose in this regard.

Nations need public commitment

Finally, the nations that are publicly committed to partnership and dialogue among civilizations must live up to this challenge. They should make clear that no state or people, as influential or powerful as they may be, can use the paradigm of dialogue to justify a strategy or policy of cultural superiority. The threat of culture wars and conflicts due to civilizational exceptionalism must be ended once and for all. The unity of humankind can only be preserved, and peace can only be maintained, through the recognition of the diversity of the human race with all that this entails in terms of an integrated policy of economic, social and cultural cooperation.

Notes

1 It was originally composed in Bengali possibly in 1900 under the title "Prarthana", meaning prayer. It appeared in the volume called 'Naibedya' in 1901. Later in 1911 Tagore himself translated the Bengali poem into English and that translation appeared as poem 35 in his Nobel-winning anthology "Gitanjali" (Song Offerings) published by the Indian Society, London in 1912.
2 *Human Development Report*, New York: Oxford University Press, 1994, p. 22, accessed 20 June 2018.
3 *Ibid*.
4 Barry Buzan, "New Patterns of Global Security in the Twenty-First Century", International Affairs, vol. 67, no. 3, 1991, pp. 432–433, accessed 25 June 2018.
5 Bill McSweeney, "Identity and Security: Buzan and the Copenhagen School", *Review of International Studies*, vol. 22, no. 1, 1996, pp. 81–96, accessed 30 June 2018.
6 See William T. Tow, "Alternative Security Models: Implications for ASEAN", in Ramesh Thakur and Edward Newman (eds.), *Broadening Asia's Security Discourse and*

Agenda: Political, Social, and Environmental Perspectives, Tokyo: United Nations University Press, 2004, accessed 15 June 2018.

7 *Ibid.*

8 See Benedict Anderson, *Imagined Communities: Reflections on the Origin and Spread of Nationalism*, London: Verso, 1983, accessed 20 June 2018.

9 See, for example, Syed Aziz-Al Ahsan, "Burma's Iron Hands Towards Ethnic Minorities: The Rohingya Plight", *Asian Profile*, vol. 21, no. 4, 1993, accessed 25 June 2018.

10 Muthaiah Alagappa, *Asian Security Practice: Material and Ideational Factors*, Stanford, CA: Stanford University Press, 1988, pp. 30–31, accessed 25 July 2018.

11 See Barry Buzan, "Human Security in International Perspective", a paper prepared for the ISIS Malaysia 14th Asia-Pacific Roundtable on *Confidence Building and Conflict Reduction*, Kuala Lumpur, 3–7 June 2000, accessed 10 August 2018.

12 For a detail report please see, www.un.org/en/sections/issues-depth/water/, accessed 15 August 2018.

13 *Ibid.*

14 www.worldbank.org/en/news/feature/2012/10/22/food-security-south-asia, accessed 15 September 2018.

15 *Ibid.*

16 *Ibid.*

17 http://siteresources.worldbank.org/EXTPOVERTY/Resources/336991-131196 6520397/Food-Price-Watch-August-2012.htm, accessed 12 October 2018.

18 www.worldbank.org/en/news/feature/2012/10/22/food-security-south-asia, accessed 30 October 2018.

19 *Ibid.*

20 https://businessjournalist.blogspot.com/2012/10/food-security-in-south-asia-worsening. html, accessed 14 August 2019.

21 www.worldbank.org/en/region/sar, accessed 15 November 2018.

22 *Ibid.*

23 *Ibid.*

24 www.wfp.org/sites/default/files/Bangladesh_Strategic_Review_Summary.pdf, accessed 25 November 2018.

25 *Ibid.*, p. 4.

26 www.emeraldinsight.com/doi/abs/10.1108/14468951211241146?journalCode=ijdi, accessed 15 December 2018.

27 *Ibid.*

28 https://docs.wfp.org/api/documents/WFP-0000039591/download/, accessed 15 January 2019.

29 *Ibid.*

30 http://in.one.un.org/un-priority-areas-in-india/nutrition-and-food-security/, accessed 20 January 2019.

31 http://naco.gov.in/hiv-facts-figures, accessed 25 January 2019.

32 *Ibid.*

33 *Ibid.*

34 *Ibid.*

35 www.avert.org/professionals/hiv-around-world/asia-pacific/india, accessed 27 January 2019.

36 www.commondreams.org/headlines06/1009-06.htm, accessed 29 January 2019.

37 "Climate Change and Bangladesh: A Perspective on Where Are We", 14 December 2007, http://archive.thedailystar.net/newDesign/news-details.php?nid=15364, accessed 29 January 2019.

38 Barry Buzan, Ole Waever and Jaap de Wilde, *Security: A New Framework for Analysis*, Boulder: Lynne Rienner Publishers, 1998, pp. 36–37.

4

HUMAN SECURITY IN SOUTH ASIA

The locus of a cooperative context

I. P. Khosla

Introduction

It is most appropriate to define *human security* by quoting from the United Nations Development Programme (UNDP) report of 1994, which said,

> Human security is the sense that people are free from worries, not merely from the dread of a cataclysmic world event but primarily about daily life. Human security is people centered while being tuned to two different aspects: it means, first, safety from such chronic threats as hunger, disease and repression. And second, it means protection from sudden and hurtful disruption in the patterns of daily life – whether in homes, in jobs, or in communities.[1]

So there were two early components of human security, freedom from want and freedom from fear.

Origins and evolution

The concept of security has evolved through four stages since the 1960s. Before that, security in its origins meant the safeguarding and protection of the sovereignty of the nation state from external threats, all of which were from one or more other nation states. In the Westphalian international order prevalent till then, each nation state was on its own and had to look for its security either singly, by arming itself, and/or through alliances which it might formulate against other nation states or groups of nation states, in its own best judgement. The theory for this international arrangement was realism or neo-realism. This aimed or hoped to formulate objective and universally applicable laws that would, in brief, remain unchanged by temporal or contextual variations. In the 1940s this essentially anarchic situation was given some shape by the emergence of the UN, which promised to unite the participating nations to maintain international peace and security, while under the relevant provisions of that organisation, collective security arrangements were created between different groups of nation states. But essentially this was based on the same theoretical foundations: both the target of threat and the source of threat to security remained the nation state.

Then in the 1960s, the first ideas emerged that the target of threat might be the individual or a community of individuals other than the nation state, such as a group of persons defined by language or religion or culture and the source from which they were threatened might be not only violence but also a lack of development, economic distress, hunger, disease and even a lack of political opportunity. For instance, Robert McNamara's writing in 1968 on "The Essence of Security" linked this concept closely with the economic, social and political progress that comes with development. There were others who postulated a similar concern to expand the scope of this concept. In brief, the concept of security was both widened by including sectors other than the military such as human development, economy, health and even education within its scope and was deepened by including, other than the nation state, individuals and other collectivities of people such as ethnic or linguistic or religious groups. This was the first stage in its evolution; it was a significant widening and deepening of the concept, but it was not yet called 'human security'.

That phrase came into use in the second stage of the evolving concept from the 1990s. One of the earliest examples was the Bonn declaration issued by the European Parliamentarians Conference on Building Human Security held in 1991. Global human security is, it said, "the absence of threat to human life, lifestyles and culture through the fulfillment of basic needs".[2] Taking this further, in January 1992 the UN Security Council issued a declaration recognising that economic, social, humanitarian and ecological sources of instability have become threats to peace and security. The same year UN Secretary-General Boutros Boutros Ghali called for an integrated approach to human security in his 'Agenda for Peace'. Another example was the Ramphal Commission on Global Governance, which issued a report in 1995 called 'Our Global Neighbourhood' which said "global security must be broadened from its traditional focus on the security of states" to include the security of people and the security of the planet,[3] thus presaging the intensive link that was to develop between security and the environment.

In the 1990s, in fact, human security moved towards centre stage among the various ideas of security, such as the earlier 'collective security', which continued its dominance within the UN system; cooperative security, which was about rivals working together rather than in competition; and comprehensive security, which sought to include other elements, still not well defined, within the concept. In any case, there was, in regard to human security, a multiplicity of pronouncements about what it could be, by political leaders, intellectuals, non-governmental organisations (NGOs) and the corporate sector, with groups and institutions set up to study it. Ideas about it were almost as diverse as the leaders, groups and institutions, although

50 I. P. Khosla

the defining ideas were still those of the UNDP report of 1994; most discussions of the subject would begin with the sentences of that report and elaborate from there. And it was further elaborated.

In 1999 the UNDP's human development report referred to seven threats: "The many threats to human security, differing for individuals at different times, fall into seven main categories: Economic insecurity, food insecurity, health insecurity, personal insecurity, environmental insecurity, community and cultural insecurity, and political insecurity".

The UN Secretary-General also elaborated in an interview to 'Choices' in 1999 and said,

> Human security, in its broadest sense, touches on the respect for the human rights of an individual and his or her personal dignity . . . ensuring that the average person- the individual the UN puts at the centre of everything that it does – has the basic necessities . . . health, education, and the possibility of living life to the fullest . . . human security also touches on the question of peace, which is more than the absence of war . . . we should be focusing on the security of the individual within the state, not on state security per se.[4]

Comparisons were made between the different approaches:

> [T]he UNDP and Canada are in agreement on 'security by what means'. They are in agreement in their discomfort with the traditional instruments of security of security – force, deterrence, balance of power. However, at a deeper level, they are in fairly strong disagreement. The UNDP's far greater emphasis on economic development contrasts with Canada's much greater accent on political development.[5]

Human security rapidly became one of the fastest growing areas for work by academics, NGOs, governments and even the corporate sector. A chairman's summary issued in May 2000 after the second meeting of the newly established Human Security Network Ministerial meeting "stressed the crucial role of NGOs as key non-state actors partners in developing, advocating, building and implementing human security" and "highlighted the role of the private sector . . . to enhance the value of good 'corporate citizenship' as a way to promote human security".[6]

There were many others. Harvard University set up a programme on the subject; institutions dealing with issues of governance, energy or the environment, poverty, health or education and a host of issues which had for years been on the international agenda tagged the term *security* or *human security* to their work, their books and articles and their speeches.

However, this subject was also looked on with some suspicion by those whose primary focus was on collective security through the system of military alliances, as it was felt that it would divert attention from the central threats that faced the world and that arose from ideological and great power rivalry.

The third stage included two developments. One was that ideas about human security matured and gained wider respectability even among those who have thus far been doubtful about their utility. Second, there was a definitive elaboration of the elements that would go into implementing the concept on the ground.

The three freedoms

This began with the 2000 Millennium Summit where the then UN Secretary-General Kofi Annan called on the world to advance the two aims of freedom from fear and freedom from want. The same year the government of Japan and the UN Secretariat launched a United Nations Trust Fund for human security, and by 2001 Canada and Norway sponsored a human security network to include all those countries which wanted a concrete action to get the concept implemented on the ground. Another step in the wider respectability that it gained during this stage was the establishment of a human security unit within the UN Secretariat. Then there was a Commission on Human Security, established in January 2001 in response to the UN Secretary-General's call at the 2000 Millennium Summit for a world "free from want" and "free from fear".

Broadly, different nation states emphasized different components. The Japanese and the UNDP have focused on freedom from want. In this context they have made several proposals which cover economic security, food security, the security of health and education, among others, and remedial actions would include debt relief, trade liberalization and an increase in aid disbursement for purposes such as health and education services. There is also an obvious link between such proposals and the achievement of the Millennium Development Goals (MDGs) such as the reduction of extreme poverty, so, in effect, human security has been tied to the achievement of the MDGs.

Freedom from fear has been emphasised by Canada and some others. This includes making the world safer by improving collective security arrangements, not the traditional ones based on alliance systems but initiatives to prevent catastrophic terrorism and the proliferation of weapons of mass destruction. Proposals in this regard include the need for a universal definition of terrorism as well as comprehensive convention against terrorism, for which, of course, India has been campaigning hard at the United Nations. Such a convention against nuclear terrorism has already been approved. There are other aspects such as support to countries during the transitions from armed conflict, action against organized crime, containing the illicit trade in small arms and implementing effectively the universally accepted ban on landmines.

Universal endorsement came in the fourth stage with the 2005 World Summit, which adopted an outcome document, paragraph 143 of which stated,

> We stress the right of people to live in freedom and dignity, free from poverty and despair. We recognize that all individuals, in particular vulnerable people, are entitled to freedom from fear and freedom from want, with an equal

opportunity to enjoy all their rights and fully develop their human potential. To this end, we commit ourselves to discussing and defining the notion of human security in the General Assembly.[7]

So we see that apart from the two freedoms specified earlier there is also a third: the 'opportunity to enjoy all their rights' for all individuals. This now, adding the call for 'freedom to live in dignity', therefore became a three-pronged approach to collective action. One of the central thoughts was that all three prongs were deeply intertwined, that there can be no development without security, no security without development, and neither without the universal application and protection of human rights. In order to reinforce this, the Secretary-General announced the creation of an independent and self-financing Democracy Fund to help governments strengthen their democratic practices and institutions. Other things were also done to pursue such ideas, including a call for the acceptance of a universal principle of the responsibility to protect civilian populations from crimes against humanity when governments are unwilling or unable to do so, strengthening the office of the UN High Commissioner for Human Rights and the creation of a new Human Rights Council, whose membership would be subject to approval by two-thirds of the General Assembly.

A common understanding

The adoption of General Assembly resolution 66/290 on 10 September 2012 was a significant milestone for the advancement of human security. In paragraph three of that resolution, the assembly agreed on a common understanding of human security which included the following:

(a) The right of people to live in freedom and dignity, free from poverty and despair. All individuals, in particular vulnerable people, are entitled to freedom from fear and freedom from want, with an equal opportunity to enjoy all their rights and fully develop their human potential;

(b) Human security calls for people-centred, comprehensive, context-specific and prevention-oriented responses that strengthen the protection and empowerment of all people and all communities;

(c) Human security recognizes the inter-linkages between peace, development and human rights, and equally considers civil, political, economic, social and cultural rights;

(d) The notion of human security is distinct from the responsibility to protect and its implementation;

(e) Human security does not entail the threat or the use of force or coercive measures. Human security does not replace state security;

(f) Human security is based on national ownership. Since the political, economic, social and cultural conditions for human security vary significantly across and within countries, and at different points in time, human security strengthens national solutions which are compatible with local realities;

(g) Governments retain the primary role and responsibility for ensuring the survival, livelihood and dignity of their citizens. The role of the international community is to complement and provide the necessary support to governments, upon their request, so as to strengthen their capacity to respond to current and emerging threats. Human security requires greater collaboration and partnership among governments, international and regional organizations and civil society;

(h) Human security must be implemented with full respect for the purposes and principles enshrined in the Charter of the United Nations, including full respect for the sovereignty of states, territorial integrity and non-interference in matters that are essentially within the domestic jurisdiction of states. Human security does not entail additional legal obligations on the part of states.[8]

It is important to bear four characteristics of this concept in mind, as it has developed over the years, and has been underlined by different institutions and bodies. One is that it is people-centred, which means that you have to start thinking about security as being about people or individuals, who may then be grouped into ethnic, religious, language or national groups, but it will be the individual at the centre of the thought, not the social entity and not certainly the abstract entity called 'state' or 'nation'. People and the groups that they form themselves into, need their security to be assured. This does not mean that state security is omitted, but it derives from the need to give security to individuals, not from the need to protect the state; national or state security is then a component of human security, which takes primacy, not the other way around.

The Commission on Human Security (CHS), for example, in its final report Human Security Now, defines human security as "to protect the vital core of all human lives in ways that enhance human freedoms and human fulfilment".[9]

People-centred also means the need to build on people's strengths and aspirations. Thus, people have a definite role in assuring or delivering human security. When NGOs or other civil society groups are formed or ethnic, language, religious or other groups are formed and wish to work to enhance human security, they need to be assured a suitable role by state organs and by the international community. In this version, human security is about protection as well as empowerment, it is top down as well as bottom up.

The second characteristic is that it has to be comprehensive, meaning, first, that it covers all aspects, all threats to security, whether economic, environmental, health, education, physical threats and threats to rights and dignity, and these are just a few of the examples, and, second, that all these threats could be interconnected: environmental threats can lead to economic threats, and those, inturn, could even lead to damage to people's dignity or physical safety. This will also involve, among other things, creating political, social, environmental, economic, military and cultural

54 I. P. Khosla

systems that together give people the building blocks of survival, livelihood and dignity. The CHS has highlighted this aspect in particular.

Third, it is context-specific. As such, human security acknowledges that insecurities vary considerably across different settings and advances contextualized solutions that are responsive to the particular situations they seek to address.

Fourth, it is prevention-oriented; in other words, it works towards conflict prevention and peace building strategies in order to find sustainable solutions to those problems, both structural and immediate, that cause fear, want and humiliation, violations of the three freedoms that lie at the heart of the concept.

The first two of the preceding four characteristics are widely accepted, and generally without controversy, but the third has been the subject of much debate, and here theory and context, both for assessing threats as well as possible actions to deal with them have been largely developed in the West, while the fourth is also of doubtful applicability or validity as far as the South Asian region is concerned.

Relevance for South Asia

In brief, these contexts and prevention-oriented actions are often not relevant for South Asia. Three examples may be given by way of illustrating this, though it applies to many other areas of human security, and here the following parameters for the implementation of human security measures in our region are important. First, in the evolving paradigm the state has often been counter posed to the individual; indeed, it is sometimes argued that it is the main threat to human security. Such an approach cannot be applied in South Asia where state building is a work in progress and modes of strengthening it are dominant considerations in political life. Second is the increasingly important role for international actors through peacemaking, peace building and even peace enforcement, with or without the consent of the state concerned.

Of notable importance here is the Outcome Document of the 2005 United Nations World Summit (mentioned earlier), which was followed up and formulated in the Secretary-General's 2009 *Report on Implementing the Responsibility to Protect*. The three pillars of the responsibility to protect are

> First, the State carries the primary responsibility for protecting populations from genocide, war crimes, crimes against humanity and ethnic cleansing, and their incitement; Second, the international community has a responsibility to encourage and assist States in fulfilling this responsibility; And third, the international community has a responsibility to use appropriate diplomatic, humanitarian and other means to protect populations from these crimes. If a State is manifestly failing to protect its populations, the international community must be prepared to take collective action to protect populations, in accordance with the Charter of the United Nations.[10]

Of these three pillars the first is acceptable as far as conditions in South Asia are concerned, and even the second may, under appropriate circumstances, be applicable. As for the third, this is not applicable in South Asia, where there is widespread mistrust of the motivations of international actors, up to and including the United Nations and its organs. For prevalent conditions in our region, it needs to be established that it is the government of a country that bears the primary responsibility to protect its citizens; the international community may provide assistance, but this can only be at the request of the concerned state authority; it cannot be violative of the necessary respect for sovereignty or amount to interference in internal affairs. Furthermore, it cannot, for the time being, have a standard formula in terms of implementation. It is still a concept, not a norm of international law; there are still different interpretations, if not controversies regarding many aspects of this. So, in considering this whole question, it is, by consensus, reached through negotiation and discussion that agreement can be reached, not by the imposition of ideas which may have the appearance but not the reality of international law.

Third, at the other end of the spectrum, an increasingly important and even independent role is being assigned to non-state actors, civil society, NGOs and even multinational corporations. In our region, such actors may have a role to play but it is and will remain a small one firmly subordinate to the state.

We need to pinpoint specific contexts in which human security may be promoted in our region, as a whole, through cooperative action, as well as how cooperative action may be promoted by joint regional approaches to human security. For this purpose, several parameters need to be established. The four parameters recounted in the following are only illustrative, not exhaustive. First, that the state will be the lead actor (although others could also have a role) which contrasts with suggestions which are often heard about the need to curb the role of the state. Second, the international (in this case, the regional) community, through state or non-state actors, will have only a subordinate role to play; there is justifiable distrust, based on historical experience, of the hidden agendas of such actors. Third, all action has to be cooperative, with none disagreeing, which rules out the possibility of the military option while implicitly insisting on wide consultation with all stakeholders both about the outlines of a joint approach and the kind of action to take. Fourth, areas of activity should be those where cooperative action has already been successful.

Human security in South Asia

There are many such areas and many agreements that illustrate that cooperation can be successful though most commentators would assert that it goes forward much too slowly. Indeed, the very founding charter of SAARC can and should be seen as a call for the promotion of human security.

The principal goal of the charter in Article II is to place people at the centre of development, while the highest priority shall be accorded (Article III) to the alleviation of poverty in all South Asian countries. Other aims are there: promoting the health of the population; education, human resource development and youth

56 I. P. Khosla

mobilization; promotion of the status of women and of the rights and well-being of the children; all these are, of course, crucial elements of human security.

The sixteenth SAARC Summit, Thimphu, 2010, adopted climate change as its theme, along with a statement on climate change. There are many others: the trafficking in women and children, food security; there is also a SAARC Social Charter setting out goals in all such cases. Furthermore, there is now increasingly successful coordination on international issues, with regular regional ministerial meetings before international gatherings for this purpose, indicating that the prospects for cooperation, despite the many who are sceptical, do exist and can be strengthened.

We can examine some of these in more detail.

There are a number of broad socio-economic goals adopted by SAARC which serve national, regional and international purposes or commitments, and all of these go to enhance human security. The goals include, *inter alia*, the areas of poverty eradication or alleviation, wider social improvement, agriculture and climate change. These goals are often adapted to the region from prior international commitments; they are common to the region, to be pursued by national means, but the very fact of regional adoption gives added impetus and urgency to those responsible for achieving them. Furthermore, mutual regional commitment to them adds to the sense of regional solidarity, a process which is reinforced by the frequent ministerial- and official-level meetings (apart from those by NGOs) held to assess and evaluate progress in achieving them. Such meetings add to the social learning process.

Some of the most important such goals are given here.

Poverty alleviation came on to the SAARC agenda at the sixth summit. There had previously been a decision to develop a regional plan with specific targets, a basic needs plan, but it was only at the sixth summit that the leaders homed in on poverty as important enough to deserve more special attention. Now the Independent South Asian Commission on Poverty Alleviation (ISACPA) was established to report to the seventh summit. This it duly did and said poverty in the region should be eradicated by 2002, so the leaders decided to commit their governments to this goal 'unequivocally' through an Agenda for Action, a good example of the way a regional goal can give urgency to national goals. This was also the reason for a number of meetings: 1995 was declared the year of poverty eradication; a three-tier mechanism was set up; nodal agencies were designated by the governments, which also held meetings; then there were dialogues with regional and international funding institutions, to which the Asian Development Bank, the World Bank and others contributed, which led to more meetings, now often outside the region.

Eradication remained the goal until 1998, and then there was the UN Millennium Summit of 2000 which suggested world poverty be, not eradicated, but reduced by half and not soon but by 2015, as one of the MDGs. So then the SAARC goal was also suitably modified; it was decided to reinvigorate SAARC activities in the context of regional and global commitments to poverty reduction. A new and reconstituted ISACPA was agreed on. This submitted its report in 2004, with a 'Road Map towards a Poverty Free South Asia', strategic priorities, core targets and a list of six initiatives.

Another example is the SAARC Social Charter, which was inspired by the World Summit for Social Development, Copenhagen, 1995, where it was decided to put people at the centre of development, create the environment to enable people to achieve social development and eradicate absolute poverty; each of these aims accord well with those of human security. The successful adoption of collective SAARC positions prior to this led to the idea that the region should have its own social development goals, translated and modified versions of the world goals. An inter-governmental Expert Group was set up; the SAARC Secretary-General drafted a paper and gave it to the experts, which was ready by 2004 for signature, signed and hailed as 'a historic development, which would have a far-reaching impact on the lives of millions of South Asians'. Thereafter, National Coordinating Committees were set up in each member state for its implementation, and then an annual meeting of the heads of those committees (along with delegations from different ministries concerned) was agreed on, as well as Expert Group meetings. A large number of meetings came out of the Social Charter.

The third example is the Charter of Democracy. This goes back to the Agenda for Democratization presented in December 1996 by the UN Secretary-General to the 81st session of the UN General Assembly (UNGA) and to the Universal Declaration on Democracy adopted by the Inter-Parliamentary Union in September 1997. Then, ten years later, the UNGA resolved to observe 15 September each year as International Day of Democracy. In that resolution, it is affirmed that 'there is no single model of democracy' and that democracy does not belong to any country or region, nor does the resolution have specific items on the independence of the judiciary or unconstitutional changes of government. But when translated and modified for South Asia, and Bangladesh was the initiator of the move, those specific items were included.

This was done at the sixteenth summit, 2010, a time when all member states could take pride in having evolved into multiparty democracies but still faced problems in ensuring good governance. So the Bangladesh idea was that a SAARC Democracy Charter should be drawn up, for which it offered to circulate a concept paper. And it was; based on the Bangladesh paper, a tentative charter was drafted and even placed on the SAARC Secretariat website. However, its contents, including the commitment to reinforce democratic practices, guarantees for the independence of the judiciary and renunciation, 'unequivocally' of any unconstitutional change of an elected government, proved too big a pill to swallow for some governments; no more was heard about it.

Success of broad goals

By contrast, some of the broad goals were resoundingly successful, not always in achieving their aims, which are often too lofty, but in getting enthusiastic agreement among all the member states. Two examples are given in the following.

One is in the area of the environment, another key element in the context of human security. The third SAARC summit, 1987, first took cognizance of the need for regional cooperation in this area by commissioning a study on the causes and consequences of natural disasters and the Protection and Preservation of the Environment; this was completed by 1991. In parallel, the fourth summit, in 1988, commissioned a study on the greenhouse effect, which was completed by 1992. So there was now a large number of recommendations regarding regional action to be taken on the whole subject. Accordingly, a technical committee was set up to oversee how these recommendations could be implemented and began functioning from January 1993. SAARC environment ministers started meeting from 1992 and have, since then, met regularly, about once every two years, thus further elaborating regional action as well as consolidating the common or collective positions taken by the member states in international negotiations on the subject.

As for regional action a SAARC Environmental Action Plan adopted by the ministers in October 1997 led to the establishment of a SAARC Coastal Zone Management Centre, or SCZMC in 2004, a Forestry Centre, SFC, in 2007 as also action on climate change, specifically a Dhaka Declaration and SAARC Action Plan on Climate Change adopted by the ministers in July 2008 and endorsed by the summit a month later. A number of studies were commissioned: a Marine Initiative, a Monsoon Initiative, a Mountain Initiative and a Climate Related Disasters Initiative. All this also led to a SAARC Convention on Cooperation on Environment, signed in Thimphu at the sixteenth summit (which had as its theme 'Towards a Green and Happy South Asia') 2010, as well as a Thimphu Statement on Climate Change, which set up an expert group on the subject and a SAARC Goodwill Ambassador for Climate Change, appointed for two years, 2010–12.

It has also been possible to coordinate collective positions at international conferences on the subject, based on the adoption of a rights-based approach, convergence of per capita emissions of the developing and developed countries on an equitable basis and recognition of historic responsibility.

There was also action on disaster management. Having commissioned a study on the subject in 1987, the leaders saw the urgency of the matter at the May 1994 World Conference on Natural Disaster Reduction, at Yokohama which had decided, given the increased impact of natural disasters in recent years, that disaster prevention, mitigation, preparedness and relief, the four central elements, be incorporated into development plans at community, national, subregional and international levels, all of which went into a Yokohama Strategy and Plan of Action for a Safer World, which was reviewed in 2000. Meanwhile, the UNGA had declared the 1990s as the International Decade for Natural Disaster Reduction; another World Conference on Disaster Reduction followed in 2005, leading to a Framework for Action, 2000–2015. SAARC developed regional versions of all this. A SAARC Disaster Management Centre was established in New Delhi in 2006, while a Natural Disaster Rapid Response Mechanism or NDRRM was mandated by the fifteenth summit, 2008; and a regional Agreement on Rapid Response to Natural Disaster was signed at the seventeenth summit in 2011.

The second example is from the general area of food and agriculture. This has been a key component of regional cooperation. As early as September 1981 the regional study group on agriculture convened in Dhaka; then there were the working group meetings in 1982 and the technical committee meetings in 1983; at the same time meetings at the expert and technical levels were held on specific subjects, for instance, the application of statistics in agricultural research; the exchange of technical information; and on potato cultivation, all even before the launch of SAARC in 1985. The technical committee met often, seventeen times between 1983 and 1999; a regional centre SAARC Agricultural Information Centre (SAIC) was set up in 1988, which brought out a number of publications, which has been its major strength, although the ministers did not meet that often, once in 1996, then in 2002 to prepare for the World Food Summit and then in 2006.

In the area of food security, a major initiative was the establishment of a food security reserve by an agreement signed in 1987, to provide a cushion against regional food shortages. Each member state contributed to it, and the total reserve stood at 241,000 tonnes in 2002. The idea behind this was not that member states put this somewhere central but keep it as a reserve for regional use so that member states could draw on it in case of such calamity that its own food reserves were insufficient. But it was never used, despite the frequent occurrence of food shortages in one member state or another after it was established. So then an agreement on a SAARC Food Bank was signed in 2007 to act, again, as a food security reserve in case of food shortages. The total held was increased and the agreement was ratified by all member states (including Afghanistan, the new member) by July 2012. A Food Bank Board has also been set up.

Notes

1 UNDP Human Development Report 1994, New Dimensions of Human Security, New York: UNDP, 1994, http://hdr.undp.org/en/reports/global/hdr1994, accessed 9 May 2019.
2 P.R. Chari and Sonika Gupta (eds.), *Human Security in South Asia: Energy, Gender, Migration and Globalization*, New Delhi: Social Science Press, 2003, p. 25.
3 *Our Global Neighbourhood: The Report of the Commission on Global Governance*, Oxford: Oxford University Press, 1995, http://clclibrary-org.tripod.com/cgg2.html, accessed 25 June 2019.
4 Interview to Choices, www.undp.org/dpa.choices.december99/kofi.htm, accessed 15 December 2014.
5 Kanti Bajpai, "Human Security, Concept and Measurement", Kroc Institute Occasional Paper, No. 19, p. 35, August 2000.
6 Second Ministerial Meeting of the Human Security Network, Lucerne, 11–12 May 2000, Chairman's Summary.
7 UN General Assembly, 2005, World Summit Outcome, para 143. UNGA Res. A/60/1 of 24 October 2005.
8 *Human Secuirty Handbook*, New York: United Nations, January 2016, pp. 6–7.
9 www.humansecurity.chs.org/final report/pdf, accessed 14 November 2012, cited in Human Security in Theory and Practice, by the Human Security Unit of the UN, p. 5, 2009.
10 Report of the Secretary-General, *Implementing the Responsibility to Protect*, 12 January 2009, http://responsibilitytoprotect.org/SGRtoPEng%20(4).pdf, accessed 25 June 2019.

5

IS THE REGION READY?
CAN THE STATE DELIVER?
ESSAY FROM INDIA

D. Suba Chandran

Introduction

The concept of security has been on a roller roller-coaster ride since the 1980s. Major international developments during the last four decades have impinged substantially on the expansion of security concept at times and its narrow interpretation. If the post–Cold War 1990s witnessed a particular trend in making the idea of security elastic to include multiple issues, the post-9/11 2000s saw a cautious approach in that expansion.[1] The emergence of human security within the security discourse as an independent sphere should be seen in this context.

Recent developments in West Asia, especially Iraq and Syria, and the subsequent refugee crisis have brought back the expansion process. Human security as an approach is likely to receive more attention not only in West Asia but also in South and South-East Asia.

As a concept, human security also became a part of an expansion at the regional levels as well. South Asia witnessed a series of studies on the subject during the 1990s and the following decades. As an independent line of inquiry within the security fold, although the concept of human security entered South and South-East Asia later than in the developed world, as a field, it has already witnessed indigenous literature on the subject.[2] In fact, a later discourse attempted to even "reintroduce" the debate on human security in South Asia.[3]

Despite "introduction" and "reintroduction", is "human security" as a concept and an independent security discipline placed well within the larger security discourse in South Asia? Or is it too early to expect the state to deliver on human security? This chapter looks into two primary questions – whether the region is ready to address human security issues and whether the state can deliver.

I. From global to regional: the expansion of security studies

Although a section in South Asia would like to attribute and trace the concept of human security to Mauryan, and even the mythical Mahabharata and Ramayana, as an independent security discipline, it evolved in the West. Even in the West, it did not appear on its own and suddenly; there has been gradual progress since the end of Second World War.

After the Second World War, "security" as an independent discipline focused mainly on the state. The security of the state was seen as primary importance; hence, the definition centred on it. Securing the state from external threats was seen as a primary focus of security studies in this phase. As Walter Lippman defined it "a nation is secure to the extent to which it is not in danger of having to sacrifice core values, if it wishes to avoid war, and is able, if challenged, to maintain them by victory in such a war".[4]

The preceding definition led the security discipline for the next five decades. Since external security was perceived as a primary threat, securing the state from the same became the primary objective. External security in this context was further defined primarily from a military perspective. As a result, the state became the central and dominant element of the security discourse.

The preceding trend continued during the Cold War; this phase, at least until the 1980s, continued with no major challenge to state as the dominant actor in the security studies. As David Baldwin explained, during this phase,

> security studies were composed mostly of scholars interested in military statecraft. If military force was relevant to an issue, it was considered a security issue; and if military force was not relevant, that issue was consigned to the category of low politics.[5]

During the 1990s, there was a steady questioning of the preceding approach. Although one could identify this trend in the 1980s itself, the end of the Cold War and the new problems fastened this process. Scholars started questioning whether the state should be the only attention of security studies and whether such an approach is adequate to deal with contemporary problems. A series of studies emphasised the need for an expansion of security studies.[6]

The end of the Cold War made many realize that military power was "not the only source of national security" and military threats were "not the only dangers that the states face". It was felt that security studies of the Cold War were inadequate or narrowly focused; hence, a need arose to redefine or revision the concept of security. This initiated a debate on whether the ambit of security studies needs to be enlarged. Although a section cautioned against such an expansion, the trend towards an expansion of security studies continued. For instance, Stephen Walt warned that such an expansion of security concept "would destroy

62 D. Suba Chandran

its intellectual coherence and make it more difficult to devise solutions to any of these solutions".[7]

The previous change in approach during the 1990s again was led primarily by scholars from the West during the initial period. However, this phase also witnessed scholars from South Asia started focusing on the subject. The following reasons could be identified for the emergence of human security as a research focus, if not an independent discipline. First, developments within South Asia, especially related to ethnic conflicts and the (in)ability of the state to deal with the situation at least during the initial phase accentuated this approach. For instance, India witnessed a violent armed struggle led by the militant groups in Jammu and Kashmir (J&K) and in the Northeast, so, too, did Sri Lanka. Second, non-state actors became a reality for the region, with groups with sectarian and criminal backgrounds using violence against the state, but in the process civil society bore the primary brunt. Pakistan, for instance, in the 1990s witnessed a series of sectarian violence all over the country, while the ethnic conflict in Sindh, especially in Karachi, saw increasing human casualty. India witnessed a series of terror attacks in Mumbai led by criminal groups, with common men becoming the victims. Third, the state in South Asia, for the first time became more embroiled with conflicts within than outside. While the state had a clear approach towards its external conflicts, it lacked a strategy to deal with internal conflicts. Besides, the use of the military to address internal conflicts did pose a huge challenge for the organization; while the military was trained to address challenges externally, their ability to deal with domestic conflicts facing their own citizens had its own repercussions in terms of direct damage and the collateral. As a result, human rights violations of citizens became an important discourse in South Asia during the 1990s.

Until then, as newly independent countries, most of South Asia during the Second World War pursued the same trend that the West witnessed since the 1940s. The partition in 1947; the first and second India–Pakistan wars during 1947–48, 1965 and 1971; break up of Pakistan; the Soviet invasion of Afghanistan – all these developments had a crucial impact in state-centric security pursuits. Besides external threats, problems of nation building and ethnic conflicts within most of South Asia had its own implications on the security discourse.

To conclude, in South Asia, the following developments impinged on the evolution of human security studies as an independent discipline. Although some scholars would like to extend the argument to *Vasudhaiva Kutumbakam* – that the world is one family as explained in ancient Indian text, human security as a discipline and a study entered into South Asia only recently. The following aided its growth in the region.

> First, the role of the military in politics and civil–military relations played a substantial role in the centricity of state. Pakistan, Bangladesh and Nepal, in particular, have witnessed the military and monarchy playing a substantial role in civilian administration either directly or indirectly. As a result, the security narrative in these countries was built predominantly with the state as a central actor.

Second, most of South Asia still remains afflicted with ethnic conflicts internally. Pakistan, India, Nepal and Sri Lanka witnessed the emergence of ethnic conflicts; while some of them got addressed, most of them continue even today. Bangladesh and Bhutan also had their own problems with the ethnic issue, though they were addressed by the state. Sri Lanka witnessed the end of war, with the collapse of the Liberation Tigers of Tamil Eelam, but this has not brought the ethnic conflict to an end. The minority community still feels the issues are to be settled politically. Nepal saw the end of Maoist insurgency but coinciding with the emergence of another conflict in the Terai region with the Madhesis. Although a new constitution is in place, the Madhesis are not satisfied yet. In India's Northeast and in J&K, the violence have come to an end but not the conflicts. So is the case with Baluchistan in Pakistan.

Besides the ethnic conflicts, in recent years, one could also see an ascendancy of sectarian violence. India, in particular, has also been witnessing Naxal violence. As a result, the state in most of South Asia remains in firefighting mode than a welfare one.

Third, the emergence of political parties, parliamentary politics and constitutions in South Asia has been stunted. Except for India, the rest of South Asia has not experienced a prolonged parliamentary rule as enshrined by a supreme constitution and protected by an independent judiciary. A functional parliament, strong constitution and independent judiciary for the state, if the concept of security has to expand and convert the former into a welfare one. Most of the developed world has succeeded in having the preceding three in place, which has further provided the space for the expansion of security, including human security.

Fourth, security as an independent academic discipline in South Asia is yet to find its roots. Security is studied and taught either as a part of political science or international relations. Even those institutions that teach political science and international relations rely more on the West for literature, as the region is yet to produce a coherent security thought of its own.

Fifth, the role of non-governmental organizations (NGOs) and think tanks in South Asia – is slowly taking root but is far from becoming strong, as has been the case in the West. As a result, the security debate is predominantly shaped by the state and those institutions supported by various governmental institutions. Even within the state, the "security" establishment led by the military and the Ministry of Home/Internal Affairs have a disproportionate contribution to the debate on security. The preceding institutions define and interpret what the security threats are and propose how they could be addressed.

Sixth, the role of institutions of democracy both at the national and provincial levels – the national and state legislatures – do not play a lead role in defining and shaping the security discourse. As mentioned earlier the "security" establishment has taken a role, but the democratic institutions need to

64 D. Suba Chandran

take the blame, for they have abdicated their responsibility to the security forces. In terms of fighting militancy, the security forces to have a major role, but once the violence is addressed, the "political" establishment has failed to move in. As a result, one could see a trend in Baluchistan, J&K, Nepal, the Northeast and Sri Lanka; the political leadership in these regions still prefers to fire from the shoulders of the security forces instead of taking direct action.

II. Human security in South Asia: emerging trends and challenges

Undoubtedly, recent years have witnessed a renaissance in human security studies in South Asia, within a larger ambit of non-traditional security. Led by independent think tanks and research institutes, scholars from South Asia have been increasingly focusing and writing on human security issues from a regional perspective.

Increasingly, research studies on the environment, health, poverty, food security, water security and so on have been directly and indirectly focusing on human security. But an important aspect of this growth/renaissance has been – its limitation. The expansion is taking place more at the academic level, led by independent think tanks and research institutes, than at the governmental levels. Scholars from the academic discipline in South Asia have a larger exposure to global literature on the subject and have been writing profusely underlining the need for South Asia to address human security issues. As a result, civil society is ahead the state in understanding and projecting the human security needs in South Asia.

Second, as a result of the previously mentioned imbalance, the harsh reality for South Asia is reflected in its budget allocation for issues that would address human security issues. From education to health, major sectors of human security received insufficient attention and allocation. A cursory look at the budget expenditure over the last two decades and its breakdown in terms of individual sectors would underline the low focus that the government in South Asia has towards human security. Alternatively, defence expenditure all over South Asia remains high.

Third, in South Asia, a section has been building a narrative pitching military security against human security. This debate with an "either–or" focus will neither help reduce the defence expenditure nor pressure the state into spending more on developmental projects. Given the recent trends, the state in South Asia is unlikely to yield to any pressure to divert military expenditure into developmental activities. Such pressure is likely to backfire.

In short, although the idea of human security in South Asia has considerably grown, the state is yet to seriously pursue it. Worse, a section within the state sees the idea of human security as driven by a Western agenda, and those who are propagating it as agents of external actors. Fears of the state, however, are not truly unfounded. Many within civil society do agree that there are few NGOs in South Asia, driven by financial reasons than humanitarian, projecting a particular image of the state. However, the state views all the NGOs that are working on non-traditional security issues with the same prism. This approach does not give enough space for the debate on human security to be carried into the state discourse.

Does the preceding mean the debate on human security will remain outside the state's focus? It need not be.

The debate on human security cannot be either or projection. Both the state and civil society will have to work together. While civil society may be well aware of the problems of human security, the solutions are with the state. The civil society cannot expect the state to deliver on human rights yet pitch the latter as the problem.

Civil society should understand the recent changes at the South Asia level. For the first time in recent decades, the region has become democratic, with elected representatives having the power to legislate and execute. During the last few years, all countries of South Asia witnessed democratic elections, resulting in having an elected legislature.

Civil society should ensure that elected governments take responsibility for governance and delivery instead of abdicating their responsibilities to the security forces. Unfortunately, this trend continues, despite civil society providing a clear mandate to the governments. Consider the following developments during 2016–17 in the region. Pakistan has been delaying the census survey for the seven years for political reasons; when it decided in 2017, after being pressured by the Supreme Court, it had asked the military to assist the census process! Similarly, both the federal and provincial governments in India have been reluctant to pursue a political process in post-violence societies in J&K and the Northeast. Instead of minimizing the footprints of the security forces and allowing the political processes led by the state governments, both provincial and federal actors prefer that the security forces continue. The recent deterioration of the situation in J&K during 2016–17 is a result of this approach. Similarly, in Sri Lanka there is debate about engaging the security forces in civilian administration. While such an option may be tempting and even pragmatic to a section in the government, the state should desist "civilianizing" the security forces, for the dangers of government getting "militarized" is greater.

III. Human security in South Asia: the road ahead

To conclude, South Asia today is better placed to address issues of human security, than during the earlier decades. However, this has to be a partnership between the state and society; if this has to be the case, then the human security debate should certainly avoid state vs society debate.

Second, given the inherent weaknesses of the state, perhaps some in the region may pursue the human security approach faster than the other. For instance, Bhutan, given its tradition and culture, and the population may be better placed to take the lead than, for example, Bangladesh in the immediate future. In fact, Bhutan has already started the process with its emphasis on "Gross Domestic Happiness" project. The civil society in South Asia will have to be patient and try to learn from each other instead of asking for a copy-and-paste process.

66 D. Suba Chandran

Third, civil society and the academic community also will have to relook the process of securitization overdrive in South Asia. Today, invariably every issue is brought under the "security umbrella" in the contemporary discourse. From the sharing of waters within and outside the national boundaries to managing fishermen's livelihood – issues are increasingly getting placed in a different paradigm with security as the primary driver. Such an elevation also ultimately leads to dangerous theories (such as the Water Wars), undermines the role-played by different civil society organizations and places the state (especially the federation) at a predominant position. "Bringing the state in" and "securitizing" issues complicate the human security dialogue process.

Fourth, the judiciary is becoming extremely active in South Asia. One could even say that there is an element of judicial activism in the region. Learned courts, in recent years, have been interpreting the constitution and legislation not in a narrower and stricter sense but by keeping in mind the larger objective and spirit behind them. Intervention from judiciary can help the state to promote human rights situation in two ways. First, it provides an opportunity to the state for course correction; being a pillar of the governance yet outside the elected government, the judiciary not only plays an independent role in checking the role of the state but also provides valuable advice and, at times, even a road map for the state. For instance, during the recent years, much legislation by the state, especially relating to the environment – in terms of addressing pollution came through judicial interventions. Second, the judiciary also plays an important role for the state by ensuring the public faith in the system. In a region like South Asia, it is pertinent that the civil society, especially the youth have faith in the system.

Finally, the new media poses both an opportunity and a challenge to the state in dealing with human security issues. Given the recent revolution in communication, media, especially the role of social media, has become important. However, it can become a tool and a thorn for the state to address human security issues. Whether it is a failure of justice or disaster management, social media is extremely powerful in sharing the news and building public opinion. For instance, an abuse of authority by police in the street can become national and global news in real time, even before the officer could realize it. At the same time, it can help the state to convey, for instance about relief operations and availability of resources during a flood situation. This new media, thus, has both positive and negative roles to play in addressing human security in South Asia. The state has to make positive use of this medium and negate the other side.

Despite bilateral tensions between India and Pakistan, war as an option has greatly come down in South Asia, reducing external threats to the state. However, ethnic conflicts within and non-state actors pose a threat to the state; as a blessing in disguise, this changes the nature of threat perceptions to the state – from external to internal. For the region, threats to the state come from domestic sources than external. This means a paradigm shift in the nature of threats to the state; this change should help the state look inwards and address human security issues, as a part of it.

Is the region ready? Essay from India **67**

In terms of delivery, the state is also better placed today. The economic situation is slowly improving within the region; individual and collective initiatives, if pursued with a long-term understanding, can improve the situation even further. India has been looking towards to sustain its economic growth and aims to progress further with new initiatives such as 'Make in India'. External interests and investments in other countries of the region, for example by China and Japan, are expected to play a role in developing the economies in India's neighbourhood.

Although it is unfortunate that the region has failed to make effective use of the SAARC as an organization of regional economic cooperation, countries in the region, as mentioned above have attracted investments from elsewhere. For instance, Pakistan has succeeded in attracting more than fifty billion dollars from China as a part of China–Pakistan Economic Corridor. Nepal, Bangladesh and Sri Lanka see the One Belt One Road initiative of China as an opportunity to improve their investment opportunities. Japan, as a part of its initiative towards the Bay of Bengal region, has enhanced its investments that would benefit Myanmar, Bangladesh and India's Northeast. South Korea and Australia also have increased their economic attention towards South Asia. Russia is planning to reinvigorate its push towards a Eurasian Economic Union; South Asia can greatly benefit from such an endeavour.

During mid-2017, India and Pakistan have joined the Shanghai Cooperation Organization (SCO) led by China and Russia. The members of the SCO include most of Central Asia, besides Afghanistan. The SCO membership is likely to play a positive role in the gas pipelines and energy corridors projects of South Asia. For instance, the Turkmenistan–Afghanistan–Pakistan–India gas pipeline and Central Asia–South Asia electricity corridor linking Central Asia and South Asia are likely to get a new fillip, with India and Pakistan joining the SCO.

As a result, South Asia is likely to enhance its economic potential in the next decade. If the countries pursued a positive approach towards the SAARC, it is possible, intra-regional trade can double or triple from its existing single digit position. All the preceding would lead to an improved economic condition for the states in South Asia – an essential ingredient necessary to improve the situation on human security.

The civil society, especially the research institutes and think tanks, along with the larger academic community in South Asia should understand this new opportunity for the region, and prepare a policy draft on how the state could improve its role in enhancing human security. The state needs not only a critical approach but also a constructive one – that is actionable and implementable. The region is likely to be more ready during the next ten years than ever before to pursue the right course of action towards improving human security.

Notes

1 See the following: Stephen M. Walt, "The Renaissance of Security Studies", *International Studies Quarterly*, June 1991; Edward A. Kolodziej, "Renaissance in Security Studies? Caveat Lector!" *International Studies Quarterly*, December 1992; David Baldwin, "Security Studies and the End of Cold War", *World Politics*, October 1995; and Helga Haftendorn,

"The Security Puzzle: Theory-Building and Discipline-Building in International Security", *International Studies Quarterly*, March 1991.

2 See P.R. Chari and Sonika Gupta (eds.), *Human Security in South Asia*, New Delhi: Social Science Press, 2003; Kanti Bajpai, "Human Security: Concept and Measurement", Kroc Institute Occasional Paper 19, Notre Dame: University of Notre Dame, August 2000; Amitav Acharya, "Human Security: East versus West?", IDSS Working Paper 17, Singapore: Institute of Defence and Strategic Studies, September 2001; and Bertram Bastiampillai, "Role of Human Security in Regional Security and Peace in South Asia", *Regional Studies*, vol. 16, no. 4, 1998.

3 Rajesh Basrur and Mallika Joseph (eds.), *Reintroducing the Human Security Debate in South Asia*, New Delhi: Samskriti, 2007.

4 Walter Lippmann, *US Foreign Policy: Shield of the Republic*, Boston: Little Brown, 1943, p. 51.

5 David D. Baldwin, "The Concept of Security", *Review of International Studies*, vol. 23, 1997, p. 9.

6 See the following: Kolodziej, no. 1; Richard Betts, "Should Strategic Studies Survive?", *World Politics*, vol. 50, October 1997; Baldwin, no. 1; Walt, no. 1; Keith Krause and Michael Williams, "Broadening the Agenda of Security Studies: Politics and Methods", *Mershon International Studies Review*, vol. 40, no. 2, October 1996; Edward Kolodziej, "What Is Security and Security Studies? Lessons from the Cold War", Arms Control Today, vol. 13, 1992; John J. Mearsheimer, "A Realist Reply", *International Security*, vol. 20, no. 1, Summer 1995.

7 See Stephen Walt, "The Renaissance of Security Studies", *International Studies Quarterly*, vol. 35, no. 2, June 1991.

6

IS THE REGION READY?
CAN THE STATE DELIVER?
ESSAY FROM PAKISTAN

Salma Malik

Introduction

In the post–Cold War period, not only the nature and pattern of conflict but also the discourse on security underwent a substantial change. The growing emphasis on promoting and ensuring individual security gave rise to the notion of *human security*, which to a certain extent was a clear departure from the previously state-centric traditional discourse. The human security debate, for the first time, brought into purview concerns other than purely militaristic ones and expanded the concept of security into the people-centric sphere, relying on the universality of freedom from fear and freedom from want.[1]

Unfortunately, this change is not yet reflected in the South Asian region, where state-centred perspectives with a focus on enhancing military postures and capabilities remain deeply entrenched. The enduring tensions between India and Pakistan coupled with their prized nuclear muscle have overshadowed the non-traditional security concerns (as well as discourse) not only in their respective countries but also in the region as a whole. The key questions that would be addressed in the chapter are, with respect to South Asia, Where does the discourse on human security stand? and Does the contemporary South Asian state hold the capacity to adapt? In a changing global discourse, where the state is both a security provider and a recipient, has the South Asian state made this transition? What and how has been the role played by the public–private enterprise, as well as the impact made by the revolution in communication? Is it a bridge builder or a spoiler?

Given the traditional fault lines of amity and enmity, is the South Asian state ready for the change. Fundamentally, is there an entity in the region that can be labelled as *the* South Asian state? Apparently an abstraction – as despite seven decades post-decolonization – each South Asian country in its singular pursuit of defining (and thus asserting) its nationhood leaves little space for a collective identity.

State fragility versus state capacity

The *state* has conventionally/traditionally been regarded as an independent, sovereign, powerful actor that yields centralized command and authority, an overarching entity in a defined geopolitical domain with binding decisions and having the ultimate control over the instruments and institutions of coercion and dominance, growth and development.[2] However, despite this singular role and authority assigned, the state has not always been able to fulfil these expectations. Since the 1990s, with greater focus on the internal dynamics of states, any such actors that lack the capacity to exercise absolute sovereignty undertake the routine functions of running the state and are unable to bring about sustainable progress and development, with characteristics such as weak institutions, poverty, corruption, inequality and civil strife leading to open armed conflict are considered as *fragile states*.[3] Although these conditions may rise out of specific occurrences in the past, such as a flawed decolonization process, divided populations and so on, yet it is important to understand both internal and external factors that build onto this (somewhat) inherent fragility and in the due course of time contribute further to the process.

Can state fragility be defined? According to Muggah,[4] "[t]he phenomenon of *fragility* is more easily described than defined. Its causes and characteristics are surprisingly diverse with most descriptions focusing on the extent to which weak governments are unable or unwilling to deliver core services".[5] Whereas Ghani and Lockhart[6] describe the aspect in terms of *sovereignty gap*, that is the social distance between elite decision-makers and those on the receiving end of their decisions, as the key factor that would dominate and push the global focus towards a common security development paradigm, more so in the post-9/11 world, "an effective state is necessary for the solution of both local and global problems".[7] According to them, the state's relevance in resolving the contemporary problems has once again taken the centre stage, which was somewhat relegated during what they term as *periods of stability* that peaked and ebbed from time to time. This relegation of the state was typically marked by "a combination of sharp social and economic inequality, demographic pressures, poor governance and the instability generated by a bewildering array of *violence entrepreneurs* – from gangs and organized crime syndicates to insurgents and terrorists".[8]

Furthermore, much focus regarding state fragility has been on unstable states, whose economic life form has been severely affected by corruption, a lack of transparency, informal and liquid flow of funds and instability. According to Muggah, despite a lack of consensus over the definitional aspect of the concept, there is comparatively little disagreement over its costs and consequences. The World Bank describes 'waves' of fragility as contributing to cross-border spill-over effects through the production of 'refugees, warring groups, contagious diseases and transnational criminal networks that traffic in drugs, arms and people'.[9] These consequences are similar in severity to the impact of non-traditional security threats such as environmental scarcity and stress pose on states and add to their fragility. With triggers such as uncontrolled population growth, unequal resource access and a

Is the region ready? Essay from Pakistan **71**

decrease in quality and quantity of renewable resources lead to enhanced environmental scarcity, which has consequences as severe as ethnic conflicts, deprivation conflicts, coup d'états, decreased economic productivity, migration and expulsion leading to weakened states.[10]

The world order envisioned by the prophets of human security, comprising an existence free from any fear for life, want or persecution, despite more than two decades has still to be realized. Much more poignantly in regions such as South Asia, but even in successful models of integration such as the EU and ASEAN. As a result, economists Mahbubul Haq and Amartya Sen in 1990s[11] created the first Human Development Index (HDI) which continues to date, with the rationale to measure comparative statistics composed of four tiers of human development, namely, life expectancy, mean and expected years of schooling and education and, last, gross national income per capita indices in order to measure and rank countries' levels of social and economic development based on these four criteria.[12] The HDI makes it possible to observe and track changes in development levels over time and correspondingly compare these levels in different countries. The HDI gave rise to ideas such as putting in place human security indices (HSI), as well as human governance indices (HGI), as a means to both *quantitatively* and *qualitatively* access the measurement of security and governance in respective countries. What could such an audit yield? Amongst many things, *quantified* data help in monitoring and studying of violent crime, violence against women and children, displacement, ecological decay and government repression as well as access or denial of basic rights, internal wars and so on. measurable variables. This, in turn, helps state actors, monitors and entities looking at conflict preemption, prevention and management into carrying out adequate measures in the right direction. Furthermore, not only are these indicators different for different countries but may also vary within a state, among federating units, provinces, regions and municipalities.[13]

At the *qualitative* level, the impact of non-quantifiable variables, such as legislation, state norms, laws and policies that may positively or adversely affect the lives of citizens, whether majority or minority groups, vulnerable populations, ethnic, sectarian or religious minorities, hard-core traditional security issues, and their impact on population groups can be appraised. Bajpai, in a monograph on human security, gleans at the merits of how helpful an Human Security Index (HIS) can be in developing a *social* early warning system, targeted attention on problem concerned, setting and adjusting policy options and priorities, setting the standards according to the underlying priorities and, last, generating new social scientific knowledge in order to better understand and deal with the problems concerned.[14]

In the category of *Social* indicators, demographic pressures, group grievances, refugees and internally displaced persons and human flight along with brain drain. Whereas *economic indicators* comprise poverty and economic decline and uneven economic growth, last, the *political indicators* cover legitimacy of the state, human rights and security, as well as the public sector, external intervention, the rule of law, factionalized elites and the public sector.[15] These instruments are helpful in providing early warning and preemptive measures for social and political disasters that can

72 Salma Malik

be effectively predicted and thus duly prevented. A pertinent counter-argument also indicates that despite the presence of such indices and quantifications, state actors generally tend to disregard such paper assessments and sociopolitical disasters usually following their natural downward spiral, have not lessened by any measures despite these warning signals. Rather during times of peace and stability, it has been observed that most state actors appear rather defiant towards such trends.

Pakistan at geopolitical crossroads

In societies, such as Pakistan, that not only inherited a complex conflict structure, in the shape of external triggers such as territorial or ideological disputes with the neighbours, which after decades of non-resolution, ended up becoming not only complex but also gave birth to secondary and tertiary conflicts. In turn, these, over time, metamorphosed into independent moot points themselves. There also exist structural weaknesses, that Pakistan inherited at the time of its birth, such as unsettled and contested borders, divided populations, abysmal governance and social infrastructure, fractionalized federating units, a lack of economic resources and insufficient defence preparedness led to joining of alliance politics to counter-balance this vulnerability, as well as seek help from international financial donors, which provided short-term relief but failed to transform the economy on a sustainable basis.

The over-reliance and sustained involvement of external actors, whether in the shape of state actors as power balancers, international financial and donor agencies or the destabilizing role played by destructive/disruptive non-state actors at sub-conventional level, has not only influenced the entire politics of the country but also dominated the narrative on state fragility, which may or may not ring true with the ground realities. According to Osaghae,

> [a]s with other development concepts, fragility and its associated descriptive terms are relative . . . suggesting deviance and aberration from the dominant and supposedly universal (but Western) paradigm of the state, which played a key role in the development of capitalism. The relativity of state fragility makes it an empirical rather than normative construct.[16]

Prior to the 1979 Soviet military intervention in Afghanistan, Pakistan's threat perception and strategic concerns were almost entirely India-centric. The physical occupation of its Western neighbour by a superpower against whom Pakistan had partnered with the US in a Cold War alliance system. Also, the perceived threat of the Soviet Union using first Kabul and then Islamabad as dominos to access the warm waters of the Indian Ocean spelt greater dangers for Pakistan. Subsequently, these security calculations became more complex as Pakistan got increasingly involved with the conflict in Afghanistan. Where the 9/11 and the US-led military intervention changed the political landscape in Afghanistan, it left Pakistan, whose decades-long entanglement in the Afghan war had created many domestic transformations, with little choice but to partner with the US as a non–North Atlantic Treaty Organization ally in routing the Al Qaeda and the (Afghan) Taliban. Blamed for patronizing and being the sole supporters of the Taliban rule, despite suffering heavily from the presence of Taliban, Al Qaeda and all sorts of terrorists, Pakistan had virtually lost its voice on Afghan matters.[17] Gradually, the security narrative changed from seeking a friendly space in Afghanistan to portraying Pakistan as a "front line state" and part of an "international alliance" in the "War on Terror".

Not only Afghanistan but policies pursued by both the democratic as well as military regimes of Zulfiqar Ali Bhutto (after his re-election) and military dictator General Zia-ul-Haq of appealing to the religious lobbies for garnering popularity and legitimacy (as in the latter's case) led to a rise in extremism and religious intolerance. A tool which came handy when preparing a breed of fighters as the Mujahideen who fought very bravely in Afghanistan and were the frontline resistance to the mighty Soviet army. But after the end of Soviet occupation, where Afghanistan gradually slipped into a complete breakdown and warlordism, rising extremism and religious militancy posed a threat to Pakistan at multiple levels.

The rekindling of Kashmiri resistance struggle against Indian occupation provided a diversion to the Jihadi organizations and added a new dimension to the India–Pakistan bilateral confrontation. From a line-up of conventional weaponry, the two neighbours sought and developed nuclear weapons capability, with Kashmir dispute dubbed as a potential nuclear flashpoint between the two countries, making South Asia a highly dangerous region. Incidents such as Kargil, Mumbai and now, more than ever before, the constant low-scale military exchange across the line of control and working boundary accentuate the belligerent posturing, leading to the enunciation of doctrines such as India's Cold-Start doctrine, predicated on deployment of forces closer to the border for a quick reaction to any Mumbai-like attack to teach Pakistan a lesson, as well as entering Pakistani territory to disrupt vital infrastructure. And Pakistan's development of tactical nuclear weapons to thwart such rapid reaction and surprise strikes under "full-spectrum-deterrence".[18] The current impasse in relations and Indian intentions of unilaterally altering the disputed status of Indian-held Kashmir, widespread human rights violations in the Muslim-majority Kashmir Valley[19] and waging of water wars promises further instability and insecurity for the people of not only the two countries but the region as a whole.

The boycott of SAARC summit, indefinite postponement of bilateral Pakistan and India dialogue process, continuous cross border fire exchange, which has now claimed a significant number of civilian non-combatant causalities[20] leads to an environment in which the thought of a common regional perspective seems extremely unlikely. Unfortunately, SAARC as the sole regional institution remains ineffectual in addressing such hostilities. Chartered specifically and intentionally to disallow bilateral contentious issues to override matters affecting the entire region, over the decades SAARC's performance and role have been minimized to an expensive South Asian leaders' coffee and tea party, which is also hostage at the whims of individual leaders. Although SAARC as a sole regional forum has in the past lead to rapprochement, at worse, diplomatic impasse, yet the individual member states need to invest and honour their commitments towards the organization in order to make it credible and empowered.

There is a need for revisiting SAARC's charter, whose future viability lies on the commitments and importance each member state accords it. So long as the member states keep the process hostage to their whims, SAARC will remain ineffectual and fail to deliver even the basics. Second, member states need to iron out their bilateral differences through peaceful means, whether entering a dialogue process, reviving pre-existent non-functional networks or exploring avenues to strengthen confidence building, which, in the case of India and Pakistan, would also include steps towards nuclear risk reduction.

In the case of Pakistan, its adversarial relations and threat perception vis-à-vis India are legacies of its birth. In an effort, to counterbalance India in the region, not only has Pakistan traditionally relied on the West, but it also joined the Cold War military alliance system in the past to provide it strategic leverage beyond the region and has as a norm measured its geostrategic importance from the perspective of the West and, in particular, the US. Given the asymmetric nature of this relationship and differential strategic goalposts, the US–Pakistan relations, at best, can be described as a roller-coaster ride, with lesser upward spirals, than the low patches. Pakistan usually measures its tumultuous relations with the US as a fair-weather friendship, in contrast to its neighbour China's "all weather friendship", which not only is of a multifaceted nature but also provided Islamabad with an important anchor at worse of times.

Whereas Pakistan's relations with Afghanistan have seen many difficulties over the decades, despite that since the late 1970s, Pakistan has hosted the largest Afghan population on humanitarian ground. Afghanistan, during this period, underwent a civilian coup, Soviet military intervention and a drastic civil war post-Soviet withdrawal, which not only influenced bilateral to regional dynamics but was also a precursor to the 9/11 terrorist attacks. With divergent security perspectives, and border dispute over the Durand line, which has been politicized and manipulated from time to time, the entry of US-led international security forces as an active stakeholder, and Afghanistan's rebirth as a resource-rich area, has once again made the precarious peace between the two countries difficult. Enjoying a limited window of opportunity with Afghan president Ashraf Ghani's coming into office, eroded within a year and a half due to terrorism and security issues.

Terrorism, being an overriding concern for Pakistan, has cost the country extensively in terms of human lives, economy, domestic peace and stability, as well as made its relations and image both within and outside the region questionable. While the nuclear weapons and one of the biggest conventional military forces provides Pakistan a strong strategic defence, the biggest challenge to address overridingly remains domestic, in terms of addressing militancy, improving the economy, overcoming energy deficiencies and meeting the needs of a growing population. None of this can work but for a cohesive political structure, balanced and objective civil–military relations and a vision for stability, development and growth that extends at all levels – domestic, bilateral, regional as well as international.

Not only does Pakistan aspire to, but also due to its geostrategic location, it can and has the inherent potential to become the hub of economic and commercial activities. Yet, its strong domestic challenges, as well as its uneasy relations with India predominantly and then Afghanistan, prevent the country from exploring its potentials to the fullest. The establishment of Gwadar port and the CPEC are two mega projects which can help Pakistan realize its aspirations as an economic and trade hub. However, much depends on how the rest of the regional players, especially India and Iran demonstrate their role. The hike in terrorist activities, specifically in the province of Baluchistan, are but one of the indicators of how regional players want this economic corridor to fail and get adversely affected. With India's heavy investment in developing Iran's Chabahar port as an alternate competing hub and route to resource-rich Central Asia and a bypass to reach Afghanistan, Gwadar port and CPEC remain affected.

Unfortunately, the regional players, overcast by their bilateral confrontations, remain hostage to their long-nurtured rivalries rather than realizing and exploiting such opportunities for mutual bridge building and building a common vision of development and prosperity for South Asia by effectively linking not only Pakistan but also the region to Central Asia and West Asia. As according to Khan,

> [d]evelopment of an economic hub or interaction within a region is realized not just by one decision or declaration. It requires [a] determined and sustained policy and [a] series of decisions and actions. Otherwise, the potential does not materialize and even dissipates. . . . In terms of potential, theoretically, Pakistan could serve as a bridge for 1) energy corridors from Iran and the Gulf to India and China and from Central Asia/Caspian Basin to India or providing Gwadar as an energy port outside the Persian Gulf, in addition to catering for Pakistan domestic requirement; 2) road/rail links for Central Asian commerce to have access to the Arabian Sea, for linking overland commerce between Central Asia and West Asia with India and between West Asia and Western China (Xinjiang) or access to Pakistani sea ports for exportable goods produced in Western China specifically Xinjiang.[21]

At present, the Central Asian markets are already dominated by Russia, China, Turkey and Iran, and over the years, these countries have developed adequate road and rail links, bypassing the troubled Afghanistan route. Whereas the European and American access the rare-earth metals and minerals of Kazakhstan through the air route and plan to develop East–West Eurasian Rail links in a bid to establish the New Silk Road. However, development of trade routes such as Gwadar would at any time be welcomed by the Central Asian states, as well as China and other big trading partners, given the ease of market access and the shorter route. But much depends not only on physical security and safety but also on the political stability within and between the regional actors. Linking bilateral, as well as transit, trade and commerce to political considerations and excluding regional actors from economic partnerships and arrangements definitely help state entities in the short-term gains, such as appeasing domestic constituencies and securing electoral vote bank, but it is highly detrimental when it comes to the common South Asian vision.

How does Pakistan exactly envision its role and position in the region? Explaining the strategic vision of the government, advisor on National Security and Foreign Affairs of the former government, Sartaj Aziz, stated that it "is to turn Pakistan's strategic geographical location from liability into an asset through trade, transport and energy connectivity with China, Central Asia and West Asia. This could also rebalance our geographic and geo-economic priorities".[22] Dwelling further on the other contours of this vision, he stressed on the need for eliminating extremism, violence and intolerance, with economic revival, development and peaceful relations with the neighbouring states, especially India and Afghanistan, based on principles of non-interference and non-intervention. However, given the complex dynamics of relations that Pakistan shares with Afghanistan and India, besides the changing trends of global politics, where the established norms of sovereignty are also under review and revision, maintaining these principles is not an easy accomplishment.

As Pakistan's relation with India deteriorates, so, too, does its alienation from the regional groupings. Whether it be the sixth round of Heart of Asia summit held in Amritsar, December 2016, or the eighth Brazil, Russia, India, China and South Africa (BRICS) Summit, New Delhi does not let go of any opportunity to diplomatically isolate Islamabad or indulge in geopolitical mudslinging, which may not only serve the desired purpose but also has an impact on and stunts the growth and development of any such fora into a meaningful entity.[23] The BRICS from its last years' promising start of the BRICS Bank relegated to a paper tiger, the Heart of Asia summit, just a forum for bad mouthing and sledgehammering Pakistan, all at a cost of regional peace, development, and growth, where opportunities such as CPEC or energy pipelines can be of enormous benefit. What should Pakistan do in such a situation, is an important question to ask, as it stands at a very critical juncture. Somewhat isolated, somewhat in a circle of some new and old friends such as China and Russia, and somewhat speculative of its traditional pillars of diplomatic support, the US and Muslim world, and with domestic challenges to face as well.

Challenges and opportunities for Pakistan

Pakistan, an important South Asian country, has been a fault-line state through most of the Cold War and the successive decades. Since 9/11, its role and position in counter-terrorism activities have been both enormous as well as often questioned, mainly due to the spill-over effect of the Soviet intervention in Afghanistan through the decades of the 1980s. Acting as a conduit state in the US's proxy war against the Soviet Union with Afghanistan as ground zero, both Afghanistan and Pakistan were left with a legacy of drugs, guns, violent militancy and terrorism, which plagues the countries to date. An additional consequence was the legitimacy and recognition accorded by the US to a military regime which served the latter well, so long as its interests in Afghanistan and the greater Cold War dynamics were served. Whereas the events leading to 9/11 and after may be studied and regarded independent, they remain deeply embedded in the politics of the 1980s, and their effects still resonate at different levels, from domestic militancy to cross-border terrorism, empowered non-state actors, refugees, troubled economy and a further worsening of already-fragile civil–military relations. As a consequence, Pakistan faced yet another decade of military rule before a smooth transition to democracy, which, despite pronounced problems of governance, continues on a path of institutional strength and norms building.

Civil–military relations have been one of the most problematic and controversial aspects for the country, especially with regard to the issue of governance and strength and stability of political institutions, with a history of direct military interventions and rule, whose collective impact has been stronger and deeper than the civilian regimes and has ended up creating a sociopolitical culture, which makes the military more popular amongst the common people, and very often perceived as the ultimate saviour as well, primarily because the military has, as and when convenient, been used by the civilian authorities as an administrative reserve and active human resource base, as well as a political support base, for all democratic actors who have, openly or behind curtains, sought its support to establish themselves or consolidate their clout.

Hence, the military was given a power and image beyond its professionally defined role, which partly attributes to military's active role in politics through the various martial law regimes as well as an existential security threat and distrust which has nurtured and exacerbated over the decades. Additionally, the civilian regimes have also done little to claim or reclaim their space, using the albeit valid excuse of depleted civilian capacity, but at the same time doing little in terms of delivering good governance and consolidating political institutions. The transition to civilian power as of 2008, a very smooth electoral process which successfully brought violence and trouble-free electoral succession, as well as military's reluctance to involve itself in politics, provides the necessary confidence to a civilian regime, which can realize not only strong and stable political institutions but also through good and sustainable governance overcome issues such as a challenging economy, militant extremism and energy deficit.

These are but few of the major impediments that stint the gradual but steady strengthening of civilian institutions, especially when the country has remained in the grip of terrorism and is trying hard to rid itself of this menace. Despite the heavy presence of international security forces, Afghanistan remains a sanctuary for terrorists who fully exploit the fractious relations between the two neighbours and manipulate the border porosity to their advantage. Despite a very costly (internal) battle against terrorism, which has cost Pakistan very high in terms of material as well as human losses, it remains under pressure from India and Afghanistan regarding cross border terrorism which has had a severe impact on mutual relations. However, at the domestic level, the counter-terrorism effort, especially after the

December 2014 Peshawar school massacre remains military dominated. Whereas a civilian-led twenty points national action plan to counter-terrorism and violent extremism has, over these years not been able to deliver as desired, although certain small steps have come about. Not only the counter-terrorism operations, but also the post-conflict rehabilitation, remain in the hands of the military in the absence of a viable civilian alternative.

The state needs to build and create the space and capacity to seek ownership. Despite the predictions regarding the state becoming an abstract construct in a globalized world. The world over, and in South Asia, specifically, does not only the state remain the key guardian but also the provider of security. With security threats, other than those faced traditionally, the state remains under pressure owing to inadequate resources as well as limiting capacity to deliver. The state's capacity can and needs to be enhanced by increased public–private participation. Pakistan has a very vibrant and fast-growing media and telecom sector, it is already seeking viable and sustainable energy growth alternatives, such as solar and wind energy. The CPEC not only is enfolding as a North–South corridor but would link up East to the West as well, and if the neighbouring states of India and Afghanistan perceive its potential as one of the most economical trade routes than a parallel competitor to their exclusive efforts, all states concerned can benefit increasingly from it. Domestically, it will provide immense employment generation and uplift underprivileged sectors of provinces such as Khyber Pakhtunkhwa, Baluchistan and areas of Gilgit and Baltistan.

Conclusion

Does Pakistan have a larger world vision or suffer through a diplomacy deficit, a criticism often raised in domestic quarters? With its focus and energy spent on counter-terrorism domestically, there appears little room for a wider world vision, other than managing its relations with the regional actors, the Muslim world and greater powers such as China, US and now, to a greater extent. Russia. Pakistan needs to diversify and build stronger diplomatic clout. With many positive assets, such as trade and energy pipelines (Turkmenistan–Afghanistan–Pakistan–India Pipeline and Iran–Pakistan–India pipeline [TAPI and IPI]) being worked out, a steadily improving economic profile, proactive civil society and fast-growing private sector, the country can and has all the potential to overcome its challenges and inadequacies. But the journey to achieve these goals is arduous and long term. Where there is no dearth of institutional and infrastructure development, the need is to overcome hardline mindsets, give priority to food, health, education and societal insecurities. Although each country has to walk this difficult mile by itself, with a purpose-built organization such as SAARC, it is neither impossible nor unimaginable to make a collective effort. The civil society both within the country as well as in the region can play the role of a proactive agent of change.

Natural or man-made disasters, diseases, epidemics, spillover effects of sociopolitical instability, changing trends and tactics of non-state actors, unrestricted and global outreach and access of media, are an indicator, that if not the traditional state, then at least the challenges it faces are of a magnitude far beyond its sole capacity to handle. To overcome these problems, the state needs to partner with domestic stakeholders as much as seek regional cooperation, however progressive it may become. Good governance, better bilateral relations, economic interaction and cooperation and an amicable settlement of contentious issues are the needs of the day. Pakistan has to realize and address its over-riding domestic concerns, through political and judicial reforms, and build a sustainable vision based on good governance and economic progression. It is high time that serious and result-oriented efforts are genuinely made to settle the Kashmir dispute, for the benefit of Kashmiris, rather than hold the entire progress and development of the region hostage. Unless this realization is genuinely felt, the onus of which falls on India, the region which is home to one fourth of the global population, will lack progress and prosperity.

Notes

1 Chapter 2, "New Dimensions of Human Security", Human Development Report 1994, New York: Oxford University Press, 1994, p. 24.
2 Peter B. Evans, Dietrich Rueschemeyer and Theda Skocpol (eds.), Bringing the State Back In, Cambridge: Cambridge University Press, 1985.
3 Eghosa E. Osaghae, "Fragile States", Development in Practice, vol. 17, nos. 4/5, August 2007, pp. 691–699. www.jstor.org/stable/25548271, accessed 25 July 2011.
4 Robert Muggah, "Stabilizing Fragile States and the Humanitarian Space", in Mats Berdal and Achim Wenmann (eds.), Ending Wars, Consolidating Peace: Economic Perspective, Adelphi Series 50:412–413, pp. 33–52, http://dx.doi.org/10.1080/19445571.2010.515 143, accessed 9 May 2019.
5 *Ibid.*, p. 34.
6 Ashraf Ghani and Clare Lockhart, Fixing Failed States: A Framework for Rebuilding a Fractured World, New York: Oxford University Press, 2009, pp. 26–27.
7 *Ibid.*
8 Muggah, no. 4, p. 35.
9 *Ibid.*, p. 41.
10 Thomas F. Homer-Dixon, Environment, Scarcity, and Violence, Princeton, NJ: Princeton University Press, 2001.
11 Mahbub-ul-Haq, "New Imperatives of Human Security", RGICS Paper No. 17, Rajiv Gandhi Institute for Contemporary Studies (RGICS), New Delhi: Rajiv Gandhi Foundation, 1994. Also see Human Security and the concept of Human Development Index (HDI) proposed by Dr. Haq. See, "Redefining Security: The Human Dimension", Human Development Report 1994, no. 1.
12 Kanti Bajpai, "Human Security: Concept and Measurement", Kroc Institute Occasional Paper 19, August 2000, p. 54.
13 *Ibid.*
14 *Ibid.*, p. 55.
15 CAST Conflict Assessment Framework Manual, The Fund for Peace (FFP), 10 March 2014, http://library.fundforpeace.org/library/cfsir1418-castmanual2014-english-03a.pdf, accessed 20 September 2014, alternate url: www.files.ethz.ch/isn/179348/cfsir1418-castmanual2014-english-03a.pdf.
16 Osaghae, no. 3.
17 Riaz Mohammad Khan, Afghanistan and Pakistan: Conflict, Extremism and Resistance to Modernity, Washington, DC: John Hopkins University Press and Woodrow Wilson Center Press, 2011.

18 Prime Minister Nawaz Sharif's statement at The Hague Summit plenary on 24 March 2014.
19 Not fewer than 100 people have been killed since September 2016 in clashes and unprovoked firing by Indian security forces in the held Valley. "Fire Exchanged Across India-Pakistan Border in Kashmir", Al-Jazeera News, 2016, www.aljazeera.com/news/2016/11/deadly-cross-border-firings-india-pakistan-border-161109155002126.html, accessed 9 May 2019.
20 Hari Kumar and Ellen Barry, "3 Indian Soldiers Are Killed in Kashmir", New York Times, 22 November 2016, www.nytimes.com/2016/11/22/world/asia/indian-soldiers-killed-kashmir.html?_r=0, accessed 9 May 2019.
21 Riaz M. Khan, "Geostrategic Review and Threat Scenario", in Salma Malik (ed.), Pakistan Security Challenges and Problems in the Next Decade, Islamabad: NUST Publishers, 2015.
22 Government of Pakistan, "Press Release", Ministry of Foreign Affairs, 25 June 2014.
23 G. Pramod Kumar, "India Making Mistake by Turning BRICS Summit into Pak Bashing Programme", The News (Pakistan), 16 October 2016, www.thenews.com.pk/print/157571-India-making-mistake-by-turning-BRICS-Summit-into-Pak-bashing-programme, accessed 21 April 2019.

PART II

Environmental issues and human security

7

WATER INSECURITY IN SOUTH ASIA

Challenges of human development

Vandana Asthana

Introduction

The end of the Cold War and the disintegration of the Soviet Union brought about a shift from one's excessive preoccupation with military matters and the East–West struggle. Scholars began to shift their attention away from the established approaches of international relations and security studies that had long focused on borders, war and weapons. A renewed interest in security studies, and the core issue of what is to be secured, and how, has come to occupy our thoughts.[1] More attention came to be focused on transcending state-centric notions of security and necessitated a more inclusive definition of security in an era of global economic and ecological overdependence. The changing conceptions of security are part of the larger change in the way the working of the international system is being perceived. In particular, the state-centric security discourse can hardly capture the fundamental problems of security for the bulk of the population in developing countries. To the millions in this part of the world, efforts at ensuring state security make little meaning as long as their populations are steeped in poverty, a lack of water access and sanitation, hunger, malnutrition and illiteracy. When their very survival is at stake and their physical surroundings and economic base are severely threatened by resource depletion and environmental degradation, their daily life affected by conflict and strife, the concept of national security in its traditional sense ultimately loses its salience and importance if its own population remains vulnerable. The transition from a realist perception of security in international relations to a more novel approach began with the presentation of the United Nations Development Programme (UNDP) Report in 1994. The UNDP Report described human security as a condition in which people are given relief and safety "from such chronic threats as hunger, disease and repression. And second it means protection from sudden and hurtful disruptions in the patterns of daily life – whether in homes, in jobs or in communities".[2]

Human security, therefore, was seen as essential for human development; without minimal stability and security in daily life, there could be no development – human or otherwise.[3] Defined in more generic terms, human security encompasses human development, secured food and water, employment and environmental security. Fundamentally, it encompasses the security of people against threats to life, health, human dignity and personal safety and grants them freedom from want, deprivation and violence. Thus, human security has a preventive, integrative and intergenerational aspect that contrasts sharply with its insular, aggressive and myopic national counterpart[4] as human well-being is linked with a sustainable development process that is expected to be efficient, equitable and distributive.

In this attempt, the definition of Norman Myers brings the debate closer to the notion of human insecurity:

> [S]ecurity applies most at the level of the individual citizen. It amounts to human well-being; not only protection from harm and injury but access to water, food, shelter, health, employment, and other basic requisites that are due of every person on earth. It is the collectivity of these citizens needs — overall safety and quality of life — that should figure prominently in the nation's view of security.[5]

Thus, human well-being is linked with a sustainable development process that is efficient, equitable and distributive. Critics, however, observe that while "the discourse in human security has become dominant in international policy circles, it has had so little impact on policy outcome".[6] However, the scholarly debate on the merits and demerits of the concept should not discount the importance and privilege that human security is accorded in the international relations literature as a meaningful policy norm. Human security has seven major components as identified in the UNDP Report of 1994 comprising economic security, food security, health security, environmental security, personal security, community security and political security.

Environmental security emerged as an important concept in security studies with the growth of environmental consciousness and the rise of environmentalism that began in the developed world in the 1960s. It carved a niche for itself in the 1990s and created the intellectual and policy space for itself to enter the mainstream area of security as one of the "new" security issues.[7] While this idea is not without its contestation, there exists a sizeable literature that places environmental concerns as a central issue on the security agenda. A literature review in this area reveals that the discourse on environment and security is an area of rich and lively debate that has earned scholarly and policy salience.[8] Two schools of thought figure prominently in this discourse: (1) environmental change and violent conflict and (2) environmental change and human security.

Environmental change and violent conflict

This school of thought seeks to answer the critical question of whether environmental change contributes to armed conflict. Its predominant focus has been to reveal causal links between environmental degradation and violent conflict. Various case studies[9] by Myers, Boge, Homer Dixon, Peter Gleick and others have tried to demonstrate that resource scarcity is a contributing factor to interstate conflict. The literature on resource scarcity provides evidence for introducing the element of non-military threats into the modern conception of security. Food, water and oil are examples of resource scarcity that play an important role in precipitating a conflict. In the early writings of this school, Myers linked population growth, environmental change and violent conflict, although he argued that the links between them are not straightforward.[10] Gleick argued that there were clear connections between environmental degradation and violence where resources could be strategic goals or tools, while resource inequalities could trigger conflicts.[11] The pioneering work of Homer Dixon in the Toronto Project uses selective case studies in the developing world (e.g. South Africa and Pakistan) to demonstrate how environmental change leads to conflict.[12] However, this link alone could not directly substantiate the causal connection between environmental change and conflict. Homer Dixon's theory was critiqued for lacking evidence to support the scarcity/conflict theory. Critics argued that he downplayed natural factors like climate change and ozone depletion that would also be the driving factors in the future. The literature in this school has evolved over the years to redefine the paradigm of security, focusing principally on the potential of environmental change to generate and/or amplify conflict.

Environmental change and human security

An emerging trend within this evolution has been a move towards greater emphasis on the concept of human security.[13] This second school of thought represented by the works of Mathews, Mische, Renner and Myers argues[14] that because "security implies freedom or protection from serious threats to human well-being . . ., whatever poses such a threat, be it in military, economic, resource, food, or environmental realms, becomes a security problem". Many analysts argue that despite the traditional state-centric focus of security, in essence, the quality of life of individuals is bound to be affected by the depletion or degradation of environmental resources. Mathews's work on *Redefining Security* refers to human activities that have transformed the Earth and the ecosystem. Using environmental variables, she centres her environmental security concerns on population increase, deforestation, global warming and greenhouse gases and ozone depletion.

Environmental balance is therefore essential to people's quality of life, and

> an individual's personal protection and preservation comes not just from the safeguarding of the state as a political unit, but also from access to individual welfare and quality of life. Human security, in short, involves the security of individuals in their personal surroundings, their community, and their environment.[15]

Thus, environmental change has a direct relationship with human security, and it is due more to anthropogenic activities than to natural biocentric or environmental changes:

> The essence of this global problématique is that human beings, by virtue of their numbers and the magnitude of their activities are causing biogeochemical

changes in the earth's system that is taking place many times more rapidly than those occurring naturally.[16]

The linkage is obvious and beyond debate. Suhrke (1999) argues that

> the central task of a policy inspired by human security concerns would therefore be to protect those who are most vulnerable. . . . It is self-evident that those exposed to immediate physical threats to life or deprivation of life-sustaining resources are extremely vulnerable. . . . Other persons can be placed in equally life-threatening positions for reasons of deep poverty or natural disasters.[17]

Although the concept of human and environmental security may be limited in its philosophical and theoretical status due to a lack of consensus in the intellectual discourse, it has emerged as a comprehensive, salient and urgent term in the global and regional policy circles charged with solving real-life challenges threatening society.

Water security

Against this background, what does "security" mean in relation to water in India and South Asia? Quite simply, water has been and remains one of the most persistent sources of stress at every level: international, national, community and even individual. From a different perspective, the deterioration of water quality – whether in the form of urban pollution, run-off contamination or soil degradation – highlights the water and human security links and the deep relationship between water quality and human health and well-being. The chair of UN-Water and Secretary-General of the World Meteorological Organization, Jarraud, commented that

> security has now come to mean human security and its achievement through development. Water fits within this broader definition of security – embracing political, environmental, health, economic, personal, food, energy and other concerns – and acts as a central link between them.[18]

According to the United Nations Environment Programme (UNEP),

> "[w]ater security represents a unifying element supplying humanity with drinking water, hygiene and sanitation, food and fish, industrial resources, energy, transportation and natural amenities, all dependent upon maintaining ecosystem health and productivity"[19]

Contemporary framings of water security vary in emphasis from water quality to water rights, to protection from floods and droughts, and variation in scales from community, watershed or national and transboundary scales. In a comprehensive review of the water security literature, Cook and Bakker identify four interrelated themes that dominate the published research on water security: water availability and quantity, human vulnerability to hazards, human needs (development-related) and sustainability.[20]

To the Global Water Partnership (GWP),

> [w]ater security at any level from the household to the global means that every person has access to enough, safe water at [an] affordable cost to lead a clean[,] healthy and productive life, while ensuring that the natural environment is protected and enhanced.[21]

This framing includes seven variables: meeting basic needs, securing food supply, protecting ecosystems, sharing water resources, managing risks, valuing water, and governing wisely.[22] Indian geneticist Swaminathan draws on the GWP definition and states that water security "involves the availability of water in adequate quantity and quality in perpetuity to meet domestic, agricultural, industrial and ecosystem needs".[23]

Water security framework thus includes water availability and access, which includes water needs for diverse purposes (adequacy, reliability, dependence, vulnerability, etc.); water quality challenges (prevention or control of pollution and contamination including point and nonpoint sources of pollution); water abundance, disasters and the need for flood damage preparedness and control; international context of water management in India; and water sharing among basin states.

Water availability, however, does not automatically constitute water security. The availability of water for use at the right place, time, quantity and quality and the ability of people within a particular country or region to actually receive or gain access to clean freshwater constitutes some of the key variables while defining water security.[24] The quality of these resources affects both availability and access. These seemingly three distinct types of problems can all be present in a region experiencing water stress or water scarcity, although availability may be more dependent on physical or environmental factors, whereas access may be more dependent on social or political factors. "Perfect storm of food, water and energy shortages – caused by a combination of population growth, triggering new rural and urban demands, and global climate change which threatens to decrease the net available supply in many areas of the globe and to aggravate already contaminated supplies"[25] can be characterized as a state of water insecurity that is currently becoming a global concern and challenge.

Few people actively engaged in South Asia water sector would deny that the Indian subcontinent faces serious problems in the sustainable use of water resources for human development. The different countries in South Asia are beginning to experience moderate-to-severe water shortages, brought about due to simultaneous effects of growth in agriculture, industrialization and urbanization. The overexploitation of water, along with improper management practices, has set a dangerous trend that threatens the very availability of water resources for future generations.

88 Vandana Asthana

This chapter raises the following questions: What are the factors that drive water insecurity in India? How do South Asian water resources and their availability, access, quality, and transboundary character affect the parameters of water security? and How can we manage these resources for a secure water future?

The United Nations World Water Development Report mentions that water use has grown more than twice the rate of population increases in the last century.[26] By 2025, an estimated 1.8 billion people will live in areas affected by water scarcity, with two-thirds of the population living in water-stressed regions as a result of use, growth and climate change. The report revealed that nearly half of the global population (about 4 billion people) would be living in regions of high-water stress by 2030. The fact that the percentage of population affected by water scarcity will increase from a mere 8 percent in 2000 (508 million people) to 47 percent within nearly three decades has dire consequences for global water security. The report also stressed that increasing demands for food, water and energy will strain resources in almost all regions of the world, especially in the developing world. This impact is largely going to be felt in the developing countries of Asia and Africa already experiencing various forms of water stress, leading to a rise in consumption patterns.

South Asia hosts 24 percent of the world's population (1.64 billion people) and nearly half of the world's poor. Such a scenario poses the greatest challenge facing humanity for providing energy, food and clean water to every person. The global water challenge thus lies in not only providing access and availability to safe drinking water to people but managing issues of the food–water–energy nexus and increasing the security and resilience of a country to meet water needs. India and South Asia face similar challenges of environmental change and water security. The challenges to human development are common to the region. From a human development perspective, the availability, access and quality of clean freshwater are increasingly characterized as security issues, especially in a region that is predominantly agricultural but heading toward industrialization and urbanization in an integrating, globalized world.

With the exception of Bhutan and Nepal, South Asia's per capita water availability falls below the world average. Annual water availability has plummeted by nearly 70 percent since 1950, from about 21,000 cubic meters in the 1960s to approximately 8,000 in 2005. If such patterns continue, the region could face "widespread water scarcity" (i.e. per capita water availability under 1,000 cubic meters) by 2025. Furthermore, the United Nations, based on a variety of measures – including ecological insecurity, water management problems, and resource stress – characterizes two key water basins of South Asia (the Helmand and Indus) as "highly vulnerable".[27]

Driving factors of water and human insecurity in South Asia

Where both water endowments and the number of consumers remain more or less fixed, there is considerably less cause for concern, but in the case of arid and semiarid regions like India and parts of South Asia, with a high population growth rate and its material, institutional and behavioural drivers, the threat of resource depletion or degradation is a constant source of insecurity precisely because of competition among an increasing number of potential users and sectors. Thus, water security is becoming an increasingly important and challenging issue for South Asia. Several factors discussed in the following are the key drivers of water insecurity in the region.

Agriculture and Irrigation Factor

Irrigation has made an enormous impact on water resource development in South Asia and contributed to the achievement of higher levels of food security in the region. The agricultural contribution to South Asian economy is about 18 percent,[28] and more than 50 percent of the population is employed in this sector.[29] In spite of the shift toward industrialization and urbanization, a large part of the rural communities in the region will remain dependent on agriculture. Increased production and food security are key drivers of poverty reduction in the region, which is highly dependent on the availability of freshwater and on the hydrological cycle.[30] Irrigated land constitutes about 40 percent of cultivated land, and rain-fed crops constitute about 58 percent. Rice and wheat are the staple foods. There is a very large population in the Indo-Gangetic plain, comprising Pakistan, Bangladesh, India and Nepal, spread over 13.5 million hectares. However, "declining productivity, ground water depletion, and declining water availability as well as increased pest incidence and salinity already threaten the sustainability and food security of the region".[31]

The Green Revolution gave an unprecedented boost to food production with the rise of new high-yielding varieties that were achieved through intensive irrigation and water use. Irrigation has been a powerful tool in providing self-sufficiency in food grain production, but the environmental and social costs of this achievement have been high in terms of demand for water and its quality. This is because agriculture is extremely dependent on an adequate freshwater supply, and South Asia uses nearly 80 percent of its water resources on agriculture. Mismanaging water resources can result in the erosion, water logging and salinization of the soil, which in turn makes the soil lesser productive. Poorly managed irrigation can also result in water pollution and waterborne diseases. The need for irrigation water is likely to be greater than currently anticipated and the available supply less than anticipated.

Most chemical fertilizers not only require more water to be effective; they also contaminate the water sources through non-point sources of pollution making the availability and quality of water a key issue. Non-point sources contribute a significant load to water pollution, especially in the rainy season. Pesticide consumption that affects water quality is about 1 million tonnes a year of which Punjab, Haryana, Gujarat, Uttar Pradesh and Maharashtra are principal consumers.[32]

Waterlogging and salinity are alarming in Sri Lanka and Bangladesh. In India, it is estimated that nearly 8.4 million ha is affected by soil salinity and alkalinity, of which about 5.5 million hectares is waterlogged.[33] The rapid increase of human activity on irrigated croplands, intensive use of agrochemicals, poor infrastructure for drainage and water supply have impacted the availability of water and led to an abandonment of at least 10 million hectares of irrigated land by farmers.[34]

Investment in drainage was widely neglected in the region. Even if such investments were made, there was a lack of follow-up maintenance, causing many drainage systems to be silted up. Experts estimate that only 30 to 40 percent of water from canals, dams and rural tube wells actually reaches the fields. The worst problem in the irrigation sector is the total lack of maintenance. Crucial but entirely unglamorous maintenance has to compete with spending on new irrigation projects. The breakdown of maintenance threatens the entire rural water Programme.

In Pakistan, agriculturally inefficient irrigation uses up 97 percent of the country's water resources to support one of the lowest productivities in the world per unit of water.[35] Pakistan's excessive cultivation of water-intensive cash crops like sugarcane has increased the stress on water. Of Pakistan's irrigated lands, 38 percent are waterlogged and 14 percent are saline, and saline water has intruded into mined aquifers in Pakistan. There exists an alarming level of decline in water tables in Baluchistan and an increased reduction in sweetened water in the lower Indus basin. It seems an accepted fact the Indus basin irrigation system the only source of water in Pakistan is vulnerable and there exists a need to explore alternative water resource development and management techniques.[36] The strategy of putting dam structures when there is no water downstream creates water scarcity. Dams are losing their ability to supply water as in the case of Tarbela Dam that has lost 30 percent of its storage capacity since the late 1970s and now retains so little water that irrigation supplies are threatened.

In Afghanistan, more than 80 percent of Afghans live in rural areas subsisting on natural resources like land and water and subsistence agriculture for their daily survival. Despite Afghanistan's more favourable position from its neighbours, Iran and Pakistan, it faces a clear shortage of water as a result of war inflicted damage to 45 percent of irrigation structures and canals. Traditional system water losses are responsible for 40 percent of total water losses and which are attributable to poor management of resources.[37]

In Nepal, too, the demand for irrigation water is increasing due to high-yielding varieties of rice, wheat and water crops. This has led to increased water conflicts between farmers where unreliable water supply; excessive use of water in the head section of the irrigation canal has increased stress on availability of water users at the tail end of the irrigation system. Ninety-six percent of water consumption in Nepal is in the agricultural sector, but the performance in the irrigation sector is disappointing. Irrigation is available only to less than 20 percent of the 2.2 million hectares of land areas that can potentially be irrigated the year-round.[38] Irrigation projects in Nepal have performed dismally relative to the resources poured into the sector. Increasing systems in Nepal have become increasingly vulnerable due to higher sediment rates and frequent damage caused by flash floods. This has led to increased watershed degradation in the country, and decreasing access to water resources is negatively affecting crop production and productivity.

Sectoral demands in irrigation will increase due to the increasing population of the region by 2025. There will be a need for more water storage projects for increased food grain production. Water, food and the general well-being of people are integrally linked. A critical relationship exists between water resource management, livelihood and food security. It is important to note that the availability of water whether in abundance or in scarcity, including its quality can pose a threat to food security. Water contributes to achieving food security by influencing the food production process. With an excessive supply of water or floods, food production is disrupted. Low water supplies, in turn, can lead to a drought situation when normal agricultural production practices are interrupted. Water therefore remains a critical link to human security because of the livelihood and survival opportunities it provides to the people of the region. Depletion and degradation of the resource due to unsustainable agronomical practices are bound to affect the livelihood of a large number of populations. This will definitely increase the stress on water.

Industrial factor

Industrial use of water depends on the degree of industrialization of the country. In developing nations, the percentage of industrial use of water is ten to 13 percent. Naturally, it can be expected that this increase in industrial activity will need more amount of water for such activities like boiling, air conditioning, cooling, processing, transportation and energy production. South Asia has seen 5.6 per cent industrial growth, which has quadrupled in the last thirty years due to a high demand of consumer products that require resource-intensive processes in the transformation of raw materials into industrial products like steel, paper and chemicals. This growth alone has contributed to 4 percent of the large-scale industrial pollution and twenty per cent of the small and medium enterprises' pollution load.[39] As a growing export market, South Asia has seen an increase in large-scale and small-scale industries in the region, but compliance among the estimated 6 million small-scale industrial units in South Asian countries is extremely low in comparison to larger firms who do possess capital, as well as have incentives, to promote greener technology and compliance.[40]

Surveys in India reveal that rivers make up 80 percent of the total surface water and are home to about 85 percent of the population. Most of these rivers are so polluted mainly in stretches near towns and industrial belts that bacteria feeding on the waste are the only things that have proliferated, their counts anywhere between 20 and 1,000 times over safe levels.[41] Most of them are dead or dying. In spite of a National Rivers Conservation Authority, the entire thirteen great river systems are endangered. They are fought over by states to provide irrigation for teeming cities and industrial estates. This combination reduces the volume of water in many rivers so drastically that the Yamuna in Delhi and Agra are left with no original water but for the streams of urban and industrial wastewater that is pumped continuously into these glorified sewers.[42] Industrial effluents and sewage continue to flood waters in Allahabad and Varanasi famous for its carpet and textile industries. Tanneries

92 Vandana Asthana

release toxic effluents in Kanpur and Kolkata. Industrial effluents are poisoning the Patna stretch.

According to the UNEP report released on the state of the environment in South Asia

> "wastewater streams also contain suspended solids, oils, waste acids, chromium salts, phosphates, ammonia, cyanides, phenols, chlorides, fluorides, sulfides, and heavy metals. Contaminated gas water, quench water and condensate are in many cases being discharged without treatment".[43]

These have grave implications for people drinking that water that contains lead, mercury and cadmium, which also enters the food chain through fish eaten by the population. Human and children's health is affected by lead contamination, causing problems in mental development, increased headaches, stomach problems, memory problems, anaemia, miscarriages and kidney diseases.[44]

Water pollution is a source of danger to the health of people living in developing countries such as Pakistan. The main industries located at various industrial zones of Pakistan cause water pollution, which ultimately result in various diseases. Studies revealed that concentrations of essential and toxic metals in the drained water of three main industrial estates of Pakistan in Peshawar, Gujranwala and Haripur.[45] The elevated concentrations of heavy metals continuously entering into the food chain through agriculture leading to serious health hazards and a threat to the sustainability of the local ecosystem. Industrial wastewater contains toxic chemicals. It is alarming that most industries have been started without proper planning and waste treatment plants. Lahore, Faisalabad, Karachi, Sialkot contribute major pollution loads into their water bodies. The work of Zehra Aftab and others concludes that industrial pollution is increasing rapidly and that the health and productivity impacts are significant and worsening. Pakistani industries are increasingly contributing to air and water pollution.[46] Unfortunately, pollution control compliance in the region is poor, and there are few incentives provided to industry to adopt efficient water-use practices. As industrialization growth becomes a priority of the states of the region, problems of water quality will be aggravated by water pollution.

Demographic factors

Growing population coupled with wasteful consumption has led to a gradual decline in per capita availability of water. However, population growth in the region is expected to keep on increasing. The demographic pressure stresses water availability. South Asia's population is set to top 2 billion people by 2025.[47] As projected by United Nations, 90 percent of population growth is likely to take place until 2050 in developing countries, and the demand of freshwater resources of these countries will make sustainable economic development increasingly difficult. The UN report also predicts that India will surpass China by 2050, and Pakistan will be the fourth-most populous state in the world. The pressure on water is bound to increase as the per capita availability declines. In addition, inequalities in water distribution will lead to decreased access. This will have huge implications in terms of water security.

While the World Bank Report (2012) claims that "the improved water source (percent of population with access) in South Asia was last reported at 90.05 in 2010", only 36 percent of South Asians have access to sanitation.[48] A World Wide Life Fund (WWF)–Pakistan report concludes that municipal sewage is a major source of pollution. About 2 million wet tonnes of human excreta are annually produced in the urban sector of which around fifty per cent go into water bodies to pollute them. National Conservation Strategy (NCS) states that almost 40 per cent of deaths are related to waterborne diseases. Domestic wastewater collects on the streets and in low-lying areas. The situation is further aggravated by the addition of untreated wastes from small-scale industries.[49] Municipal sewage is a common concern that dominates the region.

Urbanization

Urbanization is likely to be a defining process and characteristic of South Asia in the years to come, and the process is already posing a serious challenge in sustaining water resources in the region. Predictions are that by 2025, 40 percent of the region's population will be living in urban centres. Very often, rural areas adjoining the cities serve as receptacles of urban waste, while providing the much-needed land and water resources that sustain urban expansion. Cities in South Asia are exploiting the water resources of the rural hinterlands in its vicinity leading to conflicting situations and claims over the right to this resource. Increasingly, drinking water sources in the cities are drying up, and water is brought from far distances to quench the thirst of an ever-increasing urban population.

In India, metropolitan cities like Shivaji Park, Mumbai; parts of national capital Delhi; and Greater Noida and Uttar Pradesh are very deficient in domestic water supplies. Despite the claims that water will be provided two to three times a day for a few hours, the fact is that taps run dry for days. People keep buckets below the open taps in hope that water will come sometimes but in vain. If this is the plight of water supply, one can imagine what will be the situation in smaller townships and rural villages. In Pakistan, too, the situation is identical in Karachi, where an old water-supply system is inefficient to supply domestic water to the residents. Lahore is a city that relies exclusively on groundwater for drinking water needs, but as urbanization grows, water tables have fallen by roughly five feet over the last five years in several parts of Lahore and by 65 feet elsewhere in the city. This water according to reports is so highly contaminated and found to contain arsenic beyond permissible levels.[50] In many areas, access is inequitable due to the purchasing power of the people. Rich households have privately installed groundwater pumps while the urban poor especially women and children suffer most from the intermittent supplies.

In most of South Asia, domestic sewage is the major source of pollution in surface water which contributes to the main source of waterborne diseases and depletion of oxygen in water bodies. In countries such as Nepal, India and Bangladesh, the pollution of rivers is more severe and critical near urban stretches due to huge amounts of pollution load discharged by urban activities. The Bagmati, Bishnumati and Manohar river systems in the Kathmandu valley,[51] the Yamuna River at Delhi, and peripheral rivers (mainly Buriganga River) of Dhaka suffer from severe pollution these days. Analysis reveals pollution loads steadily increasing nearly in step with the trend in urbanization. Unplanned urbanization and industrialization occurring in these cities may be largely responsible for this grave situation. In urban water supplies, also 17 to 44 percent of water is wasted due to leakage in the mains and pipelines.[52] Conservation of water is of considerable importance for ensuring water security.

Climate change and water security

A major threat to the region will be the impact of global climate change and rising sea levels. Changes in climatic patterns will be disastrous for arid and semi-arid regions in India and Pakistan. Most countries of this region depend on monsoons for agricultural production that is the source of livelihood to around 70 per cent of the population in the region. Disruptions in climatic patterns are bound to create drought, floods with negative effects on food security in the region; however, a World Bank Report (2013) mentions that the effects of such extreme events will be felt differently in different parts of the region.[53] For instance, half the country in Bangladesh lies at elevations less than five meters. In the worst-case scenario of local 209-centimetre rise, 18 per cent of the habitable land would be underwater. As a result, more than 17 million people would become environmental refugees. By 2100, the really worst-case scenario shows that 35 per cent of the nation's population – 38 million people will be forced to relocate.[54] A study of 1989 on rainfall variation estimates that there would be changes in the spatial and temporal distribution of precipitation. In Bangladesh, the study shows that the annual frequency of heavy rainfall depicts an increasing trend in rainfall areas and a decreasing trend in relatively drier areas. It is also anticipated that the country's vulnerability to climate change will force many people to migrate into other regions of South Asia or beyond. A report released by the World Bank in June 2013, "Turn down The Heat: Climate Extremes, Regional Impacts, and the Case for Resilience", predicts that

> [i]n South Asia, climate change shocks to food production and seasonal water availability appear likely to confront populations with on-going and multiple challenges to secure access to safe drinking water, sufficient water for irrigation and hydropower production, and adequate cooling capacity for thermal power production. Potential impact hotspots such as Bangladesh are projected to be confronted by increasing challenges from extreme river floods, more intense tropical cyclones, rising sea-level and very high temperature. . . . Sea-level rise is projected to be approximately 100–115 cm in a 4°C world

and 60–80 cm in a 2°C world by the end of the 21st century relative to 1986–2005, with the highest values expected for the Maldives.[55]

This will definitely destabilize the peace and tranquility of the region.[56]

Floods

Due to the seasonality of water supply in South Asia, floods are a constant recurrence in the region. Temporarily displacing large populations who have to survive in the unhealthiest environments. Annual floods occur in India, Pakistan, Bangladesh, Nepal and Afghanistan on a regular basis, leaving millions affected each year. Human-induced (anthropogenic) causes include deforestation, impeding of river flows and other such activities. Governments have created embankments and dams, but they have become rather part of the problem than the solution. Flood control has not been a feasible proposition, and every year the region sees floods and destruction on a large scale. Security in this context would mean timely knowledge of government and individuals so that appropriate measures can be taken to minimize the impact.[57] Inter-country cooperation is essential for flood monitoring and water flows. Efforts have been made in the South Asian Association for Regional Cooperation in this direction.

Challenges of human development in South Asia

Water is not just a topical subject like many other social, political or economic variables that periodically invoke furore, and as the passions die, become a part of history. Water is our life-support system, and its relevance is steadily rising with each leap in economic growth and population increase. This finite but renewable resource faces an aberrant hydrological cycle under anthropogenic impacts. For a sustained supply of water to its citizens, states are trying to manage water resources for food, energy, and survival.[58] Ensuring access to potable and quality drinking water is essential to prevent waterborne diseases prevalent in the region. One of the most important causes of mortality and morbidity in the region is poverty and its various manifestations that are seen in communicable diseases caused by the poor quality of drinking water and unhygienic sanitation. Safe drinking water and sanitation have direct linkage with the health of the people, their productivity and their quality of life. Waterborne diseases are endemic in South Asian cities, frequently assuming large-scale epidemic proportions. The loss in terms of mortality and economic injury is incalculable. Another report of the World Health Organization says that 25 to 30 percent of all hospital admissions in Pakistan are related to waterborne bacteria and parasitic conditions, with 60 percent of infant deaths caused by water infections.[59]

Arsenic contamination creates huge health problems in Bangladesh, where it is estimated that three quarters of all diseases are linked to unsafe water and inadequate sanitation facilities. Diarrhoea diseases, moreover, are prevalent in countries with inadequate sewage treatment. The challenge of securing water in parts of rural Pakistan has grown since the 2005 earthquake. High numbers of young children from waterborne diseases are on the rise in rural Pakistan due to water scarcity in Pakistan.[60] These are issues of water governance to ensure human security by proving clean and good-quality water. Human drinking requirements are estimated to be at least 50 litres per capita per day (LPCD), yet in Pakistan, the poorest urban dwellers have access to only 10 LPCD, and all of it is polluted.[61] The amount of resources dedicated to water supply and sanitation in Pakistan is less than 0.2 percent of their gross domestic product. Water Aid, an organization working in water, concludes that Islamabad spends forty-seven times more on military budgets than on water and sanitation. In India, too, a large part of water becomes a breeding ground for mosquitoes and diseases, as sewage collection is irregular and sewage stagnates in the city limits. Water quality does affect the quality of life and therefore is integral to the web of human security.

What lessons do we learn from the evidence cited earlier? The preceding examples and analysis enunciate the various ways in which water security issues tend to manifest themselves in the broader context of human development and state security. The challenge lies in reconciling these twin challenges.

The challenge of sustainable development as a new security paradigm for water

One of the major challenges of water security in South Asia needs to be contextualized in terms of sustainable water resource development and management practices. Placing water within the human security paradigm has key implications for the region. The notion of security in this region is intricately linked to the issues of food, livelihood, and survival and therefore cannot be delinked from developmental goals. In this context, water is more a component of sustainable development than a dimension of traditional national security. The discourse of development is guided by a scientific, technocratic perspective where supply-side augmentation takes precedence over all other alternatives in the decision-making process. Simply projecting demand and providing water supply through the production of water not only damage the environment but also raise issues of equity, rights and justice.[62] Sustainable development is a process that aims at using resources in a manner that there is enough for the present and future generations.

The current water resource development in South Asia is not sustainable. There needs to be a shift in emphasis on demand management practices and further incentives for conservation of water resources. Alternative discourses that focus on locally sustainable projects that are cost effective and cater to the local community should be encouraged and incorporated in the decision making. Several projects such as check dams, rainwater harvesting, and tank irrigation systems are examples of sustainable management practices in the region. Investment in water-saving techniques in irrigation, stakeholder participation and farmer organizations are also essential. An ecosystem-services approach should be adopted for better management of water resources in the region.[63] What is needed is a reorientation of priorities toward sustainable management practices to reduce the pressure on water and the services that the resource provides.

The challenge of water rights, equity and social justice

Throughout the region, we find several examples of water being an issue of social justice and equitable access. Big dams, interstate water allocations and conflict between head and tail users in canal irrigation in India, Pakistan, Nepal and Afghanistan demonstrate that there are serious issues of equity and justice common to the region. The debate on water rights is dominated by the problems of riparian users, indigenous community rights, rural versus urban access, caste and class issues, groundwater rights and so on. Privatization in the region is a new trend that is directly related to issues of access and social justice. In a region where a large population lives on less than a dollar a day, the discourse of water as a human right should acquire salience in policy making. Water resource development and planning should also be guided by considerations of equity and access.[64] Decisions on water should be guided by questions like Water for whom? Whose development are we talking about? and Who will benefit from these decisions? Such perceptions should guide water resource development and management in the region.

The challenge of good governance: accountable and effective institutional arrangements

A major challenge to the region is less a challenge of water availability than a distinct problem of institutions and good governance in water resource management. The region is governed by a highly politicized bureaucracy, a technocratic engineering bent of mind in the governance structures and a tendency toward bad management practices in water resource development. Corruption is rampant in irrigation practices, and bribes form a part of the lower bureaucratic process. Many examples of water-quality control, water rights and irrigation practices reveal that institutional and governance weaknesses lead to a significant amount of human security issues of health and water access. Almost every country in the region suffers from these problems, and therefore the solutions not only need technocratic fixes but institutional and governance reforms. Institutional arrangements need to be structured toward accountability, transparency, evaluations and penalty for officials in case they default on their responsibilities.[65] Good governance entails decentralization of roles, participatory processes, transparency in project decisions and democratic norms of policy making. In most cases, the participation of stakeholders begins only when the decision is already announced, after which stakeholders engage in activist roles and resort to collective action rather than being part of the planning process. Policy making needs to be more inclusive of other voices in the formation process, engaging civil society and moving beyond the top-down exclusionary approach.[66]

Transboundary challenges and scope for cooperation

The region faces common environmental risks as a result of rising temperatures, decreasing snowmelt, and altered weather patterns that can increase the intensity of flood cycles or create severe drought in the arid and semiarid regions of South Asia. They all share an intimate and heavily dependent relationship with the water system in the region. More than 3 billion people derive their livelihoods, either directly or indirectly, from the river systems that originate in the Greater Himalayan Watershed. The majority of them work in agriculture and rely on water from the Greater Himalayan Watershed to provide for their families. Yet, freshwater is becoming scarcer just as demand for it is rising. Inefficient irrigation systems, pollution from urban areas and industries and toxins from fertilizers are putting serious constraints on the availability of clean, usable freshwater throughout the region. The region has already experienced an increase in devastating floods.[67] There is a need to focus on the common environmental harm to the region due to issues of scarcity, pollution and climate change rather than individual gains. There are major constraints in the idea of common environmental harm because the individual impacts might be differential; however, moving beyond the narrow conceptualization of water interests toward a regional focus might lead us to the path of sustainable growth and prosperity.

The politics of water, instead of being bogged down in the pursuit of narrow political gains, should look at the core issue of water insecurities in the resource-starved states of the region and instead achieve security and development by enhancing cooperation. The Himalayan Region could be a tower of economic growth and therefore begs for regional cooperation and strong management institutions. The South Asian Co-operative Environmental Programme was created to promote regional cooperation in South Asia in both natural and anthropogenic contexts of sustainable development and management of resources of the region and to work closely with national, regional, international, governmental and non-governmental institutions, as well as groups engaged in cooperation and conservation efforts.[68] South Asia needs to move forward with a cooperative and participatory approach on river basins and water sharing. There needs to be regional awareness that rivers can be better harnessed through collective efforts and recognition that cooperation is essential to alleviate threats to water security. A cognitive connection and trust building can lead to institutions of regional water governance with a set of rules and mechanisms to mitigate conflict and disputes. A regional information base where all countries can have access to information and take adequate steps to mitigate damages can be made to remove problems of data secrecy. De-escalation of tension through increased interaction can also be a positive pathway to increased cooperation and peace building.[69] Cooperation on information sharing, disaster management, and advance warnings have been discussed in the SAARC environmental committees. Since agriculture and fisheries are the main sources of livelihoods, integrated development and management of water resources in the region can actually alleviate poverty and create sustainable levels of comfort, health, and well-being amongst the people of the region. States need to rationalize and depoliticize water in the region to pave the way for integrated water resource management in South Asia.

The issue of complementarities in the water and hydropower sector suggests that an optimum development of the resources of the region is necessary to get the maximum benefit from the proposed cooperation to ensure the security of supply. Negating the complementarities of geographical proximity, economic benefits, and integrated infrastructure is to deny the benefits of the economic prosperity in the region. A resource pool that could move these countries from poverty to prosperity, development and improved quality of life gets entangled in distrust, suspicion, and politics and thus impinges upon the expected pace of progress in the region. Until these hurdles are overcome, the process of constructing a resource security community in South Asia through a water-and-energy paradigm will remain a mixed bag of conflict and cooperation. Peacemaking can lead to the creation of shared regional identities and institutionalize cooperation on several issues common to the region to reconcile human development challenges and national security concerns.

Are there straightforward solutions?

Water issues in the region thus constitute another example of "wicked problems" that society may not completely understand.[70] From a waterscape perspective, "wicked problems" are ones that are multicausal and have a systemic effect. They require a keen grasp of the larger context as well as an understanding of the interrelationships among the full range of underlying causal factors. They often require long-term, holistic, collaborative and innovative approaches. The complexity and dynamics of wicked problems are such that a lack of understanding of these issues may result in the occasional failure of policy change or adjustment.

A sense of despondency descends as these multiple stressors discussed earlier impact water security in the region. The case is not monolithic but complex, and "no one size fits all" solution exists for management of water. Among the pool of different policy resources available, one set of policy options may be valid on one scale while a different set of management options may apply at another scale. Even in problems of similar scales the solutions may vary based on availability, geography and feasibility.

In a region where the availability of water is limited in time and space primarily during the four months of the monsoon, there will always be different collaborating solutions towards water security. The policy makers seem to face a fork. There are decisions in policy and investment that can lead the country in the direction of water security, while other decisions will lead to increased vulnerability and poverty. What policy makers need to do is to calibrate the leverage in policy tools to move the system forward. Steps toward a future of water security will have enormous benefits for people's quality of life and well-being, but by contrast, failure to implement reforms or make adequate investments can cost enormously in terms of human misery and economic growth.[71] As a society moves forward and modernizes, there will be trade-offs in certain places, and policy makers will need to experiment and see what works and what doesn't and adapt and repurpose policy tools towards the end goal – that is water security – because in essence, water touches the lives of billions of people, and issues surrounding its access, availability and quality are fundamental to the human security process.

Notes

1 A. Collins, Contemporary Security Studies, New York: Oxford University Press, 2007.
2 UNDP Report 1994, Human Development Report, New York: Oxford University Press, 1994, p. 23.
3 A. Suhrke, "Human Security and the Interest of States", Security Dialogue, vol. 30, no. 3, 1999.
4 S.R. Khan, "Environmental Security in Pakistan: Are there Grounds for Optimism?", in Adil Najam (ed.), Environment, Development and Human Security: Perspectives from South Asia, Lanham: University Press of America, 2002, p. 69.
5 Norman Myers, Ultimate Security, New York: Norton, 1993.
6 D. Chandler, "Review Essay: Human Security: The Dog that Didn't Bark", Security Dialogue, vol. 39, 1994, pp. 427–438.
7 S. Dalby, "Security, Modernity, Ecology: The Dilemmas of Post-Cold War Security Discourse", Alternatives, vol. 17, no. 1, 1992, pp. 95–134.
8 A. Najam, "Environment and Security: Exploring the Links", in Najam, no. 4, pp. 1–23.
9 N. Myers, Not Far Afield: U.S. Interests and the Global Environment, Washington, DC: World Resources Institute, 1987; V. Böge, "Proposal for an Analytical Framework to Grasp Environmental Conflict", Occasional Paper No. 1, Environment and Conflicts Project, Bern and Zurich: Swiss Peace Foundation and Center for Security Studies and Conflict Research, 1992; Dixon T. Homer, "On the Threshold: Environmental Changes as Causes of Acute Conflict", International Security, vol. 16, pp. 76–116, 1991; P. Gleick, "Environment and Security: The Clear Connection", Bulletin of the Atomic Scientists, 17–21 April 1991.
10 Gleick, no. 9.
11 *Ibid.*
12 Dixon, no. 9.
13 G. Dabelko, S. Lonergan and R. Mathew, State of the Art Review on Environment, Security and Development Co-operation, Paris: OECD Development Assistance Committee, 2000.
14 J.T. Mathew, "Redefining Security", Foreign Affairs, vol. 68, no. 2, 1989; P. Mische, "Ecological Security and the Need to Reconceptualize Sovereignty", Alternatives, vol. 14, no. 4, 1989, pp. 389–427; M. Renner, "National Security: The Economic and Environmental Dimensions", World Watch Paper No. 89. Washington, DC: World Watch Institute, 1989; Myers, no. 9.
15 G. McLean, The Changing Concept of Human Security: Coordinating National and Multilateral Responses, 2013, www.anac.org/canada/security/maclean.html, accessed August 2012.
16 M. Soroos, "Global Change, Environmental Security, and The Prisoner's Dilemma", Prepared for the XVth World Congress of the International Political Science Association, Buenos Aires, July 1991.
17 Suhrke, no. 3.
18 M. Jarraud, "Water Security: Experts Propose a UN Definition on Which Much Depend", Press Release, 2013, www.unwater.org/other-resources/for-the-media/all pressreleases/water-security/en/, accessed 10 March 2014 cited in V. Asthana and A.C. Shukla, Water Security in India: Hope, Despair, and the Challenges of Human Development, New York: Bloomsbury, 2014.

19 Cited in Asthana and Shukla, *Ibid.*, p. 10.
20 C. Cook and K. Bakker, "Water Security: Debating an Emerging Paradigm", Global Environmental Change, vol. 22, no. 1, 2012, 94–102.
21 Global Water Partnership, Our Vision for Water in the 21st Century, 2000, www.gwp.org/globalassets/global/toolbox/references/towards-water-security.-a-framework-for-action.-executive-summary-gwp-2000.pdf, accessed 15 March 2019.
22 Cook and Bakker, no. 19, p. 97.
23 M.S. Swaminathan, "Ecology and Equity: Key Determinants of Sustainable Water Security", Water Science and Technology, vol. 43, 2001, p. 35.
24 A.R. Regmi, "Water Security and Farmer Managed Irrigation Systems in Nepal", in Fiona Rotberg and Ashok Swain (eds.), Natural Resources Security in South Asia: Nepal's Water, Sweden: Institute for Security and Development Policy, 2007.
25 D. Tarlock and P. Wouters, "Reframing the Water Security Dialogue", Journal of Water Law, vol. 20, nos. 2–3, pp. 53–60, 2009.
26 UNWWDR, Water in Changing World, United Nations World Water Development Report, Paris: UNESCO, 2009.
27 S. Kamal, "Pakistan's Water Challenges: Entitlement, Access, Efficiency, and Equity", in Michael Kugelman and Robert M. Hathaway (eds.), Running on Empty: Pakistan's Water Crisis, Washington, DC: Woodrow Wilson Center for International Scholars, Asia Program, 2011.
28 World Bank, Turn Down the Heat; Climate Extremes, Regional Impactsand Case for Resilience, vol. 2, 2013, www.worldbank.org/content/dam/Worldbank/document/Full_Report_Vol_2_Turn_Down_The_Heat_%20Climate_Extremes_Regional_Impacts_Case_for_Resilience_Print%20version_FINAL.pdf, accessed 5 August 2017.
29 *Ibid.*
30 H. Jacoby, M. Rabassa and E. Skoufias, "Distributional Implications of Climate Change in India", Policy, Research Working Paper Series 5623, Washington DC: The World Bank, 2011.
31 R. Wassmann, S.V.K. Jagadish, S. Heuer, A. Ismail, E. Redonna, R. Serraj and R.K. Singh et al., "Climate Change Affecting Rice Production: The Physiological and Agronomic Basis for Possible Adaptation Strategies", Advances in Agronomy, vol. 101, no. 8, 2009, pp. 59–122.
32 R.C. Trivedi, Water Quality Issues in India, swm-report4, 2004, www.indiawaterportal.org/articles/water-quality-issues-india, accessed 1 August 2017.
33 H.P. Ritzema, T.V. Satyanarayana, S. Raman and J. Boonstra, "Subsurface Drainage to Combat Waterlogging and Salinity in Irrigated Lands in India: Lessons Learned in Farmers' Fields", Agricultural Water Management, vol. 95, no. 3, March 2008, pp. 179–189.
34 J. Razaqque, Public Interest Litigation in India, Pakistan and Bangladesh, Netherlands: Kluwer Law International, 2004, p. 9.
35 Kamal, no. 26.
36 *Ibid.*, p. 29.
37 A. Qureshi, Water Resources Management in Afghanistan: Issues and Options, Lahore, Pakistan: International Water Management Institution. June 2002.
38 S.G. Shah and G. Singh, Irrigation Development in Nepal Investment, Efficiency and Institution, Research Report Series 47, Kathmandu: Winrock International, 2001; World Bank, Environment at a Glance, Washington, DC: World Bank, 2004.
39 SESA, State of the Environment South Asia, United Nations Environment Programme, 2001, www.rrcap.ait.asia/Publications/southasia%20soe.pdf, accessed 7 July 2017.
40 *Ibid.*
41 Personal interview with R.K. Jaiswal, 28 August 2009.
42 V. Asthana, "Conflict Over Water Resources: Implications for National Security", in V. Ragahvan (ed.), Environment and Security, New Delhi: Delhi Policy Group, 2005.
43 Carter Brandon and Ramesh Ramankutty, *Towards an Environmental Strategy for Asia*, Washington, DC: World Bank, 1993, p. 69.
44 SESA, no. 38.

45 Rehman, W.A. Zeb, N. Noor and M. Nawaz, "Heavy Metal Pollution Assessment in Various Industries of Pakistan", Environmental Geology, vol. 55, no. 2, July 2008.
46 Z. Aftab, L. Ali. A.M. Khan. A.C. Robinson and I.A. Irshad, Industrial Policy and the Environment in Pakistan, UNIDO: United Nations Industrial Development Organization, 11 December 2000, http://climateinfo.pk/frontend/web/attachments/data-type/UNIDO%20(2000)%20INDUSTRIAL%20POLICY%20AND%20THE%20ENVIRONMENT%20IN%20PAKISTAN.pdf, accessed 7 May 2019.
47 GWP, "From Risk to Resilience: South Asia Regional Framework for Sustainable Water Management", Proceedings Report, www.gwp.org/globalassets/global/gwp-sas_files/events/india-water-week-2015/iww-2015---proceedings-report-of-regional-day-program-of-gwp-south-asia.pdf, p. 5, accessed 15 July 2017.
48 World Bank, Percentage of People with Improved Sanitation Facility, 2012, www.worldbank.org/en/topic/sanitation, accessed 1 October 2013.
49 A. Raza, "Six Districts Throwing Untreated Waste in Chenab", www.thenews.com.pk/archive/print/163140-six-districts-throwing-untreated-waste-into-chenab, accessed 12 August 2017.
50 A. Chaudhary and R.M. Chaudhary, "Securing Sustainable Access to Safe Drinking Water in Lahore", in Michael Kugerman and Robert M. Hathaway (eds.), Running on Empty: Pakistan's Water Crisis, Washington, DC: Woodrow Wilson Center for International Scholars Asia Program, 2009.
51 B.R. Upreti, "Changing Political Context, New Power Relations and Hydro – Conflict in Nepal", paper presented at the Nepal Water Security Forum organized by the Silk Road Studies Program, Sweden: Uppsala University, 27 March 2007.
52 Government of India, National Commission on Integrated Water Resources Development Plan. A Plan for Action, New Delhi: Ministry of Water Resources. Government of India, 1999.
53 World Bank, no. 13.
54 N. Gaan, Environment and National Security in South Asia, New Delhi: South Asian Publishers, 2002, p. 67.
55 World Bank, no. 27.
56 Q.K. Ahmad and A.U. Ahmed, "Social Sustainability, Indicators and Climate Change, in Climate Change and Its Linkages with Development, Equity, and Sustainability", in M. Munasinghe and R. Swart (eds.), Intergovernmental Panel on Climate Change, Switzerland: Geneva, 2000, pp. 95–108.
57 R.R. Iyer, "Special Articles – Inter-State Water Disputes Act 1956: Difficulties and Solutions", Economic and Political Weekly, vol. 37, no. 28, 2002, p. 2907.
58 Asthana and Shukla, no. 18.
59 Raza, no. 47.
60 S.J. Halvorson, "Intersections of Water and Gender in Rural Pakistan", in Michael Kugerman and Robert M. Hathaway (eds.), Running on Empty: Pakistan's Water Crisis, Washington, DC: Woodrow Wilson Center for International Scholars, Asia Program, 2009, pp. 105–117.
61 J.L. Westcoat, "Water Shortages and Water Conserving Urban Design in Pakistan", in Michael Kugerman and Robert M. Hathaway (eds.), Running on Empty: Pakistan's Water Crisis, Washington, DC: Woodrow Wilson Center for International Scholars, Asia Program, 2009, p. 15.
62 V. Asthana and A.C. Shukla, "Sustainable Development as a New Security Paradigm for India", in Adil Najam (ed.), Environment, Development and Human Security: Perspectives from South Asia, Lanham: University Press of America, 2003, pp. 25–27.
63 Asthana and Shukla, no. 56.
64 V. Asthana, "Water Security in South Asia", South Asia Journal, no. 37, September–October 2012.
65 *Ibid*.
66 V. Asthana, Water Policy Processes in India: Discourses of Power and Resistance, London: Routledge, 2009.

67 W. Goodyear, The Water Security Gamble in the Greater Watershed, http://southasia journal.net/the-water-security-gamble-in-the-greater-himalayan-watershed/, accessed 17 July 2017.
68 SACEP, South Asia Co-operative Environment Program: Mission, www.icriforum. org/about-icri/members-networks/south-asia-co-operative-environment-programme-sacep%20Accessed%20September%2015, accessed 17 September 2018.
69 Asthana and Shukla, no. 56.
70 H. Rittel and M. Webber, "Dilemmas in a General Theory of Planning", Policy Sciences, vol. 4, 1973, pp. 155–169.
71 Asthana and Shukla, no. 56.

8

CLIMATE CHANGE AND HUMAN SECURITY

A case study of the Maldives

Rabindra Sen

Introduction

This chapter seeks to undertake a case study of the Maldives to bring out the magnitude of the problems of climate change and sea-level rise faced by the island nation. The rationale behind the choice is quite obvious because for the Maldives the crisis is of such proportions that its very survival is at stake. The Maldives, as Damian Carrington has rightly pointed out, is on the environmental front line.[1]

In the first of the three sections of the chapter, the context would be established through a general discussion of climate change and sea-level rise. The thrust of the discussion in the first of the two sections on the Maldives would be on the challenges and problems emanating from climate change. And subsequently, attention would shift to the policies adopted by the Maldives in dealing with these problems. Also worth highlighting are the diplomatic efforts of the Maldives through the United Nations and other organisations, especially the Alliance of Small Island States (AOSIS), to influence the global debate on the issue and generate international action and support.

Climate change and sea-level rise

Far from being separate challenges, global warming and sea-level rise should be viewed as an integrated environmental issue confronting humankind.[2] Fifteen of the sixteen warmest years on record have occurred since 2001.[3] Evidence shows that 2000 to 2009 was hotter than any other decade in at least the past 1,300 years. This warming is altering the Earth's climate system, including its land, atmosphere, oceans and ice in far-reaching ways.[4] In recent years, these extreme weather conditions have become increasingly prevalent in South Asia and will only become more so in the absence of strong and urgent climate measures.[5]

Climate change has long been considered a global security threat as it gravely endangers the climate and ecosystems of the Earth.[6] The problem is not confined to the developing and small states. Among the examples of its devastating effects on the developed countries are Storm Desmond and Hurricane Katrina, respectively, hitting the UK and the US. The Arctic has warmed more than any other region on Earth.[7] The UN's climate science panel says melting glaciers will account for a quarter of the total sea-level rise, pegged at 26 to 98 centimetres by 2100.[8] Global sea levels have risen by 20 centimetres since records began in 1880, buoyed by melting ice and water expansion caused by rising temperatures.[9] The worst predictions of further rises are just under 2 metres by the end of this century – ominous enough to trigger panic reactions from nations like the Maldives.[10] Sea levels are likely to rise between 26 and 82 centimetres by the late twenty-first century, after a rise of 19 cm since 1900.[11]

Scientists say quick action is needed to prevent the worsening floods, droughts and violent storms that would impact billions of people worldwide in a warming world.[12] According to a report in 2015 in *The Lancet*, more people will be exposed to floods, droughts, heat waves and other extreme weather conditions associated with climate change over the next century than previously thought. Peter Cox, one of the authors of the report, said, "We have to move away from thinking of this as a problem in atmospheric physics. It is a problem for people".[13] Scientists have also pointed to the danger of ocean acidification.[14] They said,

> It is now nearly inevitable that within fifty to hundred years, continued anthropogenic [man-made] carbon dioxide emissions will further increase ocean acidity to levels that will have widespread impacts ... on marine organisms and ecosystems and the goods and services they provide.[15]

The experts have sounded a special warning for tropical coral reefs already affected by warmer seas. The risks "are of great concern, since the livelihoods of around 400 million people depend on such habitats", they said.[16] Also worrisome is a steep rise predicted in the number of people rendered homeless and stateless by weather disasters. The Environmental Justice Foundation estimates that as many as 500 to 600 million people – nearly 10 per cent of the world's population – are at risk of displacement.[17] Not surprisingly, concerted action through regional and global cooperation is necessary to deal with the enormous challenge.

Although the increasingly serious problem would affect all the nations, according to the Intergovernmental Panel on Climate Change (IPCC), small and low lying Island states like the Maldives will be affected most adversely in spite of being the least responsible for climate change.[18] Small Island Developing States (SIDS) are not only among the smallest countries in the world but also among the most vulnerable.[19]

Impact on the Maldives and gravity of the problem

The Maldives faces perhaps one of the most severe potential effects of climate change: the complete, or near complete, submersion of its national territory.[20] It is hard to be Maldivian and not care about climate change.[21] None of the coral islands measures more than 1.8 metres (6 ft) above sea level, making the Maldives especially vulnerable to sea-level rise associated with global warming.[22] The lowest-lying country in the world is not even built on sand but on the planet's most endangered ecosystem, coral reefs.[23] For the Maldives, the threat posed by climate change is already as clear as the water off its beaches.[24] Symbolically pointing to the looming threat in 2009, then president Mohamed Nasheed had, in utter desperation, convened an underwater cabinet meeting to sign a document demanding cuts in carbon emissions before the UN Climate Change conference in Copenhagen. "This is what will happen to the Maldives if climate change is not checked", he had warned.[25] In 2011, in an article in *Sydney Morning Herald*, Nasheed drove home the urgency of the matter by pointing out, "I lead an island nation that may slip beneath the waves if all this talk on climate does not lead to action soon. For the Maldives, further delay is a luxury we cannot afford".[26]

In 1987, Malé, the capital, was inundated by tidal waves, giving rise to fears that the atoll country might one day go down under the sea. The fears are quite understandable in view of the results showing that the Maldives' coastal sea level is rising in the same way as the global sea level.[27] The mean tidal level at Male showed an increasing trend of about 4.1 mm/year and at Gan registering a positive trend of about 3.9 mm/year.[28]

Being the flattest country on earth, the Maldives is extremely vulnerable to the effects of global warming and the most vulnerable to global warming and sea-level rise in South Asia.[29] It is, therefore, only natural for Maldives to be deeply concerned about climate change. Given mid-level scenarios for global warming emissions, Maldives is projected to experience sea-level rise of as much as half a metre and, as a result, lose more than 70 percent of its land area by about 2100. In the worse scenario of a sea-level rise of 1 metre, the Maldives could well be almost wholly submerged a decade and a half earlier.[30]

In 2009 at the United Nations Climate Change conference in Copenhagen, then president Mohamed Nasheed had said that climate change could "wipe our country off the map".[31] He said it could happen in a matter of years and called for urgency in fighting global warming.[32] Thoriq Ibrahim, former Maldivian minister of environment and energy, said that climate change already had a significant impact on his country.[33] Commenting on the paucity of freshwater resources in the Maldives, the former minister said, "We don't have good drinking water sources, so we have to harvest rainwater, but the dry season lasts much longer now".[34] Ibrahim said, "We have ample solar energy. We want to harness as much of it as possible".[35] According to CBS News correspondent Mark Phillips, the Maldives may be the first to feel the climate change pain.[36]

Climate change and Maldivian diplomacy

Maldives had a taste of disaster when the 2004 tsunami swept over the islands, killing close to a hundred people. The multifaceted danger threatening Maldives on account of global warming and rising sea levels has been brought up again and again at international conferences. The Maldives indeed has a long record of taking the lead on climate change issues.[37] Former president Maumoon Abdul Gayoom was the first world leader to address the United Nations General Assembly on the issue of climate change. In his "Death of a Nation" speech at the United Nations in 1987, he had noted that global warming, if not checked, would lead to the death of the Maldivian nation and others like it.[38] Gayoom was also instrumental in founding the Alliance of Small Island States (AOSIS) which has incessantly campaigned internationally against global warming.[39] The Maldives was the first country to ratify the Kyoto Protocol, the first international agreement on combating climate change.[40]

In November 2007, the Maldives hosted a Small Island States Conference on the Human Dimension of Global Climate Change with the objective of placing the people at the core of international climate change policy.[41] The Male Declaration on the Human Dimension of Global Climate Change, adopted at the conference, emphatically stated that "climate change has clear and immediate implications for the full enjoyment of human rights".[42] Also noteworthy in this context is the success of the Maldives and a group of like-minded friends in March 2008 in securing the adoption, by consensus, of United Nations Human Rights Council Resolution 7/23(co-sponsored by the Maldives) on "Human Rights and Climate Change", unequivocally linking climate change and human rights for the first time in an official UN document.[43] The Maldives called on the world to explore and define the human rights implications of climate change as a way of putting a human face on the problem and ultimately of enhancing the moral and ethical imperative for the world to act.[44]

For a considerable time, the AOSIS states, many of them low-lying states in the Pacific and Indian Oceans, campaigned for a UN-sponsored climate change agreement to try to restrict average global temperature rise to 1.5 °C above pre-industrial levels.[45] In 1989, in fact three years before the Rio Earth Summit when 'climate change and global warming' became a part of the everyday lexicon, the Maldives had hosted the Small State Conference on Sea-Level Rise.[46] It was at this conference that AOSIS countries formally came together and subsequently engaged themselves in various activities in support of their demands.[47] The inclusion of the 1.5-degree limit at the Paris Climate Conference in 2015, albeit not a firm target, was a remarkable victory indeed for the AOSIS countries, especially keeping in mind that notwithstanding their efforts, the 2009 Copenhagen Climate Conference had utterly disappointed them.[48]

Under the historic Paris Agreement, the parties were to try to hold temperature increases to 'well below' two degrees and at the same time continue trying to restrict temperature increase to 1.5 degrees.[49] The agreement, considered path-breaking, was welcomed by many countries including the Maldives. Thoriq Ibrahim responded saying, "We're happy with this".[50] In the midst of hope and expectation, however, there was skepticism too about the goal.[51] Robert Falkner rightly observed, "Paris was a breakthrough event, but it did not fix the climate problem. [It] is not the end of this journey, in many ways it is only the beginning".[52]

108 Rabindra Sen

The key policies of the Maldives for dealing with the challenges are Strategic National Action Plan for Disaster Risk Reduction and Climate Change Adaptation 2010–2020.[53] Among the policy recommendations in the 2001 national report to the United Nations Framework Convention on Climate Change, particularly noteworthy are engagement in international advocacy, the inclusion of climate change concerns into regulatory policies, the establishment of financing mechanisms for implementing climate change programmes, enhancing capacity to adapt to climate change and developing strategies for the mitigation of greenhouse gas emissions.[54]

Conclusion

The need of the hour is concrete action, not simply in the form of an agreement, regional or global, to significantly reduce emissions worldwide but to see to it that the agreement is properly implemented for the benefit of all. As Dieter Helm and Cameron Hepburn have aptly put it, "[w]e broadly know what has to be done. Doing it remains the difficult part".[55]

What has been the progress in terms of action by the Maldives in dealing with the problem looming large on the horizon? Notably one will not miss the inherent contradictions in the Maldives either with regard to the nature of the problem or the ways of tackling it.[56] Although the alarm bells about climate change as an already existing phenomenon have increasingly become louder and more convincing, dissenting opinion might continue to push it to the realm of conjecture. Debatable though it still may be, although not to the extent as previously, the answer to the reservations expressed by those who associate climate change with futurology would be that the present cannot be divorced from the future and hence the need for contingency planning. Mohamed Aslam, a former environment minister, emphasized the dire necessity of efficacious measures at home as well as garnering external support before it is too late, saying, "Just because you are not dead now doesn't mean you are not dying".[57] Asked for the odds of his grandchildren inheriting an inhabitable Maldives, Mohamed Nasheed said, "50–50".[58] Nobody perhaps can be sure about how long the Maldives will remain in a twilight zone of existence and extinction. Whether there is going to be a further deterioration or improvement in the situation and whether the island nation succeeds or fails in shaping its destiny remain to be seen.

Notes

1 Damian Carrington, "The Maldives Is the Extreme Test Case for Climate Change Action", 26 September 2013, www.theguardian.com/environment/damian-carrington-blog/2013/sep/26/maldives-test-case-climate-change-action, accessed 24 April 2019. In February 1998, former president Maumoon Abdul Gayoom had said, "Few states stand to lose as much from the adverse effects of global warming and subsequent sea level rise." Speech on the occasion of the inauguration of the Kaashidhoo Climate Observatory on 23 February 1998, http://www-indoex.ucsd.edu/news/speech/index.html, accessed 24 April 2019.

Climate change and human security **109**

2 For details see, Tariq Masood Ali Khan, Dewan Abdul Quadir, T.S. Murty, Anwarul Kabir, Fahmida Aktar and Majajul Alam Sarker, "Relative Sea Level Changes in Maldives and Vulnerability of Land Due to Abnormal Coastal Inundation", Marine Geodesy, vol. 25, nos. 1–2, 2002, pp. 133–143.
3 Damian Carrington, "2015 Smashes Record for Hottest Year, Final Figures Confirm", www.theguardian.com/environment/2016/jan/20/2015-smashes-record-for-hottest-year-final-figures-confirm, accessed 24 April 2019.
4 Melissa Denchak, "Are the Effects of Global Warming Really that Bad?" 15 March 2016, www.nrdc.org/stories/are-effects-global-warming-really-bad, accessed 24 April 2019.
5 Kamal Madishetty, "Climate Change: Can India Take the Lead in Paris?", The Diplomat, 24 July 2015, http://thediplomat.com/2015/07/climate-change-can-india-take-the-lead-in-paris/, accessed 24 April 2019.
6 As former president of the Maldives Abdulla Yameen Abdul Gayoom put it, "The Maldives believes that climate change poses as the most pressing developmental and security challenge of the 21st Century." See "President Abdulla Yameen Abdul Gayoom's Message for the Opening Day of the 21st Session of Conference of the Parties (COP)", 30 November 2015, http://foreign.gov.mv/index.php/en/mediacentre/news/2221-president-abdulla-yameen-abdul-gayoom-s-message-for-the-opening-day-of-the-21st-session-of-conference-of-the-parties-cop, accessed 24 April 2019. According to Charles Bolden, the NASA head, "Climate change is the challenge of our generation". Carrington, n. 3. Bob Ward, at the Grantham Research Institute on Climate Change at the London School of Economics, has said: "The warming is already affecting the climate around the world, including dangerous shifts in extreme weather events. Those who claim that climate change is either not happening, or is not dangerous, have been conclusively proven wrong by the meteorological evidence around the world." Ibid.
7 Celine Serrat, "Adapt or Die: Arctic Animals Cope with Climate Change", The Daily Star, www.dailystar.com.lb/Life/Environment/2015/Sep-02/313596-adapt-or-die-arctic-animals-cope-with-climate-change.ashx, accessed 24 April 2019.
8 Ibid.
9 Simon Usborne, "Is it Too Late to Save the Maldives from Climate Change and Islamic Extremism?" 6 December 2014, www.independent.co.uk/news/world/asia/is-it-too-late-to-save-the-maldives-from-climate-change-and-islamic-extremism-9901424.html, accessed 24 April 2019.
10 Ibid.
11 Alister Doyle, "Antarctic Ice Shelf on Brink of Unstoppable Melt that Could Raise Sea Levels for 10,000 Years", www.huffpost.com/entry/antarctic-ice-melt_n_5263660, accessed 24 April 2019.
12 See Usborne, n. 9.
13 "Climate Change Would Spell Health Doom", The Hindustan Times, 24 June 2015, p. 9.
14 "Scientists Sound Alarm Over Ocean Acidification", www.gmanetwork.com/news/scitech/science/382658/scientists-sound-alarm-over-ocean-acidification/story/, accessed 24 April 2019.
15 Ibid.
16 Ibid.
17 John Vidal, "Global Warming Could Create 150 Million 'climate refugees' by 2050", www.theguardian.com/environment/2009/nov/03/global-warming-climate-refugees, accessed 24 April 2019.
18 Alexander Voccia, "Climate Change: What Future for Small, Vulnerable States?", International Journal of Sustainable Development & World Ecology, vol. 19, no. 2, 2012, p. 101, www.tandfonline.com/doi/abs/10.1080/13504509.2011.634032, accessed 24 April 2019. Although contributing least to the emission of greenhouse gases, the LDCs are the most vulnerable to the effects of climate change and have the least capacity to adapt to these changes. See Saleemul Huq, Atiq Rahman, Mama Konate,

YoubaSokona and Hanna Reid, "Mainstreaming Adaptation to Climate Change in Least Developed Countries (LDCs)", April 2003, p. 12, http://pubs.iied.org/pdfs/9219IIED.pdf, accessed 24 April 2019.

19 *Ibid*.

20 The island country's average height is 1.5m. As much as over 80 per cent of inhabited land is less than 1m above sea level. See Michal Nachmany, Sam Fankhauser, Jana Davidová, Nick Kingsmill, Tucker Landesman, Hitomi Roppongi, Philip Schleifer, Joana Setzer, Amelia Sharman, C. Stolle Singleton, JayarajSundaresan and Terry Townshend, "Climate Change Legislation in Maldives: An Excerpt from the 2015 Global Climate Legislation Study, a Review of Climate Change Legislation in 99 Countries", www.lse.ac.uk/GranthamInstitute/wp-content/uploads/2015/05/MALDIVES.pdf, accessed 24 April 2019. While an expansive coral reef surrounding the island country provides protection against most oceanic storms, rising sea levels pose a real threat as regular tidal flooding may have the effect of wiping out dry land. *Ibid*.

21 Gwynne Dyer, "In Maldives, Politics, Greed Trump Climate Change", Japan Times, 2 December 2015, www.japantimes.co.jp/opinion/2015/12/02/commentary/world-commentary/maldives-politics-greed-trump-climate-change/#.WbtcSfkjG1s, accessed 24 April 2019. In June 2008, former Deputy Foreign Minister of the Maldives, Duniya Maumoon had observed, "Climate Change is the defining issue of our time and the fundamental global challenge of the 21st century." See Speech by former Deputy Foreign Minister of the Republic of Maldives, Ms Duniya Maumoon on "The Role of the Maldives in Promoting Human Rights and Environmental Advocacy", University of Iceland Reykjavik, Monday 16 June 2008, p. 2, https://studyres.com/doc/4643079/speech-by, accessed 24 April 2019. In 2007, then foreign minister of the Maldives Abdulla Shahid had said, "For us climate change poses the most immediate and far-reaching danger to our natural systems. The degradation of these systems threatens the prosperity of our people and the very survival of our nations." Seestatement by Abdulla Shahid, the Minister of Foreign Affairs of the Republic of Maldives on "Human Dimension of Global Climate Change" at the Commonwealth Foreign Ministers meeting organized in conjunction with the United Nations General Assembly, 28 September 2007, http://maldivesmission.com/statements/statement_on_the_human_dimension_of_global_climate_change_by_he_mr_abdulla_shahid_minister_of_foreign_affairs_of_the_republic_of_maldives, accessed 24 April 2019. Speaking in the UN General Assembly in 2016, Mohamed Asim, Minister for Foreign Affairs of the Republic of Maldives, said, "The Maldives is one of the countries that is most vulnerable to environmental shocks and one of the most exposed to the impacts of climate change. Climate change is an existential threat to our country." See, General Assembly Official Records, Seventy-first session, 21st plenary meeting, 24 September 2016, A/71/PV. 21, p. 21, https://digitallibrary.un.org/record/848334/files/A_71_PV-21-EN.pdf, accessed 24 April 2019.

22 "Maldives Country Profile", www.bbc.com/news/world-south-asia-12651486, accessed 24 April 2019.

23 See no. 1.

24 See, "Helping Maldives Combat the Effects of Climate Change", www.unops.org/news-and-stories/news/helping-maldives-combat-the-effects-of-climate-change, accessed 24 April 2019.

25 Dyer, no. 21. "That's where we will end up. In many senses that might be where we will be having our cabinet meetings in the future", he said. See, Mark Philips, "Climate Change Threatens Maldives", 7 December 2009, www.cbsnews.com/news/climate-change-threatens-maldives/, accessed 24 April 2019. "We've had it. There's no debate, there's no question," said Nasheed. *Ibid*., Sea levels are predicted to rise by as much as 23 inches this century according to the UN's Climate Change Panel. Other more recent studies have warned the world's oceans may rise even higher. *Ibid*.

26 Mohamed Nasheed, "Carbon Delay Is a Luxury the Maldives Cannot Afford", The Sydney Morning Herald, 27 October 2011, www.smh.com.au/politics/federal/

carbon-delay-is-a-luxury-the-maldives-cannot-afford-20111026-1mk25.html, accessed 24 April 2019.

27 See no. 2.

28 *Ibid*. The dreadful impact of a rise in sea level on the Maldives may be thought of as real and undisputed, but the following completely contrasting views and puzzling assessments about the impact of temperature and sea-level rise give us an inkling of the extent of variations in views on the issue concerned and the debate on climate change, in general. According to O.P. Singh, Tariq Masood Ali Khan, Fahmida Aktar and Majajul Alam Sarker, "Maldives . . . is extremely vulnerable to the impacts of Sea Level Rise (SLR) due to its low altitude from the mean sea level. Results show that recent sea level trends in the Maldives coast are very high." O.P. Singh, Tariq Masood Ali Khan, Fahmida Aktar and Majajul Alam Sarker, "Recent Sea Level and Sea Surface Temperature Changes Along the Maldives Coast", Marine Geodesy, vol. 24, no. 4, 2001, p. 209, www.tandfon line.com/doi/abs/10.1080/014904101753227851, accessed 24 April 2019. Niels-Axel Mörner, on the other hand, holds a diametrically opposite view arguing that while in a common greenhouse-gas globalwarming scenario the Maldives have been condemned to become flooded in fifty years or, at the most, a hundred years, "our study of past and present sea-level changes shows no sign of any sea-level rise." Mörner, in fact, takes one step further to argue that the Maldives has instead seen a sea-level fall in the last few decades. "We are confident that the people of the Maldives are not condemned to become flooded in the near future." Niels-Axel Mörner, "The Maldives Project: A Future Free from Sea-Level Flooding", Contemporary South Asia, vol. 13, no. 2, 2004, p. 149, www. tandfonline.com/doi/abs/10.1080/0958493042000242936, accessed 24 April 2019.

29 Climate Hotmap, Republic of Maldives, www.climatehotmap.org/global-warming-locations/republic-of-maldives.html, accessed 24 April 2019. Sea level rise is likely to worsen existing environmental stresses in the Maldives, such as periodic flooding from storm surge and a scarcity of freshwater for drinking and other purposes. *Ibid*. This explains the opening of a new Integrated Water Supply System by former president Abdulla Yameen Abdul Gayoom in a move to protect freshwater resources. See William Brittlebank, "Maldives Opens New Landmark Clean Water System", 26 February 2016, www.climateaction.org/news/maldives_opens_new_landmark_clean_water_system, accessed 24 April 2019.

30 See Climate Hotmap, no. 29. The Maldivian government has identified many potential strategies for adapting to rising seas, but the degree of concern can be gauged from a desperate inclusion of even relocation of its people to a new homeland as one of the options considered. *Ibid*. Also see Mark Phillips, "Climate Change Threatens Maldives", 7 December 2009, www.cbsnews.com/news/climate-change-threatens-maldives/, accessed 24 April 2019. At less than 2 metres above sea level on average, the Maldives is especially susceptible to flooding, which, combined with the porous soil, makes seawater intrusion into the country's limited groundwater a constant threat. See, "Helping Maldives . . .", no. 24.

31 Kim Se-jeong, "Maldives Calls on Developed Nations to Help Fight Climate Change", http://m.koreatimes.co.kr/phone/news/view.jsp?req_newsidx=192838, accessed 24 April 2019.

32 *Ibid*.

33 Kim Se-jeong, no. 31. In 2008, then Deputy Foreign Minister of the Maldives, Duniya-Maumoon, said, "Climate Change should not be seen as a future prediction, or as some kind of doomsday scenario decried by far-sighted scientists. Climate change is real; it is happening now; and its effects are being felt at this very moment in every country in the world – but especially in Small and Vulnerable States such as the Maldives." Speech by Deputy Foreign Minister of the Republic of Maldives, Duniya Maumoon, no. 21, p. 3.

34 Kim Se-jeong, no. 31.

35 *Ibid*.

36 Philips, no. 30.

112 Rabindra Sen

37 Dyer, no. 21.
38 *Ibid.*
39 *Ibid.*
40 *Ibid.*
41 Speech by Duniya Maumoon, no. 21, p. 8. In 2007, former foreign minister of the Maldives Abdulla Shahid cogently observed, "Today the issue of climate change is more than environment, more than science, and more than politics. It is fundamentally a human issue as it threatens human prosperity, human rights, and human survival. It is already interfering with human rights, including, the right to life, the right to take part in cultural life, and the right to use and enjoy property." See n. 21. For a discussion of the linkage see, Dinah Shelton, "Human Rights and Climate Change", Working Paper No. 09–002, December 2009, pp. 1–45, http://buffett.northwestern.edu/documents/working-papers/Buffett_09-002_Shelton.pdf, accessed 24 April 2019. Also see, Matthias Mueller, "Climate Change and Human Rights Agenda-Setting Against the Odds, 2017/01, Global Governance Institute, pp. 1–16, www.ucl.ac.uk/global-governance/sites/global-governance/files/Mueller_Working_Paper_Climate_Change_and_Human_Rights.pdf, accessed 24 April 2019.

In the words of Mary Robinson, climate challenge is the greatest threat to human rights in the 21st century. "Climate Change: The Greatest Threat to Human Rights in the 21st Century", 2 September, 2016, www.ucl.ac.uk/global-governance/news/2016/sep/climate-change-greatest-threat-human-rights-21st-century, accessed 24 April 2019.
42 "Malé Declaration on the Human Dimension of Global Climate Change", www.ciel.org/Publications/Male_Declaration_Nov07.pdf, accessed 24 April 2019.
43 Speech by Duniya Maumoon, no. 21, p. 9. Also UN General Assembly, A/HRC/7/78, 14 July 2018, pp. 65–66, https://www2.ohchr.org/english/bodies/hrcouncil/docs/7session/A-HRC-7-78.doc, accessed 24 April 2019.
44 Speech by Duniya Maumoon, no. 21.
45 Eric Reguly, "Small Island States Make Waves at Paris Climate Conference", The Globe and Mail, 13 December 2015, www.theglobeandmail.com/news/world/small-island-states-make-waves-at-paris-climate-conference/article27742043/, accessed 24 April 2019.
46 *Ibid.*
47 The small island states have argued that some of them will be doomed unless planet-warming greenhouse-gas emissions are significantly reduced. *Ibid.*
48 *Ibid.*
49 *Ibid.*
50 Under the agreement the countries were also to fulfil their individual carbon-reduction plans submitted prior to the conference and to periodically review them. *Ibid.*
51 Dyer, no. 21. Since the entire negotiation was based on each country's voluntary commitments on emission reductions, Dyer apprehended there could be 140 different ways of sabotaging whatever was agreed upon at Paris. *Ibid.* It is noteworthy that the Maldives was the fourth country to ratify the Paris Agreement. Ed King, "Maldives Becomes Fourth Island State to Ratify Paris Climate Deal", 6 April 2016, www.climatechangenews.com/2016/04/06/maldives-becomes-fourth-island-state-to-ratify-paris-climate-deal/, accessed 24 April 2019.
52 Robert Falkner, "The Paris Agreement and the New Logic of International Climate Politics", International Affairs, vol. 92, no. 5, 2016, pp. 1107–1125, https://static1.squarespace.com/static/538a0f32e4b0e9ab915750a1/t/57d3dfc646c3c43b079d1c59/1473503175245/Falkner_2016_TheParisAgreement.pdf, accessed 24 April 2019. Referring to the Paris agreement, former UN Secretary-General Ban Ki-moon said, "I am encouraged and hopeful that the whole world will be united in moving ahead with this . . . agreement. This is the political and moral responsibility of our political leaders". See "Let's Unite in Moving Ahead with this Paris Climate Change Agreement", 23 October 2017, https://bankimooncentre.org/lets-unite-in-moving-ahead-with-this-paris-climate-change-agreement, accessed 24 April 2019.

53 See, Nachmany et al., no. 20, p. 2. The Ministry of Environment and Energy is the main government body responsible for climate change in the Maldives. See in this connection, "Maldives Climate Change Policy Framework", 2014, www.preventionweb.net/english/professional/policies/v.php?id=39744, accessed 24 April 2019. This framework prescribes the Government and the people of Maldives strategic polices for responding to climate change impacts from 2014 to 2024. The policy defines five thematic goals and strategies that have been prioritized for implementation to ensure that safety and resilience are achieved.

54 Nachmany et al., no. 20, p. 3.

55 Dieter Helm and Cameron Hepburn (eds.), The Economics and Politics of Climate Change, Oxford: Oxford University Press, 2009, pp. 1–5. As already noted, *Gwynne Dyer* painted a grim picture of the future saying that not all the promises made in Paris would be kept. Dyer, no. 21. The crux lies in implementation and the time to act is now. See, "Climate Change: The Greatest Threat to Human Rights in the 21st Century", no. 41. The world risks crossing the point of no return on climate change, with disastrous consequences for people across in the world and the natural systems sustaining them, the UN Secretary-General Antonio Guterras warned. "There is no more time to waste. . . . Every day we fail to act is a day that we step a little closer towards a fate that none of us wants – a fate that will resonate through generations in the damage done to humankind and life on earth", he said. See, "'Direct Existential Threat' of Climate Change Nears Point of No Return, Warns UN Chief", 10 September 2018, https://news.un.org/en/story/2018/09/1018852, accessed 24 April 2019. As nations gathered in Poland in early December 2018 to discuss their plan to avert the environmental catastrophe, UN Climate Chief Patricia Espinosa said, "Climate change impacts have never been worse. This reality is telling us that we need to do much more." "Climate Change Threat Has 'never been worse', says UN Climate Chief", www.sbs.com.au/news/climate-change-threat-has-never-been-worse-says-un-climate-chief, accessed 24 April 2019.

56 We need to compare amplification of climate change risks for international audiences and attenuation of the same for audiences at home. See, for details, Aishath Shakeela and Susanne Becken, "Understanding Tourism Leaders' Perceptions of Risks From Climate Change: An Assessment of Policy-Making Processes in the Maldives using the Social Amplification of Risk Framework (SARF)", Journal of Sustainable Tourism, vol. 23, no. 1, 2015, p. 65, www.tandfonline.com/doi/abs/10.1080/09669582.2014.918135, accessed 24 April 2019. The total dependence of the people on diesel for generators, the expenditure as high as over a quarter of the gross domestic product on fuel, and the huge subsidies for keeping the energy bills affordable are worth mentioning in this context. Carrington, no. 1. Solar power would certainly minimize costs, but the Maldives is handicapped by a lack of capital or expertise for the flow resource. The negative effects of tourism, the mainstay of the economy, contribute directly or indirectly to a worsening of the situation, and troubling contradictions can also be found in fishing – the island nation's second-biggest industry. And ironically again, for most Maldivians, the problems are out of sight and out of mind. *Ibid.*

57 Carrington, no. 1.

58 *Ibid.*

9

DANGERS OF ELECTRONIC WASTE IN INDIA

A concern for human security

Gopalji Malviya

Introduction

The Western model of development through aggressive industrialisation and consumerism has already invaded urban India; rural India is not far off. Industrial waste, medical waste, plastic filth and nuclear waste threaten the health of the common man. Now e-waste casts its dark shadow on India. The boom in the use of electronic gadgets has revolutionised lives, but it has also created a new peril to human health and the environment. The problem is growing as rapid innovations quickly render electronic products obsolete. These products are among the fastest-growing category of municipal garbage. Devices such as computers, fax machines, mobile phones, music players and a host of others open possibilities for individuals and businesses alike. Yet there is a downside to this digital era: the growing mountain of electronic waste or e-waste.

E-waste is a term to describe old or obsolete, end-of-life electronic appliances that have been disposed of by their users. E-waste encompasses computers, servers, mainframes, monitors, TVs and display devices, cellular phones and pagers, calculators, audio and video devices, printers, scanners, copiers and fax machines besides refrigerators, air-conditioners, washing machines, microwave ovens and industrial electronics such as sensors, alarms, sirens, security devices and automobile electronic devices. Thus, e-waste comprises extremely diverse substances; it varies from products across different categories. More than 1,000 substances fall under hazardous e-waste categories. Broadly they consist of ferrous and non-ferrous substances. If elements like lead, mercury, arsenic, cadmium, selenium, hexavalent chromium and brominated flame retardant are present, the e-waste is classified as hazardous. Technically, however, e-waste is only a subset of WEEE (Waste Electrical and Electronic Equipment).

According to a study of The Associated Chambers of Commerce and Industry of India (ASSOCHAM), India has surely emerged as the second-largest mobile market, with 1.03 billion subscribers, but also the fifth-largest producer of e-waste in the world, discarding roughly 18.5 lakh metric tonnes of electronic waste each year, with telecom equipment alone accounting for 12 percent of the e-waste. Total WEEE generation in India was about 1.5 lakh tonnes in 2012 and was expected to generate nearly 8 lakh tonnes of e-waste by the end of 2012. The top states in order of contribution are Maharashtra, Andhra Pradesh, Tamil Nadu, Uttar Pradesh, West Bengal, Delhi, Karnataka, Gujarat, Madhya Pradesh and Punjab. The city-wise rankings are Mumbai, Delhi, Bangalore, Chennai, Kolkata, Ahmedabad, Hyderabad, Pune, Surat and Nagpur.

The rapid growth and rising redundancy of electronic equipment is a major health and environmental challenge to developing countries. India is witnessing an explosive consumption of electronic goods and is becoming a major destination for manufacturing these goods. It has also been short-listed by the US and European countries to dump their e-waste. More than 50,000 tonnes of e-waste comes into India every year under the pretext of charity and donation.[1] Hazardous waste imports are monitored under the Basel Convention of 1992, which regulates country-to-country movement of hazardous waste. But the norms are seldom followed.

In India, e-waste management assumes greater significance because it has a direct impact on the environment. The four metros are at higher risk of environmental pollution from e-waste. Delhi's computer waste is stored in a yard in Tughlak-abad. Scrap bidders divvy up the units and sell the parts among neighbourhoods with different recycling specialities. Workers in Ferozabad, for example, recover the glass from monitors (a process that risks exposure to lead), while those in Mandoli recover copper. Many people in Mandoli are affected by asthma, bronchitis and chronic lung infections. Mumbai, Bangalore, Chennai, Hyderabad and Delhi face grave health and environmental risks posed by a whopping more than 40,000 to 50,000 tonnes of electronic waste produced in these cities. The State Pollution Control Board of these respective cities provide annual data; however, these fluctu-ating data are not actually validated by any competent agencies.

Chennai has no proper facilities to recycle the waste. Uncontrolled burning, disassembly, disposal and poor processing are threatening both the environment and human health. Areas like Perungudi, Perungalathur, Medavakkam, Madipakkam and Kodungaiyur are being used as dumping yards for solid waste, biomedical waste and electronic waste. Land filling e-waste, one of the most widely used methods of disposal, is the most dangerous as this waste contains substances such as mercury, cadmium and lead, which are among the most toxic agents and can cause a wide variety of human ailments if they leach into the soil and water. In addition, landfills are also prone to uncontrolled fires, which can release toxic fumes.

The rate of respiratory diseases in metros like Delhi has been medically assessed to be eight to nine times higher than the national average. This is not only partly because of automobile and other 'normal' pollutants but also partly because of the substances found in e-waste. Inhaling and coming into contact with them on a regular basis can damage the brain, the nervous system, the lungs, the kidneys and the reproductive system. Innocent people become victims of what can only be described as environmental crimes. Working in poorly ventilated or enclosed areas without masks and technical expertise results in exposure to death by slow poisoning.

Lead poisoning could be silently corroding India's vast human resource pool. However, health officials remain in the dark about the threat, not to mention being clueless on how to tackle the silent terror that shows no initial symptoms. Even among the medical fraternity, it seems there is an amazing lack of awareness about the health hazards of e-waste. So even if the symptoms are present, doctors may not recognise it as the impact of e-waste. The time has come for India to wake up to the alarm bells that are ringing loud and clear.

Electronic waste is a subject that is rarely on anyone's radar. Although there are millions of users and some of the products are extremely hazardous, municipal waste managers seem to be blissfully unaware of the dangers. As a result, there is no coherent policy to dispose of it even though the waste grows exponentially.

In this context, there are a number of questions. Is mishandling e-waste a crime? If so, how does it affect the environment? Who are the victims? Is there any legislation that specifically deals with its management? Are enforcement mechanisms in place? Is technical expertise available with the state to meet this challenge? What are the punitive measures to combat e-waste? Could any lethargy and indifference in this regard be seen as a threat to the common man and hence a serious concern to human security? Do we have an e-waste disposal policy in India?

The challenges of managing e-waste in India are very different from other countries, developed or developing, because of its cultural diversity and economic disparity. The volumes are increasing rapidly, both domestically generated as well as through imported goods. These imports are often disguised as second-hand computer donations to bridge the digital divide or simply as metal scrap.

No accurate estimates of the quantity of e-waste generated and recycled are available. A lack of awareness among manufacturers and consumers of the hazards of incorrect e-waste disposal is a matter of concern. The potential for severe environmental damage is huge, given the crude techniques used in the informal sector to recycle e-waste. The methods include acid leaching and open burning. Workers in the sector have little or no knowledge of the toxins in e-waste and are exposed to serious health hazards. Inefficient recycling leads to substantial losses of material value. Rampant corruption in government departments means there is no way of getting a hold on the problem.

The first thing is strong regulation. The lack of deterrent laws is a serious barrier to the proper disposal of e-waste. It is made worse by the corrupt practices of manufacturers, contractors and recyclers, on one hand, and bureaucratic indifference, on the other. Unfortunately, there is no specific legislation on the management of e-waste in India. At present, its management is governed by the following environmental legislation: the Municipal Solid Wastes (Management and Handling) Rules, 2000; the Hazardous Wastes (Management and Handling) Rules, 2003; Draft Hazardous Materials (Management, Handling and Transboundary Movement) Rules, 2007; The Public Liability Act, 1991; and the Batteries (Management and Handling)

Rules, 2001. But all lack teeth and are still too much in the formative stage to meet the formidable challenges posed by the growing mountain of e-waste.

It is essential to restructure the recycling process. Some of the existing processes require improvement, and others must be abandoned altogether due to the risks to health and the environment. Legislation on the handling and recycling of e-waste is also necessary, not only as an environmental protection measure but also to keep pace with legislation such as the WEEE directive in the European Union. Led by the Central Pollution Control Board, this covers the issue of developing national guidelines for formal recycling operations, developing WEEE rules, formulating standards and licensing procedures.

So far, however, policy makers have shown little interest in drafting or implementing environmental legislation, especially for e-waste management. An alternative response to the proliferation of e-waste is to require manufacturers to develop and fund programmes to collect and recycle the devices they produce. Manufacturers should be designing and creating products with reuse or recycling in mind.

The benefits of information and communication technology cannot be ignored and dispensed with, in the contemporary world, but a sound and effective policy is required to dispose of its products safely. Thus, the imperative is for an early formulation of a holistic e-waste legislation that will evolve a policy. Such a policy must reflect the concerns of various stakeholders and the views of practitioners in the field, both in the organised and unorganised sectors. Coordinated efforts between various authorities responsible for e-waste management are essential for transparency. In this context, even the municipal corporations should treat city e-waste differently, just as they do biomedical waste. The Ministry of Environment, Forest and Climate Change has notified e-waste management rules, 2016, in which producers are for the first time covered under extended producers' responsibility. The rules prescribed stringent financial penalties for non-compliance. However, the implementation of these rules has not yet been followed in real terms. Given the huge user base and vast reach of telecom in India, it is practically difficult and expensive for handset manufacturers to achieve the targets prescribed in the rules from the first year.

To combat the ever-growing e-waste menace India needs to have strong regulations, deterrence and strict enforcement. While some initiatives towards an ambitious e-governance plan by India is a good sign, civil society would be properly served if e-waste management finds priority with the government.

Note

1 See https://www.sarcajc.com/july-2009-newspaper-watch.html, accessed 25 June 2019.

PART III

State, development and displacement in South Asia

10

CORRECTING ANOMALIES OF A DYSFUNCTIONAL STATE THROUGH CIVIL SOCIETY

Initiatives to complement global attempts for human security

C. K. Lal

Introduction

This chapter argues, with experiences from Nepal – a country with characteristics of a dysfunctional state[1] – that improving governance is the key to ensuring human rights and human security in South Asia. Governance is primarily a function of the government, but other 'actors' such as the instruments of the market, the international community and the civil society, too, play important roles not only in increasing effectiveness but checking the excesses of the state. A robust civil society can prevent a failing state from completely failing, but its absence can be felt even more acutely in countries with fragile systems of governance.

The concept of human security[2] is either very realistic or very idealistic, the characterization depending on the perception of the person assessing its various components. Some pragmatists still hold that the Darwinian dictum of "Survival of the Fittest" applies to the life chances of two-footed thinking animals too. For them, the idea of human security is mere idealism – the weakest have to suffer and often disappear for the survival of the strongest. Even for the believers of fatalism, anything that has to do with changing the verdict of destiny is bound to be pointless. However, human life is all about pursuing a course that can improve the living conditions of the many. It implies engaging constantly with the question of human needs at every ladder of the Maslow's Hierarchy.[3]

On a practical level, human security implies, but is not limited to, freedom of an individual to pursue a path that ensures fulfillment of basic needs of every member in the family at various stages of life that vary from the newborn to the aged and the dying. Nutritious and filling food, basic sanitation, primary healthcare, essential education and everyday skills and an environment for general well-being are indispensable components of human life. It requires freedom from fear and a general amity in society to enable a person to pursue the path of peace and prosperity. Since contestations are inevitable when resources to be shared are limited – and resources, as Mahatma Gandhi famously said in his oft-quoted quip ("Earth provides enough to satisfy every man's *needs*, but not every man's *greed*"), are never enough to fulfil human greed that comes to the mind disguised as natural wants to those with fulfilled needs – conflict resolution mechanisms are inalienable parts of social life.

Idealistically, human beings do not live by bread alone: camaraderie sans profit and loss calculations are essential for a "good life" in any society. Creating conditions for companionship in plural and heterogeneous societies, however, is fraught with innumerable challenges. It is still widely believed that democratic practices of periodic, free and fair elections combined with robust institutions of guaranteeing human rights ensure peace and prosperity even in countries with multiple nationalities. Elections, no matter how free and fair, are prone to majoritarian swings where minority voices are lost. Governments with brute majorities do not always honour human rights concerns. Governance is perhaps the key element.

Unfortunately, the record of governance in South Asia collectively fails to inspire confidence, at least among minorities. Intolerance is on the rise throughout the South Asian region. Unable to ensure even internal physical security for all – let alone human security – states then fall for the cheap rhetoric of external threats and spend an enormous amount of physical, emotional and monetary resources in either fighting or preparing to fight the 'enemy' they have created to justify their existence. Little wonder, in recently published Fragile State Index of 2015,[4] all South Asian countries figure quite low on the list with only India escaping with mere 'Warning' as others are termed with 'Alert' (Bangladesh, Nepal and Sri Lanka) and 'High Alert' (Afghanistan and Pakistan) tags.

The capacity of the state to ensure governance is a necessary, although arguably not sufficient, condition for human security. Dysfunctional states fail to inspire confidence. Flailing states lack the wherewithal to have their will obeyed. While a lot of attention has been paid to rebuilding 'failed states'[5] in the post-Soviet world – almost invariably with not much to show for all the efforts made – relatively very little interest seems to have been made in making 'flailing states' more representative and accountable, hence acceptable by every section of population, through civil society initiatives.

Governance conundrum

The concept of a government that governs, rather than just rules over the realm under its control, comes with the existence of a 'state'. The 'state', in the sense of a nation or territory considered as an organized political community and recognized to be so by other similar entities, is more or less a post-Westphalian[6] creation of the mid-seventeenth century. Although the role of some form of 'authority' has always been important in the evolution of the two-footed thinking animal; the imagination of a state with responsibilities to create a better society through proper governance is still an evolving idea.

Anomalies of a dysfunctional state **123**

The ruler as a person or an institution was the creation of human groups consisting of several individuals, some of which may have shared blood relationship. At various stages in human history, physical strength, organizational ability and the mental acumen to claim spiritual power have all been used as sources of authority.

There is a reason *hunter-gatherer* is a hyphenated term. Both occupations were perhaps necessary to sustain an animal-like existence of foraging human ancestors. In tropical climates with high plant biomass, gathering was rewarding and hunting was fraught with risks. At higher altitudes and colder climes where plants withered but birds and animals coped relatively well, fishing and game may have proved to be more reliable sources of sustenance. It is possible that the main provider of some – and the chief protector in other groups – came to claim the right to exercise decisive authority in hunting-gathering societies.

Perhaps the tribal leader was assumed to have divine sanction because of physical power rather than deriving the authority to preside directly from divinities. Gender roles came into play due to compulsions of existence in hunting and gathering societies, and most tribal chiefs turned out to be men in due course of time.

Development of agriculture required some form of stability. Even slash-and-burn farming necessitates staying more or less in the same place for a few years. The Hobbesian fears of a "solitary, poor, nasty, brutish and short" life may be a slight exaggeration, but the necessity of a central authority came to the fore with warring groups declaring ownership of more productive resources. Land grabs, the capture of crops and contestations over prime farmland may have created conditions for the emergence of councils of elders for conflict resolution.

Keepers of record could have appropriated collective memory and claimed divine right to meditate and mediate over issues of contestation. Surplus product and the ability to exchange and barter might have led to wealth creation and the necessity of security of person and property. Along with peasants, priests and the propertied class, perhaps a group of professional warriors, too, formed under the command of the feudal lords that found it convenient to function under the sovereign authority of a temple or a king. Empires soon followed with rival kings competing with each other to expand their domains. Colonialism was the degeneration of empires into commercial enterprises that put profit rather than glory above all else. Governance still implied more or less what was called the "law and order" to maintain control.

Evocations of justice-loving emperor Vikramaditya of Ujjain and his Throne of Wisdom[7] notwithstanding, the idea of governance is a post-colonial construction in much of South Asia. That could be the reason there is no exact term that captures the essence of governance in the sense of the "social contract"[8] between the people and the government. There are words for reign, rule, and administration, but all these terms put the ruler at the centre and are not based on ideals of equality. However, a system with written or unwritten rights and responsibilities is the key to understanding complex relationships that exist between an individual and his or her surroundings.

124 C. K. Lal

Even though governance[9] is often understood as an effort; it usually happens when "systems and processes" begin to work in ways that can be better felt than understood. That could be the reason governance is sometimes simply defined as things that governments do. Probably the project of "good governance" has failed to make much impact in most developing countries despite donors' conditionality and coercion for that very reason: the inner workings of systems and processes have been neglected and state-centric prescriptions prioritized over other elements.

For governance to happen, at least three kinds of relationships come into play – power, influence and exchange. Exercise of power involves will to dominate, vigour to resist and compulsions of submission. *Exchange* is exactly what the word implies and occurs when something is given in return of something received or expected and construed as more or less a just transaction. *Influence* is a little more complex to define, but in essence, it is the capacity to have a desired effect on the character or behaviours without resorting to inducements or threats. Influence is the subtlest form of power and arises out of status, contacts, wealth, knowledge or sometimes the ability to persuade that comes from a combination of all these factors with a hint of an indefinable characteristic called charisma.

According to Bertrand Russell, the fundamental concept in social science is power, in the same sense in which energy is the fundamental concept in physics.[10] The power relationship between the state and the citizen prepares the ground, which is the most important component of governance. That is could be the reason governance is often understood merely as a *function* of government. The primary purpose of the state is the maintenance of law and order, of which the explicit (through the constitution and laws of the country) or implicit (recognized by the parties as such) contract with the citizen is power-based.

The state demands that citizens grant it monopoly over organized violence; pay taxes determined with the participation of peoples' representatives in a democracy; confer it the sole right to enact laws in a transparent, logical and just manner; and participate voluntarily or with compensation for the public good such as voting, jury service or defence services. In lieu of the loyalty of the citizen, the state guarantees to protect and provide security for the life and property of the people, ensure dignity of every citizen, provide at least basic services such as clean air to breathe and potable water to drink, make sure that minimal nutritional need for survival are met, primary education and health care are accessible and affordable and conditions conducive for the evolution of fraternity and solidarity in the larger society are created. The state also commits itself to level the field and create equality of opportunity, through positive discrimination if need be, to ensure an equitable outcome for everyone.

States that have lived up to the stated or unstated contract have stable governments where governance takes place with minimum recourse to coercive forces. In most dysfunctional states, problems begin when the state demands and gets its due from citizens without delivering its side of the bargain. Most people recognize the authority of the state to legislate, its monopoly over organized violence is generally honoured, its power to tax is mostly respected despite some attempts of evasion and participation in public service is considered a matter of pride. However, dysfunctional states are unable to protect, provide or promote the existence of law-abiding citizens. Once the compact breaks, it becomes extremely difficult for the state to maintain its power – the central feature of governance.

The relationship between the consumer and the market, too, is an important component of overall governance. Unlike the power of the state, signifying the uniqueness of character and authority of the entity that exercises it, forces of the market are plural whereas consumer as a whole can be aggregated as a singular entity. Reflecting widely held view, the *Online Cambridge Dictionary*[11] posits that market forces work best independent of government. However, requirements of governance make the state regulate the market and maintain the existence of consumer as a law-abiding citizen. This leads to another implicit but well-understood contractual relationship.

Just as authority is the central concept of the power relationship between the state and its citizens, the exchange of resources runs the market, with investment and return as its main features. The exchange condition, often guaranteed by the government, implies that market forces will be entitled to recover its cost with justifiable profit for goods and services it produces and provides, the security of investment and property will be ensured by the government and due process of law will be honoured for all contractual settlements. In return, the consumer is guaranteed to get value for money, availability of goods and services and delivery of dependable quality that causes no harm. Once again, dysfunctional states can't make sure that the contractual relationship between the market forces and the consumer is maintained at a reasonable level to ensure governance. When breach of contract becomes routine, malgovernance is its natural outcome.

Breach of contract, however, is not within the boundary of the state alone. Many a time, multilateral agreements between states are not honoured for various reasons. Montevideo Convention[12] states that the state "as a person of international law should possess the following qualifications: (a) a permanent population; (b) a defined territory; (c) government; and (d) capacity to enter into relations with the other states". Flailing states often "enter into relations" but are incapable of maintaining it.

The constitutive norm of sovereignty in the international system allows states with virtually no capacity to effectively govern to exist and function.[13] The problem is compounded as the international norm of R2P[14] does not permit external intervention to ensure proper governance. The notion of sovereignty, however nebulous, allows dysfunctional states with ineffective and/or exploitative regimes to function without any international accountability.

Somewhat similar to the explicit or implicit compacts between the state and the citizen and between the market and the consumer, international commitments for governance are either ineffectual, nonexistent or liable to be used for ulterior motives as in the case of "regime change"[15] campaigns of US-led coalitions in Afghanistan, Iraq and Libya, among others. Such examples weaken the case for humanitarian interventions even when it is demonstrably necessary.

Civic initiatives

Authority of the state has existed in human civilization in some form or the other for a long time. Starting with barter, economic transactions, too, are as old as human history. Through imperial conquests or colonization drives, the intervention of an outside power has a tradition going back millennia. Civil society is also an ancient concept: the notion of working together for the good of all, or helping people in need, is an instinctive response in most people. The elders of yore exercised power that derived from religious or caste sanctions. In the age of compacts, the civil society has acceptability and responsibilities without commensurate instruments to implement its will.

Unlike the *authority* of the government and the *exchange* value of the market, power of the civil society is derived purely from its *influence*, an impact that the *Concise Oxford Dictionary* defines as "arising out of status, contacts, or wealth". Here, the idea of status perhaps includes descent, cultural position, and knowledge, which have traditionally been determinants of rank in most societies. Contact requires reciprocity, which gives birth to formal organizations or informal networks. Such ideas have influenced the definition of civil society as "[t]he population of groups formed for collective purposes outside of the State and the marketplace".[16]

The concise definition gives the location – outside of state and the market – but its importance, in the idealistic sense of the term is given by Ernest Gellner:

> What distinguishes Civil Society, or a state *containing* a Civil Society, from others is that it is *not* clear who is boss. Civil Society can check and oppose the state. It is not supine before it. . . . The broader sense of Civil Society . . . refers to a total society within which the non-political institutions are not dominated by the political ones, and do not stifle individuals either.[17]

Building on existing research, the World Bank has adopted a comprehensive definition of civil society:

> the term civil society refers to the wide array of non-governmental and not-for-profit organizations that have a presence in public life, expressing the interests and values of their members or others, based on ethical, cultural, political, scientific, religious or philanthropic considerations. Civil Society Organizations (CSOs) therefore refer to a wide array of organizations: community groups, non-governmental organizations (NGOs), labour unions, indigenous groups, charitable organizations, faith-based organizations, professional associations, and foundations.[18]

Even a cursory look at these characterizations[19] will show that the idea of civil society is different from caste panchayats, loya jirgas (the traditional grand assembly of Afghanistan, consisting of representatives of the country's constituent communities and tribes) or ganyamanya-pratishthits (acceptable and respectable) elders' forums in the Indian subcontinent. In Nepal, as in most of the non-Western world, the civil society has come to signify donor-dependent initiatives following fashionable agendas about whom Tariq Ali writes stingingly,

> The NGOs [non-governmental organizations] are no substitute for genuine social and political movements. In Africa, Palestine and elsewhere, NGOs have swallowed the neoliberal status quo. They operate like charities, trying to alleviate the worst excesses, but rarely question the systemic basis of the fact that five billion citizens of our globe live in poverty. They may be NGOs in Pakistan, but on the global scale they are western governmental organisations (WGOs), their cash flow conditioned by enforced agendas. Colin Powell once referred to them as "our fifth column".[20]

In order to avoid stigmas attached with the term and show that genuine voluntary efforts are different, some campaigners in Nepal have preferred to style themselves as civic movement (Nagarik Andolan) rather than civil society as such.[21]

Despite widespread scepticism, NGOs, along with their patrons of the international donors and lender fraternities, have done considerable work in areas such as weakening of the abominable practice of untouchability in Hindu society, empowerment of women and mainstreaming of marginalized ethnic groups and provision of services to the most neglected groups such as the drug addicts and people afflicted with leprosy. Such activities have indeed been helpful in promoting well-being. The question of human security, however, requires interventions on a scale that no NGO possesses.

Compared to the state that has its presence everywhere, at least through police posts, or the market forces that reach the remotest part of the country through their distribution networks, NGOs are relatively minor players. Trust in their capacity to improve human security is misplaced. In the case of Nepal, periodic interventions of the civil society in improving the functioning of the state has been based on the assumption that governance is key to human security and empowerment of the marginalized section. The civic activism has followed on parallel courses: traditional NGOs work with the government to improve its efficiency, while civic movements create pressure through the streets to ensure accountability. Of the five elements of civic activism, such attempts have occasionally succeeded in ensuring participation and efficiency of the state but have failed to make a mark on other criteria of effective governance – decency, fairness and accountability.[22]

When the state refuses to treat its citizen with decency, dissatisfaction spreads, which can then erupt, sometimes without advance notice. That's what actually happened during the decade-long Maoist insurgency (1996–2006) that ended up with further 'securitization'[23] of the state. The strength of the army doubled within a short period, and a paramilitary force[24] was created in a huff. Security forces have become a huge liability to the state. The denial of fairness is an equally powerful instigator. It has led to not one or two but three uprisings in Tarai-Madhesh plains of southern Nepal in 2007,[25] 2008 and 2015,[26] respectively, when aspirations of Madheshis were dismissively dealt by the state. Discontent in Tarai-Madhesh continues to simmer and has the possibility of erupting any time again with unintended consequences for peace, harmony and democracy in the country.

With impunity being the norm rather than exception, the record of accountability is even poor. More than a decade after cessation of hostilities between the Maoist guerrillas and the Nepalese army, acts related to the Truth and Reconciliation Commission and the Commission of Investigation on Enforced Disappeared Persons still remain to be amended[27] in line with Supreme Court decisions and international norms. Impunity of security agencies and their officials involved in excesses against Madheshis is even more pronounced. While a section of the civil society has been vocal in campaign against the Maoists, their silence on the excessive use of force in Tarai-Madhesh has been eloquent.

Prolonged hunger strikes by prominent orthopaedic surgeon Govinda KC[28] for reforms in medical education had rekindled hopes for civic engagement and activism in issues of public concern. However, the Kathmandu-centric civil society has lost much of its appeal due to its parochial outlook against Madheshis[29] and open support for a divisive constitution fast-tracked in the middle of aftershocks of the Gorkha earthquakes. Along with purity of intent, the practicality of means and the acceptability in society are main conditions for the effectiveness of civic activism.

Like politics, civic engagement is a practical field and not an exact and replicable science. Variations dependent on ground conditions are the norm rather than the exception. While social media has made 'flash mobs' ("A large public gathering at which people perform an unusual or seemingly random act and then disperse, typically organized by means of the internet or social media") made spontaneous protests possible, lasting change in issues as complex as correcting anomalies of a dysfunctional state, ameliorating conditions created by irresponsive government or strengthening democracy requires longer-term and sustained engagement of the civil society. And therein lies the paradox of civic activism: Long-term commitments robs intensity of effort while instantaneity lacks sustainability.

The work culture of NGOs has turned activism into a career rather than a calling or vocation. Increasingly, the Marxist view that the civil society is a component of the market ("Civil society as such only develops with the bourgeoisie; the social organisation evolving directly out of production and commerce"[30]) is turning out to be correct. Meanwhile, where crony capitalism is rampant as in Nepal, it is sometimes difficult to differentiate between the civil society and the state that work in tandem in the service of plutarchy.

Perhaps it is only the 'political society' that can bring about lasting changes in governance to ensure human security. Nonetheless, civil society has its work cut out for it: raise the voice of the voiceless through formal and *informal* channels and refuse to be silenced. The last word must go to Faiz Ahmed Faiz– *Bol* (Speak up!)[31] – for that's the only way to begin any change in the status quo.

Notes

1 According to American jurist Robert Jackson, a dysfunctional state is characterized by the growing ineffectiveness or paralysis of the administrative, legal, extractive and coercive institutions that form its essence. Some important features or syndromes found in dysfunctional states include widespread corruption; the collapse of regular channels of communication and interaction between government and state officials, between state officials and society and among state officials themselves; the fragmentation of society; and the loss of government control over the coercive institutions of the state. See, http://csis.org/files/media/csis/pubs/ruseur_wp_003.pdf, accessed 23 April 2019.

2 Human security continues to be a developmental jargon despite some very important works by academics. An introductory note to the concept, with a comprehensive list of references, is provided by Sabina Alkire. Working definition: the objective of the human security is to "safeguard the vital core of all human lives from critical pervasive threats in a way that is consistent with long-term human fulfillment." See http://www3.qeh.ox.ac.uk/pdf/crisewps/workingpaper2.pdf, accessed 7 July 2016. A version also accessible at: https://assets.publishing.service.gov.uk/media/57a08cf740f0b652dd001694/wp2.pdf, accessed 23 April 2019.

3 For a brief overview of Maslow's Pyramid, www.bbc.com/news/magazine-23902918, accessed 7 July 2016.

4 For details see, http://fsi.fundforpeace.org/rankings-2015, accessed 7 July 2016. Web archive: https://web.archive.org/web/20150622062712/http://fsi.fundforpeace.org/rankings-2015, accessed 23 April 2019.

5 Even though fixing failed states became an obsession in the US in the wake of 9/11, details of the concept continue to be debated. According to Robert I. Rotberg, "[n]ation-states fail because they are convulsed by internal violence and can no longer deliver positive political goods to their inhabitants. Their governments lose legitimacy, and the very nature of the particular nation-state itself becomes illegitimate in the eyes and in the hearts of a growing plurality of its citizens." For elaboration, www.brookings.edu/press/books/chapter_1/statefailureandstateweaknessinatimeofterror.pdf, accessed 7 July 2016. One of the early "experts" of fixing failed states was Ashraf Ghani, the present prime minister of Afghanistan. The efficacy of his theories remains to be seen.

6 For a brief overview of the concept, www.jstor.org/stable/41887235?seq=1#page_scan_tab_contents, accessed 7 July 2016. Brexit has rekindled interest in the Westphalian order, for details see, www.stratfor.com/weekly/making-sense-brexit, accessed 23 April 2019.

7 The legend has it that anyone sitting on the Throne of Wisdom could not help but be the pronouncer and protector of truth and justice.

8 Dictionary definition: "An actual or hypothetical agreement among members of an organized society or between a community that defines and limits the rights and duties of each."

9 Governance can be thought of as 'the systems and processes concerned with ensuring the overall direction, effectiveness, supervision and accountability of an organisation.' For a succinct discussion on Good Governance, www.acevo.org.uk/advice-support/governance, accessed 22 July 2016.

10 For elaboration of power in its various forms in the socio-political context, please see, Bertrand Russell, Power: A New Social Analysis, London and New York: Routledge, 2004.

11 "[T]he forces that decide price levels in an economy or trading system whose activities are not influenced or limited by government.", http://dictionary.cambridge.org/dictionary/english/market-forces, accessed 23 April 2019.

12 This treaty was signed at the international conference of American States in Montevideo, Uruguay on 26 December 1933. It entered into force on 26 December 1934. The treaty discusses the definition and rights of statehood and is perhaps regarded highly in international relations discourse due to its simplicity and comprehensiveness.

130 C. K. Lal

13 See, http://csis.org/files/media/csis/pubs/ruseur_wp_003.pdf, accessed 23 April 2019.

14 The RESPONSIBILITY TO PROTECT ("RtoP" or "R2P") is a new international security and human rights norm to address the international community's failure to prevent and stop genocides, war crimes, ethnic cleansing and crimes against humanity, www.responsibilitytoprotect.org/, accessed 23 April 2019.

15 Defined as "[t]hereplacement of one administration or government by another, especially by means of military force", www.oxforddictionaries.com/definition/english/regime-change, accessed 3 August 2016.

16 A. Van Rooy, Civil Society and the Aid Industry, London: Earthscan, 1998, cited by David Lewis, "Civil Society in Non-Western Contexts: Reflections on the 'usefulness' of a Concept", LSE Civil Society Working Paper 13, October 2001.

17 Cited by Patrick Morgan in "How Tribal Societies Operate", *Quadrant*, 1 January 2005.

18 See, http://web.worldbank.org/WBSITE/EXTERNAL/TOPICS/CSO/0,,content MDK:20101499~menuPK:244752~pagePK:220503~piPK:220476~theSitePK:228717,00.html, accessed 8 August 2016.

19 Sudipta Kaviraj and Sunil Khilnani (eds.), Civil Society: History and Possibilities, New Delhi: Cambridge University Press, 2001 gives a comprehensive overview of ideas and contestations.

20 Tariq Ali, "Bought with Western Cash", The Guardian, 7 April 2006, www.theguardian.com/commentisfree/2006/apr/07/Pakistan., accessed 8 August 2016.

21 For an evaluation of Civic Movement for Peace and Democracy in Nepal, see Celayne Heaton-Shrestha and Ramesh Adhikari, "Struggling on Two Fronts during Nepal's Insurgency: The Citizens' Movement for Democracy and Peace and the Meanings of 'civil society'", European Bulletin of Himalayan Research, no. 42, 2013, pp. 39–74, http://himalaya.socanth.cam.ac.uk/collections/journals/ebhr/pdf/EBHR_42_02.pdf, accessed 23 April 2019.

22 For a detailed discussion about civil society's role in governance, Gordan Hyden, Julius Court and Kenneth Mease, Making Sense of Governance: Empirical Evidence from 16 Developing Countries, New Delhi: Viva Books, 2005, pp. 57–75. The World Governance Survey referred in the volume lists five specific indicators – freedom of expression, freedom of assembly, freedom from discrimination, input into policy making and respect for rules – as measures of decency, participation, fairness, efficiency and accountability of the state.

23 The Copenhagen school defines securitization as a discursive process by means of which an actor (1) claims that a referent object is existentially threatened, (2) demands the right to take extraordinary countermeasures to deal with that the threat, and (3) convinces an audience that rule-breaking behavior to counter the threat is justified. Rens van Munster, "Securitization", www.oxfordbibliographies.com/view/document/obo-9780199743292/obo-9780199743292-0091.xml, accessed 31 August 2016.

24 In a way, the Armed Police Force (APF) in Nepal was a creation of compulsion. Due to duality of control over the Nepalese army, the government was not being able to mobilize its 'coercive force of last resort' against the Maoist when the king refused to give his consent as its supreme commander-in-chief. In desperation, the government formed APF through an ordinance in 2001 when the parliament stood dissolved. It was influential in checking the spread of the Maoists, but the role of the 'combat brigades' of the force in civic disturbances have remained under cloud. For an introduction to APF, see, www.apf.gov.np/pages/introduction.

25 For a preliminary backgrounder of the Madheshi issue in Nepalese politics, see K. Yhome, "The Madhesi Issue in Nepal", March 2007, http://ipcs.org/article/nepal/the-madhesi-issue-in-nepal-2228.html, accessed 31 August 2016. Also available: https://web.archive.org/web/20150503100429/www.ipcs.org/article/nepal/the-madhesi-issue-in-nepal-2228.html, accessed 23 April 2019.

26 See, "Like We Are Not Nepalese: Protest and Police Crackdown in Terai Region of Nepal", Human Rights Watch Report, 16 October 2015, www.hrw.org/report/2015/10/16/we-are-not-nepali/protest-and-police-crackdown-terai-region-nepal, accessed 23 April 2019.

27 See, www.icj.org/nepal-end-impunity-for-enforced-disappearances/ accessed 23 April 2019.
28 Subhanga Pandey, Doctor's Appointment, http://immersive.himalmag.com/doctors-appointment, accessed 31 August 2016.
29 See author's column, www.myrepublica.com/news/2615, accessed 23 April 2019.
30 See, www.marxists.org/archive/marx/works/download/Marx_The_German_Ideology.pdf, accessed 23 April 2019.
31 For the full poem and its English translation, www.outlookindia.com/website/story/speak/212905, accessed 23 April 2019.

11

HUMAN DEVELOPMENT VIS-À-VIS GROSS NATIONAL HAPPINESS IN BHUTAN

Challenges and achievements

Maitreyee Choudhury

Introduction

Bhutan, a small Himalayan state located between India and China and one of the least developed countries in the world, has become famous by adopting the unique concept of Gross National Happiness (GNH) as an alternative development strategy in place of stereotyped and traditional concept of Gross National Product (GNP)/Gross Domestic Product (GDP). The location of the nation between the two fastest-developing countries in the world has little impact on the country's aspiration to develop in its own way. The task to develop by achieving national happiness is daunting no doubt and may sound somewhat abstract or even skewed to hardcore economic policymakers elsewhere, but Bhutan strives to stand strong on its policy of bringing economic well-being by way of maintaining a high level of happiness and human security.

The state, with an area of 38,394 square kilometres, is bordered by the Tibet Autonomous Region of the People's Republic of China in the north and the Republic of India in the south. The formidable mountains in the state act as natural barriers for the country to remain isolated and, to some extent, secure. The economic and political upheavals in the two giant neighbouring countries have hardly affected the internal governance and structure of Bhutan.

Human development and the concept of Gross National Happiness

Human development is defined as the process of enlarging people's freedoms and opportunities and improving their well-being. It is about the freedom one can have to decide on matters related to one's life. Human development is interconnected with human rights and human security. The human development approach is focused on people and their opportunities and choices.[1]

The dimensions of human development are twofold: directly enhancing human abilities; creating conditions for human development

The first dimension includes a long and healthy life, knowledge and a decent standard of living

The second dimension includes participation in political and community life, environmental sustainability, human security and rights and gender equality.

Human development focuses on improving the lives of people rather than idealising that economic growth will automatically bring human well-being. Economic development is seen as a means to develop, not the end in itself. Human development means an opportunity to develop people's abilities. Once the basics of human development, viz. healthy life, access to knowledge and decent living standards are achieved, they create opportunities for progress in other spheres. Human development is about providing people with choices. Ideally, the process of development should create an environment for people to develop to their full potential.

The United Nations Development Programme (UNDP) introduced the Human Development Index (HDI) in 1990[2] as an alternative for measuring development with the traditional yardstick of per capita GDP. As opposed to GDP, the HDI measures the level of development of individual countries on the basis of three main parameters, namely, life expectancy at birth, educational attainment and average local purchasing power. The application of the first-generation HDI resulted in a very different assessment of an individual country's achievements. While the orthodox assessment of development based on per capita GDP rated most of the countries in global South as inadequately developed, the HDI assessment placed some of these countries (e.g. Sri Lanka and Cuba) in a better position compared to some oil-rich countries (e.g. Saudi Arabia and Kuwait) with high per capita income. The HDI has been refined over the last two decades and has acquired many new parameters, such as enrolment of girl children in school, availability of safe drinking water, sanitation and so on and has been widely accepted as a better alternative to gauge development. Contrary to measuring development in terms of GDP or even HDI, some countries go their own way, and Bhutan in South Asia is one of them. Even before the UN brought HDI into focus, Bhutan floated the idea of GNH[3] and the erstwhile ruler of Bhutan Jigme Singhye Wangchuk claimed that for his country and people, GNH was more important than GNP/GDP. Bhutan has nurtured the idea of GNH for nearly four decades and made the concept 'a guiding philosophy' for development. Bhutan has braced many challenges to achieve positive results by adopting the concept of GNH and to ensure maximum possible security in the context of the environment, socio-economic development, traditional culture and good governance. The country has achieved moderate success in putting the idea into practice. Some countries in global North espouse this alternative model of development in terms of human well-being, and the UN, too, recognised the model during Rio+20 Conference.

The idea of GNH is believed to have been conceived by the fourth king of Bhutan Wangchuk sometime in the 1970s, and it took the shape of a concept around 1986 by integrating Bhutanese ethos to preserve the culture and the environment with the process of development in modern life. His famous rhetoric "Gross National Happiness is more important than Gross National Product", in reply to a question by a journalist, created history and became the development philosophy for Bhutan. The then king of Bhutan made it apparent that Bhutan's development policy should just not mean economic prosperity but also create a sense of happiness by ensuring political stability, social harmony and cultural integrity. The concept of 'Gross National Happiness' and its application as the 'guiding principle' for Bhutan's development was not readily understood and took time to sink in the psyche of the common people of Bhutan. The king himself perhaps did not realise the gravity of his own remark at the time of making the statement, but his aspiration snowballed into an acclaimed and elaborate concept.

The concept of GNH is strongly influenced by Buddhist concepts and Bhutan's cultural ethos. It emphasises the need to bind material well-being with spiritual and cultural well-being, and gives a holistic idea of "development that seeks to maximise happiness rather than economic growth".[4] Bhutan's Seventh Five Year Plan (1992–1997) for the first time initiated the process to implement GNH principles. The plan proposed the development objectives of, *inter alia*, increasing income at the household level, ensuring the spiritual and emotional well-being of the people and preserving cultural heritage and natural resources.[5] According to the Planning Commission of Bhutan,

> [t]he concept of Gross National Happiness rejects the notion that there is a direct and unambiguous relationship between wealth and happiness. If such a relationship existed, it would follow that those in the richest countries should be the happiest in the world.[6]

The awareness of the concept was spread effectively by Jigme Y. Thinley, who prepared a framework for it in 1998 during the Millennium Meeting for Asia and the Pacific in Seoul, South Korea. The concept expressed the idea of treading cautiously in the path of modernisation to arrest decline in the cultural values and degradation of the environment.[7] GNH became a flashpoint of development discourse internationally in the last part of the twentieth century. So far, five major international conferences on GNH have taken place, and hundreds of publications by noted development specialists and economists have come into circulation. It was made clear that GNH should be aimed at achieving "the well-being and contentment of people". The simple yet high aspiration of achieving GNH instead of GNP created ripples internationally. Despite hiccups and sharp criticisms from certain quarters, Bhutan took enormous efforts to orient its national policy and development plans towards GNH. Meanwhile, the Constitution of Bhutan, which was a 'gift from the Monarch'[8] of Bhutan to the citizens, was finalised; it directed the newly elected democratic government "to promote those conditions that will enable the pursuit of Gross National Happiness".[9] The Centre for Bhutan Studies, Thimphu took a lead role in developing a GNH index to measure GNH and making it applicable. It took more than three decades to finalise a valid index. In 2009, after prolonged research and refining, the Centre for Bhutan Studies developed comprehensive indicators of GNH and introduced the GNH index to measure happiness for the first time in 2010.

The Bhutanese concept of happiness is distinct from the Western notion of happiness, first, because it is multidimensional and, second, it is not focused only on subjective well-being. The first elected prime minister of Bhutan, Jigme Y. Thinley (2008), opined,

> We have now clearly distinguished the 'happiness' . . . in GNH from the fleeting, pleasurable 'feel good' moods so often associated with that term. We know that true abiding happiness cannot exist while others suffer, and comes only from serving others, living in harmony with nature, and realizing our innate wisdom and the true and brilliant nature of our own minds.[10]

The Bhutan model of GNH is by now well known and has been widely accepted as an alternative approach to development. The small Himalayan state lodged between China and India may seem inconsequential in world politics and global economics, but it has received wide publicity on account of its 'guiding philosophy' of GNH apropos development. For nearly four decades, Bhutan has built an image of an underdeveloped but happy country and has frequently been referred to as a model for alternative development. The model "is increasingly becoming the trademark of Bhutan to the outside world".[11] The concept of GNH is described variously as 'Bhutan's development philosophy', 'guiding principle', 'overarching goal of development' and 'new development paradigm'.[12]

It is understood that GNH is a concept of alternative development that implies all-round well-being. It means sustainable development with a holistic, humane approach. Unlike the popular concepts of development in terms of economic growth and betterment in the standard of living, the concept of GNH emphasises on non-economic aspects of well-being and quality of life. Here wellbeing refers to fulfilling conditions of a 'good life'. The concept recognises that development has many dimensions and economic goals are not sufficient for developing a nation and making the people happy at the same time. Bhutan's philosophy of development is based on the premise that all development efforts should contribute to the material, as well as the spiritual, well-being of its people to maximise happiness. It is also recognised that a wide range of factors contribute to human well-being and that it may not be possible to make an exhaustive inventory that defines happiness. For the purpose of furthering GNH, four major areas have been underscored by the policy makers in Bhutan. The areas have been identified with the broad objectives of (a) enhancing economic growth by widening the sphere of economic activities beyond traditional agriculture and allied services, (b) utilising the environmental resources sustainably by following strong ethics of conservation in the interest of every being, (c) preserving the rich cultural heritage of Bhutan to safeguard identity in a rapidly globalising world and (d) establishing a system of governance that promotes the feeling of well-being among the citizens.

The essence of the philosophy of GNH is to enhance human well-being by means of (1) sustainable and equitable socio-economic development, (2) conservation of environment, (3) preservation and promotion of culture and (4) good governance. These four principles are widely recognised and promoted as the four pillars of GNH.

The four pillars of GNH

1 Sustainable and Equitable Socio-economic Development: for a country like Bhutan, where physical survival still poses challenges, sound economic policies matter enormously to ensure equitable socio-economic development. To drive socio-economic development in GNH economy, three considerations appear to be relevant. These are (1) the means and nature of economic activities chosen are no less important than the results they bring towards economic growth. The qualitative distinctions of economic activities must be taken into cognisance; (2) the index of measurement in a GNH economy must be different and independent of conventional methods of measuring GDP. The social and economic contribution of families should be evaluated along with the contribution of free time and leisure towards happiness. Conservation of the social, environmental and human capitals are to be given due weight to ensure sustainable socio-economic development; (3) although a difficult proposition, it is imperative to pay attention to realign happiness through income redistribution. One cannot escape the reality that wealth is concentrated in the hands of few. Unless there is equity in economic opportunities and excess income is redistributed, socio-economic development cannot be equitable.

   To foster socio-economic development, the country urgently needs to provide its people with capacities that will make them more active socially and productive economically. This necessitates the judicious selection of areas that can contribute effectively to the nation's economic wealth. The first and foremost requirement in this regard is to develop human resources by means of training and capacity building in professional and special skills to manage economic activities. Apart from developing human resources, development of infrastructure (such as road connectivity, air links, telecommunications, power, etc.) is also necessary to increase economic opportunity and productivity. Bhutan has already identified some sectors of economic growth in hydroelectric power generation, tourism, mineral resources, horticulture and service sectors that can strengthen this pillar of socio-economic development.

2 Conservation of Environment: the concept of GNH is partly based on the notion that there is a definite relationship between happiness and conservation of the environment. Human health and aesthetic experiences depend on the quality of the natural environment. The natural environment is an important

asset for economic development as well. Preservation and sustainable use of the natural environment are prerequisites for sustainable development. The ethics of conservation nowadays transcend the normal sphere of simply preserving forests or biodiversity. It encompasses emerging environmental problems such as air and water pollution, waste management and so on.

In Bhutan ethics of conservation and reverence for nature are traditionally maintained. The people in Bhutan have been practising environmental ethics even before the worldwide concerns for environment and biodiversity became evident. A majority of the Bhutanese live very close to nature which has a direct bearing on their livelihood and their way of life. The rural folks, in particular, get food, medicine and other essentials from the environment for their physical well-being and draw inspirations from nature for spiritual well-being. Fortunately, Bhutan has 72 per cent forest cover, and 26 per cent of it is declared as a protected area. However, in spite of national actions to conserve the environment, Bhutan cannot escape from the effects of global warming, the signs of which are already visible in the recession of glaciers and resultant glacial lake outburst floods (GLOF). Experiences of natural disasters such as GLOFs in the recent past are lessons enough for the country to take conservation of the environment very seriously. Considering the enormous importance of sustainable use of environmental resources, conservation of the environment is considered one of the main pillars of GNH.

3   Preservation and Promotion of Culture: preservation and promotion of culture are two priority areas for GNH. Living cultural heritage is seen as a prized possession in a rapidly changing world since it helps preserve human values and beliefs that may prove to be critical for sustainable development. Traditional beliefs and customs keep people anchored to their roots. They provide identity and sense of values and promote tolerance, respect and charity. Preservation of culture also enhances social bonding by providing links between the individual and the society. The quality of social relation is said to "lie at the root of happiness throughout a person's entire life cycle, from childhood to old age".[13]

A small country like Bhutan has every possibility to be influenced by alien cultures predominantly driven by market forces. Bhutan is averse to the cultural elements that may spoil the simplicity and cultural unity of the country. The statesmen of Bhutan are cautious to keep foreign cultures at bay, since they firmly believe and advocate that "a state which does not preserve its cultural richness is one where the choices and well-being of its citizens are diminished and greatly constrained".[14] Bhutan does not subscribe to the view that cultural liberty is central to human rights. On the contrary, free choice and cultural liberty of individuals or groups are viewed as detrimental to national unity and collective happiness. But the Bhutanese do agree that choice is instrumental to pursuit of well-being and happiness. All said and done, Bhutan takes stringent measures to preserve the traditional culture and promote the same as a symbol of unity and a pillar of GNH.

4   Good Governance: the fourth and final pillar of the concept of GNH is good governance. In a sense, collective happiness depends on good governance. Good governance is achieved when the collective desire of the people is fulfilled. At the same time, an individual's quest for happiness is to be respected as it is precious for him or her. The idea of good governance should, therefore, promote an individual's endeavour for a happy life.

To ensure good governance, Bhutan's king had given its people the option for liberal democracy. A constitution was drafted and circulated among the public to galvanise their opinion and make them aware of the democratic form of government. Subsequently, realising the need to fulfil people's desire for democracy, the absolute monarchy in Bhutan made way in favour of parliamentary democracy in 2008. However, Bhutan's people are still in a transitional mode in comprehending the new form of government. The government of Bhutan has made earnest efforts to integrate the makeover with the existing GNH policies. For instance, to make GNH an integral part of governance, the government of Bhutan has renamed its Planning Commission as the Gross National Happiness Commission. Bhutan government has credibly promoted the concept of GNH not only within the country but also internationally. As a sign of recognition of the credibility of GNH, the concept was recommended by the UN in Rio+20 Conference held in Brazil in 2012, and more than sixty nations in the world have accepted GNH as a model of alternative development. The UN Secretary-General Ban Ki-moon himself has patronised the GNH model and advocated for its wider application.

The four pillars of GNH are further classified into nine domains to create a better understanding of GNH and its values. These nine domains are (1) psychological well-being, (2) health, (3) education, (4) time use, (5) cultural diversity and resilience, (6) good governance, (7) community vitality, (8) ecological diversity and resilience and (9) living standards.

Measuring happiness: the GNH index

Undoubtedly it is very difficult to put GNH principles into practice. There may be many impressive indicators of happiness, but they may not be translated into measurable units. The first attempt to discuss and promote GNH index was made by the Centre for Bhutan Studies (CBS), Thimphu in the first GNH conference held in Bhutan in 2004. Thereafter, five successive international conferences on GNH were held in Canada (2005), Thailand (2007), Bhutan (2009), Brazil (2011) and Paro in Bhutan (2015) to acquire concrete inputs on measuring happiness and to magnify the importance of GNH. To measure GNH, the GNH index[15] and a set of screening tools were developed in 2008 by the Centre for Bhutan Studies (CBS). According to CBS experts, it is possible to measure Gross National Happiness by a 'single number index' developed from thirty-three indicators covering the nine domains. The thirty-three GNH indicators serve as 'evaluative tools' to track the progress of development over time. During the fourth GNH conference, further refinement in the process of measuring GNH was announced. This time it was revealed that seventy-two variables were selected to correspond to the nine domains, and a preliminary survey on the basis of these variables was carried out. Ultimately in 2010, a national survey on GNH was conducted by using 124 variables under the thirty-three clustered (grouped) indicators.[16] These 124 indicators became the basic building blocks of GNH. Since all the indicators did not have the same weight, a threshold of sufficiency level was attached to each variable.

It is obvious that not all variables are compulsory or necessary to make a person happy; people have diverse ways of living, and they are free to choose the ways that help them to be happy. In other words, not all the 124 variables are universally applicable. In any case, it has been ascertained that happiness can be measured by using the GNH index. On the basis of a nationwide survey on GNH, the CBS has established that there are four categories of people in Bhutan: unhappy, narrowly happy, extensively happy and deeply happy. To identify the degree of happiness, the CBS has decided on three cut-off points at 50 percent, 66 per cent and 77 per cent. If the people are identified to have less than 50 per cent sufficiency, they are categorised as 'unhappy'. If the people have sufficiency in the range of 50 to 65 per cent of the domains, they are 'narrowly happy'. Those who have achieved sufficiency in the range of 66 and 76 per cent in six to seven domains are 'extensively happy'. Finally, the people enjoying a sufficiency rate of 77 per cent or more, which is equivalent to seven out of nine domains, are identified as 'deeply happy'. CBS has also proposed to use one overall index for which the cut-off has been set at the middle, that is at 66 per cent of the variables. People can be considered happy if the level of sufficiency is above 66 per cent, but below that level, people will be considered not so happy/unhappy. The cut-off makes a difference in the GNH index as the middle cut-off gives a low score of GNH for the country as a whole.

The GNH index is still in the stage of experiment. Till date, two nationwide surveys based on samples have been conducted. The GNH policy too is being tested by screening tools. The Planning Commission of Bhutan has internalised the task of implementing GNH policies, so much so that the commission is renamed as Gross National Happiness Commission. However, it has been observed, although the government of Bhutan actively promotes GNH and promises to create the conditions under which people can seek happiness, that does not mean 'guarantee' for the people's happiness.[17] Bhutan is yet to confirm acceptance of all its policies by every community/sector. Besides, all the domains are not equally addressed. For example, it is a difficult proposition to ensure blanket psychological well-being since every individual has a different set of problems and attitudes.

Bhutan's GNH index is built on data collected from samples drawn from districts, gender, age and rural–urban residence, among others, during periodic surveys. One major objective of the periodic surveys is to estimate the number of 'not-yet-happy' people. According to the CBS, "GNH Index is meant to orient people and the nation towards happiness, primarily by improving the condition of not-yet-happy people".[18] It has been suggested by the CBS that the government can increase GNH in two ways: first, by increasing the percentage of 'happy' people and, second, by decreasing the insufficient conditions of the people who are 'not-yet-happy'. The 'not-yet-happy' people mainly reside in a rural belt and have limited access to education, a low standard of living and a less balanced use of time. In urban areas, people are largely unhappy due to insufficiency in non-material indicators, for example, community vitality and psychological well-being, rather than educational or income deficiencies. For instance, in Thimphu, the main hindrance in the path to happiness is a low level of community vitality.

Application of the concept of Gross National Happiness

It is undoubtedly an uphill task to put GNH policy into practice. The GNH Commission of Bhutan (the erstwhile Planning Commission of Bhutan) and the think tanks are in the process of refining the indicators to measure GNH for each of the nine domains so that public policies can be evaluated on the basis of their contribution to GNH. Presumably a large section of the rural folk may not know or understand the concept, but their lives are definitely influenced by the implementation of GNH policies. For all practical purposes, since the beginning of the twenty-first century, Bhutan's development is guided by the document *Bhutan 2020: A Vision for Peace, Prosperity and Happiness* (1999). The document was prepared prior to the beginning of the new millennium after intensive consultations between government agencies, communities and non-governmental organizations. It was basically a framework for future five-year plans. Following the document, the GNH policies were initiated in Bhutan's development strategies in the ninth five-year plan (2002–2007) and were further streamlined in the tenth plan (2008–2013).

GNH policies in the ninth plan (2002–2007)

The ninth plan had five overall goals addressing the four pillars of GNH. These were the following:

- Improving quality of life and income, especially of the poor
- Ensuring good governance
- Promoting private-sector growth and employment generation
- Preserving and promoting cultural heritage and environment conservation, and
- Achieving rapid economic growth and transformation

The strategies adopted to reach the goals and implement GNH policies included infrastructure expansion, sound macro-economic policy, ensuring good governance, and improving access and enhancing social services.[19] The ninth plan accorded high priority to improve and expand road network, particularly the village roads to improve access. The plan also provided for the expansion of power transmission lines and power grids to facilitate the export of power and promote the development of power-intensive industries. The improvement of telecommunication infrastructure and information technology was the other priority area. With an eye towards improving the quality of life in rural areas, telecommunication facilities were extended to all the *Gewogs* (blocks), and the private sector was invited to participate in this sector.

Bhutan's economy depended to a great extent on foreign aid, especially from India.[20] While external aid helped in implementing major development projects, the government of Bhutan aimed to meet the entire recurrent expenditures by domestic revenue. Therefore, there was an urgent need to enhance domestic revenue earnings. Efforts were made to increase earnings through improved tax administration. To broaden the revenue base, new sources of taxation were explored. Further, to put economic growth on a steady path, macro-economic policies were formulated. A major fiscal policy was to expand bank-lending services to the private sector for domestic investment projects.

Bhutan adopted a constitution during the ninth plan which was considered as the most important reform towards good governance. For the first time in Bhutan the powers of legislative, executive and the judicial bodies, and the rights and responsibilities of the citizens were fully elaborated. The process of decentralisation was also finalised and initiated with revised *Dzongkhag Yargey Tshogchung* (DYT), or District Development Committees, and *Gewog Yargey Tshogchung* (GYT), or Block Development Committees. The revised DYTs and GYTs were granted autonomy to make plans, allocate resources, and frame rules and regulations within their jurisdictions.

Since a majority of the people in Bhutan depended on primary activities, viz. agriculture and pastoralism for their livelihoods, the ninth plan prioritised the modernisation of agriculture and improvement in rural road infrastructure with the objectives of enhancement in agricultural productivity and improved access of the farmers to the markets. Other important steps taken in this direction were creating opportunities for agrobusiness, horticulture and small-scale handicraft industries. Besides, provisions were made for access to primary education, healthcare, safe drinking water and sanitation, since all of these had great bearing on the people's quality of life.

GNH policies in the tenth plan (2008–2013)

During the plan period, a historic change was made in the form of governance. The historic general elections in 2008 and 2013 and the wide media coverage they received reflected a clear shift in preference to democracy and the state's commitment to good governance.

The core objective of the tenth plan was poverty reduction. The two main themes of the plan were a Strategic Infrastructure (SI) theme and an Innovation, Creativity and Enterprise (ICE) theme. The SI theme included various development programmes pertaining to the construction and improvement of national highways, construction and improvement of roads, hydropower projects, power transmission lines, information and communications technology and postal development

142 Maitreyee Choudhury

and development of air and surface transport. The programmes under the ICE theme were meant to expand the economic and productive base by developing various industries and trade. These programmes were conceived as the main drivers of wealth creation. The strategic programmes under ICE included the promotion of domestic and foreign trade; the development of micro, small and medium enterprises; the development and management of industrial estates; strengthening the institutional framework for industrial development; sustainable environmental management and institutionalisation of cleaner technology; and private-sector participation in industries and sustainable development of tourism.[21] The other major strategic programmes adopted during the tenth plan by the GNH Commission were Integrated Rural-Urban Development and Poverty Alleviation, National Spatial Policy, Enabling Environment, and Strategies for Knowledge, Innovation and Life-Long Learning Skills.

The tenth plan emphasised on two main pillars of GNH, viz. preservation and promotion of cultural heritage and conservation of the environment. The quality of life in Bhutan was enriched and enhanced through the preservation and promotion of the nation's rich cultural heritage and traditional values. The implementing agencies for the said purpose were the Department of Culture, Folk Heritage Museum, Culture Centre, National Museum, Trongsa Tadzong Museum, Royal Academy of Performing Arts, National Library, other units and heritage centres, DYTs and GYTs. Bhutan's development agenda always gave high priority to the country's cultural heritage. It was viewed as a "perennial source of sound human values that strengthens social bonds and harmony and provides an effective antidote to cushion Bhutanese society from some of the negative impacts of globalisation".[22]

Culture–environment–development linkages

Bhutan's rich cultural heritage has played a crucial role in protecting and conserving the country's natural environment. The local belief system and inherent spirituality of the people of Bhutan help to conserve the natural environmental resources. The cultural ethos of the Bhutanese has always been a driving force behind the country's environmental sustainability.

The promotion of cultural heritage within modern development policies has certain advantages. The people of Bhutan who are largely guided by sociocultural values feel at ease if they find the development models are in consonance with tradition and do not go against their culture and sentiments. Development models without care for cultural tradition are likely to face resistances that may prove detrimental to the nation's pursuit for GNH.

Bhutan's environment has a profound influence on the well-being of the communities living in the country. The National Environment Commission in Bhutan is responsible for mainstreaming environmental concerns into the development process. The National Environment Commission was established in 1992 to make environmental concerns integral to the development agenda including Millennium

Development Goals and the Sustainable Development Goals. The specific goals of the commission linked with the eradication of poverty, hunger and environment are to ensure environmental sustainability, to maintain an acceptable level of forest cover, having an acceptable level of water and soil quality, air quality, the conservation of biodiversity, wetland conservation and a ban on dumping of hazardous waste. The implementing agencies for the previously mentioned goals are the National Environment Commission Secretariat, Environmental Units, DYTs and GYTs. The National Environment Commission in Bhutan maintains that

> conservation of environment is extremely important as the progressive and sustainable development of human society fundamentally depends on viable and healthy eco-system. It is also essential condition for the fullest possible satisfaction of human needs and wellbeing.[23]

The GNH Commission in Bhutan has made it clear that national planning for poverty reduction and strategies of development should be closely linked with environmental sustainability.

Environmental sustainability has been given priority in Bhutan since the very beginning of the first socio-economic planning. The Royal Government of Bhutan's policy claims to have maintained that the process of development should be 'holistic and consistent' with the environmental and cultural integrity of the country. To this goal, Bhutan has adopted the principle of "The Middle Path" as a development strategy to conserve the environment and traditional culture.[24] The government of Bhutan has promulgated "The Middle Path" as a National Environment Strategy to ensure the material well-being of the people without damaging the natural environment and compromising with their spiritual well-being. Owing to such an environment-conscious approach, Bhutan has been able to maintain 72 per cent of forest cover, 29 per cent of land dedicated as a protected area and 9 percent as a biological corridor.[25] The National Environment Commission of Bhutan has institutionalised environmental assessment processes and dissemination of information on the environment. The key strategic activities of the commission are to institutionalise and decentralise environmental assessment process, mainstreaming environmental issues into development planning process through awareness and capacity building and drafting environmental legislation.

Although Bhutan relies heavily on international aid for the implementation of its economic programmes, the state has taken a policy to implement only those programmes that will help to develop sustainably. Now that the public service is well established, the state is creating economic opportunities through the private sector. Service sectors such as tourism are receiving priority in the private sphere, but the state is keen to ensure that the profits accrued from tourism stay within the state. Bhutan maintains a policy of 'high value, low impact' tourism by implementing high tariffs for international visitors to restrict mass tourism and budget tourism in the country. The government has a policy for fixing the number of tourists permitted to enter the state every year. This policy serves two important purposes: first,

144 Maitreyee Choudhury

the quality of tourism is maintained, and second, the local culture and environment are less affected and less polluted.

Challenges in implementing policies

Bhutan lacks adequate manpower in implementing the framework policy and needs to train people on various development issues and effective dissemination techniques. However, regarding the conservation of forests and protected area, Bhutan has been very conscious and active for a reasonably long time. The government of Bhutan has taken the landmark policy decision to maintain minimum 60 per cent of its total geographical area under forest cover at any point of time and to meet the basic forest product requirements of the villagers simultaneously so that sustainability of both forests and livelihood operations can be ensured. As it is, Bhutan has 72 per cent of its area under forest cover. The Forest and Nature Conservation Act 1995 and the Forest and Nature Conservation Rules 2006 are the main legal instruments to implement the policies of environment conservation in Bhutan. Even before that the government of Bhutan adopted a national system of protected area in 1993. The state has 30 per cent land under nine protected areas that include four national parks, four wildlife sanctuaries and one strict nature reserve. As a special measure to connect the isolated protected areas, Bhutan's government has taken the decision to introduce biological corridors for safe passage and dispersal of animal and plant species.[26] These biological corridors not only connect the protected areas but also form a contiguous landscape for nature conservation. The Biological Corridor Rules (2007) have been added later with the Forest and Nature Conservation rules. The forest conservation rules and regulations are supplemented by National Park Management Plans, and many community-linked programmes, for example, Integrated Conservation and Development Programmes, Social Forestry, Community Forestry, and Private Forestry. In addition, there are other national policies, strategies and laws, including National Environment Protection Act 2007, Land Act 2007, National Ecotourism Strategy 2001, Vision and Strategy for the Nature Conservation Division (2003) and Bhutan Biological Conservation Complex Plan 2004.

As for the preservation of culture, it is explicit that Bhutanese society is deeply involved with its traditional culture and religion, that is, Buddhism. The Bhutanese code of conduct, *Driglam Namzha*, has been strictly enforced. Particularly, Bhutan's policies on language and dress code are strictly adhered to. The officialdom in Bhutan is bound by both. Dzongkha, the national language of Bhutan, is the main, if not the only, language in schools, colleges, universities and government offices. The dress code, too, is rigidly maintained in the workplace. Although people are free to wear non-traditional dress during leisure time, wearing the same during working hours is an offence. People, in general, have little qualms to follow the code of conduct, although the citizens of Nepali origin have grievances for obvious reasons. As for religion, with Buddhism being the state religion, it is revered by Buddhists and non-Buddhists alike, and no controversy or conflict has been observed on the issue of religion in Bhutan.

Outcome of the first GNH survey

On the basis of the first GNH index, the first survey was conducted by the government of Bhutan to understand the applicability of the GNH concept in 2010. The first-ever survey of GNH was conducted with samples taken from different districts and regions. The survey used questionnaires to gather relevant data from 7,142 respondents, out of which 6,476 or 90.7 per cent furnished sufficient information suitable for GNH index in the scale of 0 to 1. The methodology provided information on three levels – headcount, intensity and the overall GNH index. Headcount gave the percentage of respondents who are happy, while intensity showed the average sufficiency in terms of well-being. If the headcounts indicated sufficiency in six or more domains of GNH, then the situation was considered as happy. The lack of sufficiency in four or fewer domains indicated unhappiness.

During the 2010 GNH survey, as per the middle cut-off, or 66 per cent sufficiency, the headcount of happy persons in Bhutan was 41 per cent. The intensity revealed that 59 per cent of Bhutanese were not considered happy. However, according to degrees of happiness in stage-wise cut-off, 10.4 per cent of the population in Bhutan was 'unhappy', 48.7 per cent was 'narrowly happy', 32.6 per cent was 'extensively happy' and 8.3 per cent was 'deeply happy'. A higher number of GNH indicated a happier state. According to the survey, the GNH index in Bhutan stood at 0.743. The value of 0.743 on a scale of 0 to 1 definitely suggested a positive trend in terms of happiness. The index varied in the districts between 0.655 and 0.807. The western districts, comprising Haa, Paro, Thimphu, Punakha, Gasa, and the southern districts of Dagana, Tsirang and Sarpang, recorded high GNH values, ranging between 0.757 and 0.807. The districts of Trongsa in central Bhutan and Lhuentse, Tashi Yangtse and Samdrup Jongkhar in eastern Bhutan recorded low GNH between 0.707 and 0.756. Rest of the districts recorded medium GNH, between 0.707 and 0.756.

The survey also revealed the following trends:

- Men in Bhutan were happier than women.
- Of the nine domains, the domains of health, ecology, psychological well-being and community vitality showed sufficiency.
- The people in the urban areas were happier (50 per cent of urban respondents) compared to rural areas (37 per cent of rural respondents)
- Urban areas fared better in the domains of health, standard of living and education, while rural areas did better in community vitality, cultural resilience and good governance.
- The level of happiness was higher among people with formal primary education or above, compared to those with no formal education. But higher education exhibited little effect on GNH.
- The happiest people by occupation were civil servants, monks/nuns and members of GYT/DYT (local governments). Strangely enough, the unemployed Bhutanese were happier than the corporate employees, housewives, farmers and national workforce.

146 Maitreyee Choudhury

- The unmarried and the young were among the happiest.
- The DYTs(districts) across the country had a lot of similarity and equality. The happier DYTs included Paro, Sarpang, Dagana, Haa, Thimphu, Gasa, Tsirang, Punakha, Zhemgang and Chukha. The least happy DYT was Samdrup Jongkhar.
- The ranking of DYTs by GNH score differed significantly from their ranking by income per capita. Sarpang, Dagana and Zhemgang scored higher in GNH index but had lower average incomes.
- In absolute numbers, Thimphu had the most happy people while Chukha had most unhappy people.
- Thimphu ranked highest in education and living standards but lowest in community vitality.[27]

Field observations on GNH achievements

To make an estimation of the applied side and achievements of GNH, selective observational studies were undertaken in different districts of Bhutan during 2011–2012. The places visited were Phuentsholing, Chukar, Gedu, Paro, Thimphu, Punakha, Wangdue, Trongsa and Bumthang. A cross section of Bhutan government officials, educators and students, as well as workers in various unorganised sectors, viz. hotels, shops, transport and tourism sectors, were interacted with. Intensive studies were made in Thimphu, Trongsa Dzong and Bumthang Dzong. In Trongsa Dzong, the concerned officials in various departments were consulted, while in Bumthang Dzong, an informal discussion on various aspects of GNH was held with the Dzongpen (governor) and other officials of the Department of Culture.

During fieldwork, it was observed that the urban people in Bhutan, by and large, were well aware of the concept of GNH. Starting from the high officials in different government establishments to the workers in the unorganised sectors, the Bhutanese people demonstrated fair to marginal knowledge of GNH. It was but obvious that all government departments were bound to follow the GNH policy of the state, and the officials therein acquired fare to an adequate understanding of the concept. The education department, in particular, was found to apply the concept right from school level. The department adopted the policy of "Educating for GNH"[28] to train the young minds on GNH. Noted Bhutanese educationist T.S. Powdyel (2010) stated, "We were on a mission no less sublime than educating for Gross National Happiness – a mission that aims to reclaim the core objective of education".[29] The vein of GNH objectives runs all along the formal education system. The students are tutored regularly on the values of GNH through different levels of education in schools, colleges and various branches of the Royal University of Bhutan. Conversations with the high school students in the remote Bumthang Valley revealed that the concept of GNH had long been incorporated into the school curriculum, and the younger generations in Bhutan were already sensitised on issues like preservation of heritage, culture and environment.

Other government departments, viz. agriculture, forest and environment, were found to apply the GNH policies in various activities. Their efforts were reflected in various publications of the concerned ministries and notably in the GNH Commission Mid-term Review Report, 2011 of the Tenth Five Year Plan (2008–2013). In a bid to preserve traditional crops and indigenous farming system of Bhutan, the Ministry of Agriculture banned the import of all genetically modified organisms (GMOs) in 2000. The government had enforced the ban as a precautionary measure for the safety of agriculture as well as health care issues. The legislation related to biosafety in Bhutan were the Plant Quarantine Act 1993, the Seeds Act 2000, the Livestock Act 2000, the Environmental Assessment Act 2000, the Biodiversity Act 2003 and the Food Act of Bhutan 2005, among others. The National Environment Commission of Bhutan had long been working towards conservation of the biodiversity. A National Biosafety Framework (2006) had also been prepared by the National Environment Commission of Bhutan. In implementing the biosafety framework, the social, economic, ethical, cultural and religious impacts, plus the benefits and risks of research and development of GMOs, were taken into consideration. One very significant step taken in this regard was the 'Principle of Subsidiarity'. It was clearly spelt out in the framework that "decisions should be made at the lowest level to involve all affected citizens regardless of their status, wealth, power, ethnicity, or gender".[30]

On another level, the workers in private sectors, for example, hotel employees, cab drivers, petty business people and so on, were found to be well acquainted with the concept of GNH.[31] During interviews conducted on the laypeople in five major urban areas in western and central Bhutan, viz. Thimphu, Paro, Punakha, Trongsa and Bumthang, it transpired that the average Bhutanese citizens in the young-age and middle-age categories were pretty much aware of the concept of GNH, and many of them took pride in it, while some were confused or not convinced. According to a key informant, the rural people in Bhutan, including his own friends and relatives, intrinsically valued religion, culture and natural environment, even more than any material possession. They did not necessarily depend on their *Gup* (village headman), GYT or DYT representatives to teach them on GNH.

However, it must be mentioned that there were some people, mostly the aggrieved citizens of Nepali origin, who were not at all convinced of GNH ideals. On the condition of anonymity, a group of educated ethnic Nepalis in Bhutan expressed that the whole GNH business was a hype to divert the attention of the world from the issues related to violation of human rights of the citizens of Nepali origin at home. This group was politically conscious and educated and did not accept the concept of GNH on its face value. Moreover, according to them, some minority groups, apparently in the grip of poverty were not at all sampled while measuring GNH, lest the whole exercise to prove Bhutan a happy country went off-balance. The issue was highly debatable, but the discontent was palpable.

There was yet another set of respondents who were sceptical of applicability of the GNH index and believed that the whole exercise involved in measuring

148 Maitreyee Choudhury

happiness was futile since the concept itself, according to them was based on abstract ideas.

Conclusion

The concept of GNH is an 'above ordinary' concept not experienced or tested before by any nation. It is understood to have been developed by the nobility, the aristocracy and the elites in Bhutan to protect Bhutanese culture and identity. The government of Bhutan has reservations in replicating the modernisation processes prevalent in other parts of the developing world. Although Bhutan has discarded the self-imposed isolation and opened up in the new millennium by allowing the entry of satellite channels and sharing cyberspace, the country is still in dilemma in adopting modern ways. To overcome the conflicting position with regard to modern development and traditional culture, Bhutan has adopted the "Middle Path" perspective in consonance with Buddhist tenets. Bhutan believes that GNH can be achieved individually, as well as collectively, by practising and cultivating Buddhist philosophy. But chunks of Bhutanese population who live in remote inaccessible villages, high altitude localities and in the margins (socially and economically), have little or no knowledge of GNH philosophy, its four pillars, nine domains and 124 happiness indicators. They are too busy to earn barely enough to sustain themselves and fight poverty day in and out. The discourse on 'Gross National Happiness' is beyond their comprehension, as is the discourse on 'poverty', and touches them only remotely.

Post-script: outcome of GNH survey 2015

During the latest International Conference on GNH held at Paro in Bhutan in November 2015, it has been revealed at the opening ceremony (3 November 2015) that 91.2 per cent of Bhutanese are happy. According to reports, "[t]he GNH index, used to provide a reliable, comprehensive and up-to-date picture of the country's overall situation and progress, is moderately higher at 0.756 this year (2015), as compared to 0.743 in 2010" (*Kuensel/The Statesman*, 4 November 2015). The CBS, Thimphu, claims that GNH in Bhutan has increased by 1.8 per cent since the last survey carried out five years ago. Of those found to be happy, 8.4 per cent are categorised as being "deeply happy",35 per cent as "extensively happy" and 47.9 per cent as "narrowly happy" while a little less than 9 per cent of Bhutanese are "unhappy". The percentage of "deeply happy" and "extensively happy" people taken together has increased from 40.9 per cent in 2010 to 43.4 per cent in 2015. The goal of Bhutan is to achieve sufficiency in all nine domains of GNH. The CBS states, "The aim is for all Bhutanese to be extensively or deeply happy. Bhutan is closer to achieving that aim in 2015 than it was in 2010". The CBS also says that the improvement in GNH is the outcome of improved living standards and service delivery, better health and more participation in cultural festivals. However, in spite of overall improvement in GNH score, there has been a significant reduction in the sufficiency of certain domains. A marked decrease has been noted in psychological well-being due to higher levels of anger and frustration and lower level of spirituality. The sense of belonging at the community level in terms of sharing time and money has also decreased. The CBS has also noted that the traditional etiquette of courtesy and effectiveness of the national code of conduct known as *Driglam Namzha* have weakened in last five years, and the compound effect of a decrease in psychological well-being, spirituality, community vitality and traditional etiquette has resulted in moderate increase in GNH. According to Karma Ura, GNH Research president, "The 2015 GNH Index provides a self-portrait and offers Bhutanese the opportunity to reflect on the directions society is moving, and make wise and determined adjustments".[32]

The 2015 GNH report shows that men in Bhutan are happier than women, with 51 per cent 'happy men' against 39 per cent 'happy women'. It has also revealed that urban dwellers are happier than rural Bhutanese, with 55 per cent happy urbanites compared to 38 per cent happy rural folks. The report clearly indicates more education means more happiness, as only 32 per cent of those without formal education are happy compared to over 50 percent of citizens having high school experience. The marital status of the Bhutanese has a considerable impact on the happiness of the average Bhutanese: it has been found that the married people are less happy compared to unmarried people. Out of the twenty-odd DYTs in Bhutan, the happiest DYTs are Bhutan, Gasa and Paro. Bhutan is striving hard to bring all the DYTs on a par in terms of happiness, but for all practical purposes, it is a difficult proposition.

Notes

1 Human Development Report 2015: Work for Human Development, 2015, UNDP.
2 The first HDI was applied to measure human development in 1990. All the countries in the world were ranked accordingly (e.g. Iceland, No. 1 to Sierra Leone, No. 177), www.measureofamerica.org/human-development/, accessed 16 April 2019.
3 Although the concept of GNH is widely recognised as a model of wellbeing and assessing quality of life, there is no single definition of GNH. The widely accepted definition of GNH runs as follows: "Gross National Happiness (GNH) measures the quality of a country in more holistic way (than GNP) and believes that the beneficial development of human society takes place when material and spiritual development occur side by side to complement and reinforce each other" www.educatingforgnh.com.
4 Akiko Ueda, Culture and Modernisation: From the Perspective of Young People in Bhutan, Thimphu: The Centre for Bhutan Studies, 2003, p. 112.
5 Planning Commission of Bhutan, 1991; cited in Ueda, *Ibid*., p. 111.
6 Planning Commission of Bhutan, 1999, p. 46, cited in Ueda, *Ibid*.
7 Sonam Kinga Kinga, Polity, Kingship and Democracy: A Biography of the Bhutanese State, Thimphu: Ministry of Education, Royal Government of Bhutan, 2009.
8 Winnie Bothe, "The Monarch's Gift: Critical Notes on the Constitutional Processes in Bhutan", European Bulletin of Himalayan Research, vol. 40, 2012, p. 27.
9 Article 9, Constitution of Bhutan, 2008.
10 Jigmi Y. Thinley, Opening address of Educating Gross National Happiness Conference, Bhutan: Thimphu, 7 December 2009.
11 Karma Phunthso, The History of Bhutan, Noida: Random House India, London: Random House Group Limited, 2013 p. 595.

12 *Ibid.*
13 "Development Philosophy", Ninth Plan Main Document, 2002–2007, Thimphu: Royal Government of Bhutan, 2008, p. 5.
14 Lyonpo Jigmi Thinley, "Rethinking Development: Local Pathways to Global Well-being", Keynote address delivered at the Second International Conference on Gross National Happiness, Canada: St. Francis Xavier University, Antigonish, Nova Scotia, 20–24 June 2005.
15 The GNH index was constructed on the basis of a highly complex, multidimensional methodology known as the Alkire–Foster method, www.grossnationalhappiness.com, accessed 9 May 2019.
16 Karma Ura, Sabine Alkire, Tshokiv Zangmo and Karma Wangdiv, A Short Guide to Gross National Happiness Index, Thimphu: The Centre for Bhutan Studies, 2012, p. 2.
17 Edahiro Junko, "Bhutan: Creating Index to Measure People's Happiness", JFS Newsletter, no. 81, May 2009.
18 Ura et al., no. 16, p. 2.
19 Ninth Plan Main Document, no. 13, pp. 49–50.
20 Dhurba Rizal, Administrative System in Bhutan: Retrospect and Prospect, New Delhi: Adroit Publishers, 2002, p. 185.
21 Tenth Five Year Plan: 2008–2013, vol. 2, Programme Profiles, 2009, Thimphu: GNH Commission, Royal Government of Bhutan.
22 Tenth Plan Document, vol. 2, Thimphu: GNH Commission, Royal Government of Bhutan, 2009, p. 191.
23 *Ibid.*, p. 339.
24 Sean Boyd Frye Hargens, "Integral Development: Taking 'Middle Path' to Gross National Happiness", The Journal for Bhutan Studies, vol. 6, no. 3, 2002, p. 46.
25 Tenth Plan Document, no. 23, p. 340.
26 Biological Corridor Strategic Plan [2008–2013], Thimphu: National Environment Commission, Royal Government of Bhutan, 2008, p. 13.
27 See, Centre for Bhutan Studies, www.grossnationalhappiness.com.
28 Nurturing Green Schools for Green Bhutan – A Guide to School Management, Thimphu: Department of Education, Royal Government of Bhutan, 2011.
29 Keynote address during the 14th Annual Education Conference, 27–29 December 2010, Bhutan: Chukha.
30 National Biosafety Framework of the Kingdom of Bhutan, 2006, p. 27.
31 The cab driver who drove me from Thimphu to Trongsa was a high school drop-out but an unusually well-informed man who became a key informant for me.
32 Kuensel, 4 November 2016, Butan's Daily News Paper online.

12

LINKAGES BETWEEN MIGRATION AND POVERTY IN NEPAL

Amrita Limbu

Introduction

Migration discourses in the twenty-first century have seen a surge in transnational labour migration from developing countries of the South to the rapidly growing economies of the South, specifically in the Middle East and parts of South-East Asia. While this migration trend has often been engulfed in debates surrounding workers' rights, protection and dignity, the earnings remitted by the migrants have resulted in substantial changes and impacts on migrant households within a short period. This chapter focuses on the latter aspect, exploring the linkages between migration and poverty, and, in particular, examines how migration has resulted in reduced poverty among migrant households in Nepal.

The South–South migration is, for the most part, driven by the labour market demand in the host countries. In line with the dual labour market approach, the initiation of migration is, therefore, a formal mechanism whereby the state plays a primary role.[1] Likewise, temporary mass migration of workers from developing countries to the countries in the Middle East and Malaysia was instigated with the adoption of guest-worker programmes and the demand for labour to work on modern infrastructures or to provide services of care and reproductive labour. Numerous factors continue to perpetuate migration to these countries that now host a large number and proportion of foreign migrant workers on temporary contracts. Wage disparities in host and origin countries and the role of migration networks of families and relatives, as well as the demographic, economic and political factors of the states, play an influencing role in the migratory trends and patterns.[2]

Although the trend of migration is predominantly directed from developing countries to the more developed countries, migration benefits both the host and the origin country. In the host countries, migrants have fulfilled labour shortages taking up jobs undesired by the locals and contributed to the rapidly growing economies, as well as towards taxes and social security payments. At the other end of the spectrum, migrants and families in migrant households have directly benefitted from remittances sent by migrants, and the states, too, have used migration as development tools, including to reduce poverty. Several studies on migration provide evidence that remittances have been instrumental in reducing the severity of poverty in developing countries with a large international migrant population.[3]

However, since remittances are often the sole sources of income for most households in the developing countries, the impact of remittances is much higher than in the developed countries. In a similar finding from a panel study of forty-six countries using data between 1970 and 2000, Portes[4] concluded that the effect of remittances is strongest in the low-income countries and weakest in the high-income countries. The study estimated 1 per cent increase in remittances increased the income of the lowest-income countries in the first decile by 0.43 per cent whereas the income of the highest-income countries in the highest decile decreased by 0.10 per cent, and remittances were also found to reduce inequality in terms of income distribution in the low-income countries.

In a study of seventy-one developing countries, Adams and Page[5] reported that a 10 per cent increase in per capita official remittances leads to a 3.5 per cent decline in the share of people living in poverty, noting that remittances contributed to a reduction in level, depth and severity of poverty in the developing countries. Similarly, the World Bank,[6] through an analysis of household surveys, estimated the reduction of poverty headcount ratio in countries such as Bangladesh by 6 percent, by 11 percent in Uganda and by 5 percent in Ghana. Another study[7] involving a survey of 1,200 households in Algeria concluded that remittances contributed to the reduction in the number of people living below the poverty line by 40 per cent.

The contribution of migration to poverty reduction also remains valid for Nepal. Sunam and McCarthy[8] reported that migration resulted in poverty reduction for a large majority of the households in the study sample in eastern Nepal. Acharya and Leon-Gonzalez[9] and Lokshin (et al.)[10] have used statistical analysis of Nepal Living Standards Surveys[11] data to draw conclusions between poverty and migration, primarily focusing on the reduction in national poverty rate due to migration. However, migration studies in Nepal have not examined the core issues surrounding migration at the household level to demonstrate their reflection on poverty reduction.

This chapter takes a micro-level approach to assess the linkage between labour migration and poverty in Nepal. Drawing on secondary literature and the experiences of migrants and migrant families, this chapter analyses the changes brought about by the migration of family member(s) and the remittances sent home at the household level and how migration has resulted in poverty reduction of migrant households. This chapter emphasises on labour migration to the Middle East and Malaysia due to the large volume of migration to these destinations and the largest share of remittances received from these destinations also discussed in the following.

Background

Nepal has faced persistent poverty over the years. It can be linked to the long-term political upheaval that the country has faced throughout much of its modern history. To make matters worse, the decade-long armed insurgency that began in 2006 was a major setback to the nascent economic growth and development. Destruction of infrastructure, insecurity, extortion and confiscation of property directly affected investments. Even as the insurgency ended in 2006, power squabble and frequent changes in the government continues to hamper growth, stability and prosperity. Unemployment, underemployment and poverty are thus long-standing problems in Nepal. Even so, the poverty rate decreased, and the economy fared better than expected. Between 1995/96 and 2003/04, the poverty rate declined from 41.8 percent to 30.8 percent and further to 25.2 percent in 2010/11.[12] Remittances sent by migrant workers is considered to be the major contributor to poverty reduction.

For the past few decades, Nepalis have increasingly sought alternate sources of livelihood in about a hundred countries across the globe.[13] The main motivating factors of migration not only are poverty, unemployment and thus aspirations to find work and generate income but also go beyond economic reasons. Labour demand, employment opportunities and the immigration policies that facilitate the transnational mobility of labour particularly in the Middle East countries and Malaysia have resulted in the movement of a large Nepali youth population driven by a desire to make decent earning. Due to employment opportunities abroad, unemployed youth face social pressure to migrate, but the overwhelming scale of migration also incites in non-migrants a desire to follow the popular trend and gain an experience of the world beyond home, perpetuating a culture of migration. Migration for the thousands of youth is also an opportunity to move away from rural life to experience modernization and life in one of the rapidly growing cities/countries.

The national population census notes that almost 2 million Nepalis are living outside the country, a threefold increase within a decade.[14] Nepal shares an open border with India, and therefore, India has historically been an important migration destination. The migration flow continues to India at an increasing rate, but as more and more Nepalis migrate beyond India to the Middle East and Malaysia, the proportion of migrants to India has rapidly declined from 89 per cent of all migrants in 1991 to 77 per cent in 2001 and 38 per cent in 2011.[15]

Migration to Malaysia, Qatar, Saudi Arabia and the United Arab Emirates accounts for 37 per cent of Nepali out-migrants.[16] Migration to these countries primarily falls under the formalised labour migration requiring work permits from the Nepali government to leave the country. This is mainly temporary short-term migration of about two to three years initially and, in some instances, may extend for up to ten years depending upon extension or continual return. The UK, the US, Australia and other developed countries also host a significant Nepali population, but the number and proportion to these countries are far lower than to the Middle East countries and Malaysia. The purpose and nature of migration are wide-ranging, but labour migrants or those leaving the country for employment purposes account for almost a quarter of the total migrants, by far exceeding the other trends including educational migration or migrating as dependent family members.[17] Therefore, the migration trend in Nepal is, by and large, dominated by labour migration especially of the youth.

A deeper analysis into the policies on migration in Nepal reveals that labour migration has been an important development tool adopted by subsequent governments to overcome poverty and unemployment in the country. In the five-year development plan of 1980–85, the government recognized the necessity of utilizing the workforce to improve the living standards of those living below the poverty line and, for the first time, initiated to send its citizens abroad for employment. The Foreign Employment Act was introduced in 1985, initiating a system of organized and registered overseas labour migration (beyond India).[18] The government's policy benefitted from the huge labour demand in the oil-rich countries of the Middle East, as well as rapidly growing economies like Malaysia, and used migration as a means to check high-scale unemployment and poverty in the country.

Linkage between migration and poverty

Contrary to the general perception, it is not only the poor who migrate. Although poverty is a major push factor contributing to migration, everyone from the poor to rich migrates. However, the destination preferences do vary by the wealth of the migrant household. Migrants from the poorest households in Nepal mainly migrate to India, and as the income level of households increases, migration is directed towards the Middle East countries and Malaysia and migration from the wealthiest households is increasingly to the developed countries in Europe, Australia and America.[19]

This trend is concurrent with the cost of migration. Crossing the border into India can be accomplished by carrying a few thousand rupees (US$10–30),[20] whereupon migrants utilize the network of their friends and families to find work and make living arrangements. Non-requirements of work permit from either the origin or the host country, or any other documents, further facilitate the migration process to India. Comparatively, the cost of migration is higher to the Middle East countries and Malaysia and increases when migration is to the developed countries. In average, migrants pay about US$1,000 to migrate to the Middle East and Malaysia[21] but could range from US$200 to US$7,000. The rigorous migration process requiring specific and numerous documentation, including visas, medical check-ups, life insurance for the duration of the contract period, orientation training certification and contracts, further adds to the migration costs beyond India.

The cost of seeking employment in developed countries is much higher with accounts of migrants paying as much as US$10,000 to US$15,000 to the agents or intermediaries alone to enter Europe. Unlike the formalized migration programmes in the Middle East or Malaysia, the pathways of migration to the developed counties are not straightforward, and migrants often channel through indirect and even irregular routes to obtain regular migration status, taking months and even years. The cost of migration also correlates to the remuneration that migrants might earn abroad. Earnings in India are comparatively low compared to the Middle East and Malaysia, and likewise, income is much higher in Europe or America. Despite the wage differences, migration to any destination, including India can add to the welfare of migrants and migrant households.[22] It is in the hope of higher earnings that migrants invest a large amount to finance their migration.

But in order to meet the high cost of migration, most migrants resort to taking loans or borrowing from family and relatives. Migrants, most of whom lack collaterals, pay interest rates as high as 60 per cent when taking loans from money lenders.[23] High-interest rate loans are often a risk, as migrants spend almost a year or two paying off their loan and, in some instances, even longer. During instances of an unsuccessful migration, the inability to make an earning and high-interest loans have proved to increase the poverty of migrant households. As a result, migration might not always have the same linear effect on poverty. While remittances receiving households fare better, the situation of migrant households who are not able to benefit from remittances for various reasons risk the negative effects of migration. Households that do not receive remittances have experienced worsened poverty.[24]

Numerous factors determine the migrants' ability or inability to remit earnings. Health and well-being are fundamental, but many migrants find themselves in difficult circumstances of not receiving remuneration or not finding work. Extensive literature on Nepali migrant workers in the Middle East and Malaysia have brought to light, the extremely unfavourable work and living situation of migrant workers in forced labour and trafficking situation.[25] Reports of ill treatment of Nepali migrant workers in the Middle East and Malaysia, physical and psychological abuses, non-payment of salary and inadequate living and working facilities are often cited realities of migrant workers abroad. Even in the country of origin, aspiring migrants risk deception by fallacious agents and recruitment agencies of numerous natures resulting in financial losses and psychological stress even before departure.[26] Despite these challenges, which are beyond the scope of this chapter, the contribution of migration in the form of remittances is vividly visible and significant.

Decent earnings are core to a successful migration. Earnings made abroad help migrants to manage their daily expenses while working and living abroad, but if they also save enough to remit to their family, the impact of migration overflows to the migrant household. Remittances are fundamental to improving the financial situation of the households. At present 25 per cent of the total population in Nepal live below the poverty line (if per capital total annual consumption is below NPR 19,261, approximately US$186). The poverty rate in Nepal would have been much higher without remittances received from abroad. As shown in Figure 12.1, poverty has declined over the years, from 41.8 per cent to 25.2 per cent within 15 years. The reduction in poverty is synchronous to the increase in the percentage of households receiving remittances. Within the same time frame, the percentage of households receiving remittances increased more than twofold, from 23.4 in 1995/96 to 31.9 in 2003/04 and to 55.8 in 2010/11.[27]

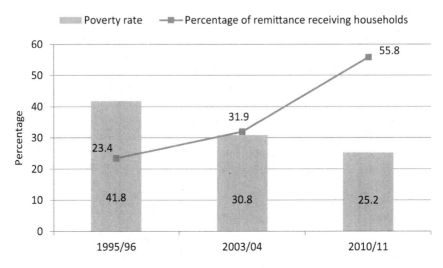

FIGURE 12.1 Poverty rates and number of households receiving remittances

Source: Nepal Living Standards Survey 2010/11[28]

Between 2003/04 and 2010/11, the amount of remittances increased by more than four times from 58.5 billion rupees (US$0.5 billion) to 253.5 billion rupees (US$2.4 billion).[29] During the fiscal year 2015/16, Nepal received more than 665 billion rupees (approximately US$6.4 billion) in remittances.[30] A remittance is equivalent to approximately 30 per cent of the total gross domestic product.[31]

The three countries that receive the largest share of Nepali migrants – Malaysia, Qatar and Saudi Arabia – account for more than half the share of all remittances from overseas, demonstrating that migrant workers are the main source of remittances for households in Nepal.[32] The remittances that the workers send home have enabled a reduction in poverty and an improvement in the living standard of even the poorest households.

Migration and poverty reduction at the household level

Migrants are often the only earning members in most migrant households across the country. Remittances received from the migrants have resulted in wider changes at the household level; it has not only increased household income but in doing so helped households to surface above the poverty line. Even the poorest households have benefitted from the migration of family member(s), an opportunity that would not have been possible without migration.

The migration of family members has contributed to increased consumption capacity of the households, investment in health care, children's education and assets. Out of the total remittances received by households, almost a quarter is spent on daily household expenses, while the remaining are utilized to pay for children's school, for health care, to keep savings, to repay loans (taken to finance migration or other loans) and to invest in land and property.[33] Despite the seemingly large spending on household consumption, studies reveal that households receiving remittances invest more in health care and children's education compared to households not receiving remittances.[34] Migrant households enrol their children in private schools, where the quality of education is considered better in comparison to public schools.

Remittances are also major source of insurance for migrant families. Remittances increase during times of financial or political crisis or natural disasters to help the family members.[35] This was also true for Nepal as remittances increased following the earthquake of 2015 that took away thousands of lives during a period marked by decreased out-migration.[36] At a time when many people lost their livelihoods, remittances were an important source of living. In fact, the dependence of migrant families on the migrant(s) increased after the earthquake, as they looked up to the migrants to overcome the then financial difficulties and for rebuilding their houses.[37]

Remittances allow households to have better saving capacity compared to nonmigrants and for investment opportunities either in land, property and other assets or in business. Migrant households have bought land and built houses mainly in semi-urban localities. Having the financial capability, migrant families have shifted to semi-urban and urban areas to provide better education to their children, as well as for an easier lifestyle. This has resulted in increasing urbanization from rural villages to more urban towns or from towns to the cities. The economic status of households with better access to services likes schools, hospitals, roads and markets are known to be better than households in remote rural areas.[38] The economy of these newly emerging semi-urban localities is mainly driven by remittances with small single ownership entrepreneurial activities mainly shops. They lack production and manufacturing activities to boost employment, investment, a larger share of financial return or even sustainability.

More important, remittances have increased the consumer culture in Nepal. Migrant households are able to afford the latest technologies and gadgets like mobile phones, televisions and motorbikes, as well as clothes and other everyday things. Additionally, migrant households are able to spend increasingly on religious and social functions.[39] This increasing consumer culture and consumption of remittances primarily in household expenses has often raised questions about the unproductive utilization of the hard-earned money by migrants abroad. Utilization of the remittances for long-term sustainable income generation should be a priority to harness the benefits of the ongoing short-term migration, but many migrant workers are unable to utilize the earnings or even skills and knowledge they acquire abroad on return to the country. As a result, the large majority of them fall into the cycle of migration, over and over again, or risk falling back into poverty.

Therefore, migration alone is not a determinant of poverty reduction. Although remittances are core to poverty reduction, factors such as a household's economic status prior to migration of family member, as well as engagement of the left behind family members in other income-generating activities, level of the migrant's earning, migration costs and the ability to leverage on remittances, are highly influential. Experience from other countries also reveals that remittances have been utilized in public welfare services, such as clean drinking water, drainage, schools, hospitals, roads and electricity, and have decreased dependence on state-provided welfare.[40] Remittances thus largely help to contain expectation and frustration with the government and the same holds true in the case of Nepal, where poverty has decreased despite the absence of employment opportunities, growth of manufacturing and service sector, local government structure or even a stable government.[41]

In reverse, migration is likely to have a negative effect on those who stay behind or those who choose not to migrate.[42] For poor households, not choosing to migrate could be a missed opportunity to overcome poverty like many of the migrant households. Although familial obligations and other circumstances play an important role in non-migration decisions, the flow of remittances from migrants to the community consequently means that the poor non-migrant households are further vulnerable to the rapidly changing economic and social setting they live in. Increased consumption practices among migrant households play a catalytic role in price hikes; more and more migrant children are enrolled in schools that provide better education, and migrant households are increasingly adopting easier lifestyles, moving away from difficult farm labour and taking up small entrepreneurial activities like shop keeping and moving to semi-urban localities with better access to transportation and other infrastructures. Although agriculture is still the main source of occupation for the majority of the people in Nepal, the abandonment of agriculture, the urbanization and the mass migration of youth have resulted in agriculture wage hikes in the rural areas mainly due to the lack of workforce. Therefore, migration could also indirectly or directly impact the non-migrant households.

Conclusion

Migration has largely contributed to improved living standards of the people and towards crucial investments mainly in human capital and land and property. However, a major challenge remains for migrant households, as well as the government, to channel remittances for sustainable livelihood sources and to overcome migrant households falling back into poverty or to the cycle of migration. The long-term impact of migration on poverty reduction is particularly a critical issue since the migration of the youth is taking place at a rapid pace, the economy is largely sustained by remittances, employment opportunities within the country are scarce, and the otherwise high dependence of Nepali households on agriculture has been rapidly decreasing over the years. Migrant households have higher incomes, a higher level of consumer spending and a lower incidence of poverty, but long-term poverty reduction depends on creating alternative sources of employment and harnessing the benefits of migration. And yet without remittances, poverty in Nepal would have been higher.

Notes

1 D.S. Massey, J. Arango, G. Hugo, A. Kouaouci, A. Pellegrino and J.E. Taylor, "Theories of International Migration: A Review and Appraisal", Population and Development Review, vol. 19, no. 3, 1993, pp. 431–466; D.S. Massey, "A Missing Element in Migration Theories", Migration Letters: An International Journal of Migration Studies, vol. 12, no. 3, 2015, pp. 279–299.
2 I. Goldin, G. Cameron and M. Balarajan, Exceptional People: How Migration Shaped Our World and Will Define Our Future, Princeton, NJ: Princeton University Press, 2012.
3 D. Ratha, "The Impact of Remittances on Economic Growth and Poverty Reduction", Policy Brief, vol. 8, 2013, pp. 1–13; R.H. Adams and J. Page, "Do International Migration and Remittances Reduce Poverty in Developing Countries?", World Development, vol. 33, no. 10, 2005, pp. 1645–1669; R.K. Sunam and J.F. McCarthy, "Reconsidering the Links Between Poverty, International Labour Migration, and Agrarian Change: Critical Insights from Nepal", The Journal of Peasant Studies, vol. 43, no. 1, 2016, pp. 39–63; L.S.V. Portes, "Remittances, Poverty and Inequality", Journal of Economic Development, vol. 34, no. 1, 2009, pp. 127–140; D.N. Margolis, L. Miotti, E.M. Mouhoud and J. Oudinet, "To Have and Have Not: International Migration, Poverty, and Inequality in Algeria", The Scandinavian Journal of Economics, vol. 117, no. 2, 2015, pp. 650–685; World Bank, Global Economic Prospects: Economic Implications of Remittances and Migration, Washington, DC: World Bank, 2006.
4 Portes, no. 3.
5 Adams and Page, no. 3.
6 World Bank, no. 3.
7 Margolis et al., no. 3.
8 Sunam and McCarthy, no. 3.
9 Chakra P. Acharya and Roberto Leon-Gonzalez, The Impact of Remittance on Poverty and Inequality: A Micro-Simulation Study for Nepal, St. Louis: Federal Reserve Bank of St Louis, 2012.
10 M. Lokshin, M. Bontch-Osmolovski and E. Glinskaya, "Work-Related Migration and Poverty Reduction in Nepal", Review of Development Economics, vol. 14, no. 2, 2010, pp. 323–332.
11 CBS, Nepal Living Standards Survey 2010/11: Statistical Report, vol. 1 & 2, Kathmandu: Central Bureau of Statistics, 2011.
12 CBS, Poverty in Nepal, Kathmandu: Central Bureau of Statistics, 2012.
13 B. Sijapati and A. Limbu, Governing Labour Migration in Nepal: An Analysis of Existing Policies and Institutional Mechanisms, Kathmandu: Himal Books, 2012.
14 CBS, National Population and Housing Census 2011: National Report, Kathmandu: Central Bureau of Statistics, 2012.
15 CBS, Population Monograph of Nepal Volume I: Population Dynamics, Kathmandu: Central Bureau of Statistics, 2014.
16 Data from the Nepal Living Standards Survey 2010/11, no. 11.
17 *Ibid.*
18 Due to the open border between India and Nepal, these policies only regulate migration beyond India. The prevailing policies governing labour migration in Nepal comprise the Foreign Employment Act 2007, the Foreign Employment Rules 2008 and Foreign Employment Policy 2012.
19 World Bank, no. 3.
20 Estimate conversion rates as of June 2017.
21 World Bank, no. 3.
22 S. Sharma and D. Thapa, Taken for Granted: Nepali Migration to India, Kathmandu: Centre for the Study of Labour and Mobility, 2013.
23 Amnesty International, False Promises: Exploitation and Forced Labour of Nepalese Migrant Workers, London: Amnesty International, 2011.
24 Sunam and McCarthy, no. 3; Margolis et al., no. 3.

25 S. Paoletti, E. Taylor-Nicholson, B. Sijapati and B. Farbenblum, Migrant Workers' Access to Justice at Home: Nepal, New York: Open Society Foundations, 2014; R. Bajracharya and B. Sijapati, The Kafala System and Its Implications for Nepali Domestic Workers, Kathmandu: Center for the Study of Labour Mobility, 2012; H. Harroff-Tavel and A. Nasri, Tricked and Trapped: Human Trafficking in the Middle East, Geneva: International Labour Office, 2013; Amnesty International, The Dark Side of Migration: Spotlight on Qatar's Construction Sector Ahead of the World Cup, London: Amnesty International, 2013.
26 Paoletti et al., *Ibid.*
27 CBS, no. 11.
28 *Ibid.*
29 NRB, Current Macroeconomic Situation: Based on Annual Data of 2011/12, Kathmadu: Nepal Rastra Bank, 2012; NRB, Current Macroeconomic Situation 2005 (Mid-December), Kathmandu: Nepal Rastra Bank, 2005.
30 NRB, Current Macroeconomic and Financial Situation of Nepal: Based on Annual Data of 2015/16, Kathmandu: Nepal Rastra Bank, 2016.
31 *Ibid.*
32 CBS, no. 11.
33 *Ibid.*
34 Ratha, no. 3.
35 *Ibid.*
36 NRB, no. 30.
37 B. Sijapati, J. Baniya, A. Bhandari, A. Bhattarai, S. Kharel, A. Limbu, D. Pathak, N. Rawal and P. Thami, Migration and Resilience: Experiences from Nepal's 2015 Earthquake, Kathmandu: Centre for the Study of Labour and Mobility, 2015.
38 CBS, no. 11.
39 C. Bhadra, "Working Beyond Borders: Push of Poverty on Migrant Women in Nepal", Pakistan Journal of Women's Studies: Alam-e-Niswan, vol. 16, nos. 1&2, 2009, pp. 225–233.
40 L. Mosley and D.A. Singer, "Migration, Labor, and the International Political Economy", Annual Review of Political Science, vol. 18, 2015, pp. 283–301.
41 A. Limbu, "Mass Exodus: Migration and Peaceful Change in Post-War Nepal", Accord, no. 26, 2017, pp. 125–126.
42 U. Kothari, Migration and Chronic Poverty, University of Manchester: Institute for Development Policy and Management, 2002.

13

SUSTAINABLE DEVELOPMENT MODEL

Experience from India

Rashmi Bhure

Introduction

South Asia today is a region of immense possibilities, complexities and contradictions. According to a World Bank report in the last quarter of 2014 South Asia was the fastest-growing region in the world.[1] As per the *South Asia Economic Focus* report the region's growth is expected to further accelerate from seven per cent to 7.6 per cent by 2017.[2] There is an overall upsurge in the growth rate of South Asian economies in the last two years.[3] In spite of these positive developments in South Asia the vital fact cannot be ignored that the fast economic growth of this region is accompanied by severe environmental problems. Additionally, the region still continues to have a high poverty rate, and an undernourished population is its dark reality. Increasing militarization, the challenge of climate change, migration, social exclusion, an infrastructure gap and energy and water crises are posing threat to human security in South Asia. Today scholars have well recognized the idea that the 'national security' and 'human security' are overlapping concepts. From this perspective for attaining sustainable national security, human security is considered to be a prerequisite.

Thirty years back South Asian countries formed the regional organisation, South Asian Association for Regional Cooperation (SAARC) broadly to address some of the previously stated challenges (though the term *human security per se* was not used in 1985) and to develop the concept of individual or citizen-centric security. Its specific aim was to improve the quality of life of the people in the region, develop economies, to promote collective self-reliance and to step up regional sociocultural cooperation and friendship. But unfortunately SAARC has not been particularly effective in achieving its objective of regional economic integration or cooperation. SAARC could not bloom fully as it was overshadowed by suspicion, mutual distrust, apathy amongst its members and the political turbulence within the states of the region. Given the lack of trust and tensions amongst the political establishments of the countries in the region, the questions that have been most juxtaposed is, What is the way forward to achieve economic cooperation, or will it remain a distant dream?

Amid this despair, in the recent past, there has been a growing sense of optimism among South Asian scholars that for closer integration of the region or for a better future of the region, it must look beyond the framework of SAARC. Simultaneously the idea of harnessing the 'natural affinities' between the South Asians which transcends beyond the governmental spectrum is also emerging.[4] This idea is gaining rising acceptance owing to the various common concerns that are emerging in the region that require regional solutions.

It is today widely acknowledged in South Asia that natural resources have increasingly become linked with matters of sovereignty and national security, particularly in the case of Brahmaputra and the Indus Basin.[5] The non-traditional security[6] or human security issues are not the problems that the region would face in the future but a present reality that is already having an impact on the lives and livelihoods of the people in South Asia. In the coming years the larger challenge for South Asia would be the way it would confront with the human security issues of air, water and noise pollution; climate change; deforestation; energy; food security; health; inequality; land degradation; man-made and natural disasters; migration; poverty; quality education; sanitation; solid waste management; and water security.

Undeniably aping the Western model of development, poor resource management, increasing population growth rate, consumerism and haphazard or unplanned economic development has made South Asia an environmentally stressed region. If the human security challenges are not addressed on an urgent basis, they can lead to instability in the region ultimately leading to a major crisis.

To address these challenges effectively the focus has to be a holistic approach towards security. Many of the human security issues in the region can be tackled if South Asian countries adopt 'sustainable livelihood' or 'inclusive development'. Sustainable livelihood is a path ultimately leading towards sustainable development. Since the concept of human security is people-centric the states singularly cannot deal with them, it is the people of South Asia who can collectively play the role of catalyst in transforming the region. By educating, engaging and empowering the people, they can turn to be partners in development. In particular, efforts will have to be made in going much beyond the conventional 'top-down' approach and implement the 'bottom-up' approach to sustainable development in the region for transforming our tomorrow.

Since every country in the South Asian region is embedded with the challenges of Human security issues, to confront them the countries in the region have to communicate, cooperate and collectively search for solutions to these problems. Sharing each other's experiences will help in a great deal to face these issues in an effective way in the near future.

The chapter focuses on the experience of sustainable livelihood or integrated development model from India by making a case study of village Hiware Bazar in

Maharashtra. The people of Hiware Bazar are known worldwide today for their success story of rags-to-riches. The chapter further argues that India and other South Asian countries need to prioritise sustainable model of development to deal with the non-traditional security issues confronting the region.

India's response to human security issues

There are certain prominent markers that show that the economic growth rate of the world's largest democracy, India, is on the rise when most of Western countries are struggling to balance their economy. India's Gross Domestic Product (GDP) grew at 7.4 per cent in 2015,[7] as compared to its Asian competitor China's 6.9 per cent in the same period.[8] China's economy is slowing down; in contrast India's economy seems to be recovering from the economic lull between 2010 and 2014 (during the United Progressive Alliance government). There are signs that investors are beginning to look at India as an island of global growth.[9] Prime Minister Narendra Modi's ideas of 'Startup India' and 'Make in India' are aimed to make India as a global manufacturing hub which would further help to build the image of India as a global power. Modi's initiatives appear very striking but these actions are not enough for transforming India. The real task is how the growth story of India would bring a sustainable growth or inclusive growth across India without compromising the environment. How the Indian policy makers would manage the multiple risks that would accompany this robust economic growth? As these challenges are not in future but is a harsh reality of today understanding these challenges and finding solutions for them has to be done on a pressing note.

Understanding human security

India is a land of contradictions. It is considered to be a country with the potential of gaining the superpower status in the next two decades, yet India ranks 130 on the Human Development Index (HDI).[10] India is bracketed in the Medium Human Development category. Education, health and environment are the crucial areas of concerns to which India will have to pay serious attention. HDI ranking of India clearly demonstrates that the significant growth of India is at the cost of degrading the environment. For India it has been like an adolescent suddenly getting freedom, then starts behaving in an absurd manner and, last, lands in an awkward situation. The path forward for India may require a deeper understanding of multiple dimensions of human security.

India, first, needs to recognize that in the twenty-first century, the concept of security has changed drastically. It is not restricted merely to the security of the nation and its territory (state-centric security/traditional security) but has broadened to include security of the human beings or individuals (human–centric security/non-traditional security). Rather, the distinction between the two is getting more and more blurred.

Second, India needs to precisely map the human security issues that it is facing currently. Indian policy makers, as well as people, should be well aware of the increasing vulnerability faced by India due to changing climate, environmental degradation, natural disasters, the impact of rapid urbanization and industrialization, water and energy deficiencies and so on.

Third, India will have a rapid population growth in the next two decades. This would mean a further burden on its sources, adding to resource scarcity that would not only slow down the economic growth of India but, if not handled proficiently, would lead to a major human crisis. Problems of providing employment and infrastructure to the rising population will also be a big challenge. The masses if left behind while India is traversing on the path of development would be further pushed in the state of poverty and hunger, creating new fault lines in India.

Fourth, India's neighbourhood is equally vulnerable to the human security issues that will in a big way affect India development. In the coming years India will continue to confront the problems of migration; food and water security, among others, that would create road blocks in developing India's relations with its South Asian neighbours. According to strategic thinker Brahma Chellaney, "[w]ater stressed South Asia will turn to be a battleground for water wars".[11]

Last, India has to understand the gravity of the challenges that human security issues are posing and act collectively with other countries in the region to save the Earth and humankind.

Sustainable development

India has a long history of being sensitive to concerns relating to poverty, environment, population growth and socio-economic irregularities, among others.[12] Since India's Independence some twenty-one poverty alleviation programmes have been launched. Apart from this employment guarantee schemes and community development programmes have been continuously implemented by successive governments. However, these issues till late were considered in India as developmental issues and not as human security issues. A holistic approach towards all these issues was not taken in India. The human security challenges have received far less attention by the government; there is somewhat of a lack of political consensus in India about what exactly should be considered as human security challenges. Critics of the concept of human security in India are of the opinion that it is a very loose concept that includes everything from water to waste management. This voice is in line with the security scholars worldwide have criticized the conceptual ambiguity of human security. Y.F. Khong argues that by broadening the concept of security to encompass anything from environmental degradation and pollution to homelessness and unemployment, we would end up prioritizing everything.[13] Due to such global and within-country debates, it becomes absolutely necessary for the government to clearly spell out its strategy to cope with human security issues.

The buzzword today in India for dealing with the human security challenges is *sustainable development*. In this context the questions that are often raised are – What is the relationship between sustainable development and human security? How would sustainable development help in putting an end to farmer's suicides in India?

Can it rejuvenate the disappeared wetlands, rivers and lakes of India? Can it change the reality of women walking for miles to fetch a pot of water? The list is long for which answers have to be searched collectively.

Sustainable development is defined as "development that meets the needs of the present without compromising the ability of future generations to meet their own needs".[14] In other words, leave the world better than you found it. The genius of 'sustainability' lies in its ability to provide 'space' for serious attempts to grapple with the real, dynamic and complex relationships among societies, economies and natural environments, as well as between past, present and the future.[15] Citizen's participation is one of the bases for a functioning democracy; sustainable growth gives the poverty-stricken and the marginalized sections of the society equitable access to resources. Furthermore, an equity-based society would strengthen the democratic political process.

As one traverses through India, we hear many success stories of common, powerless people who have become change makers and unbelievably have transformed their areas to ensure sustainable growth for their people. These success stories from different corners of India are the hope for a better tomorrow.

Sustainable development – the case study of Hiware Bazar

What is common between Golpapura, Alwar District, Rajasthan; Tilonia, Ajmer District, Rajasthan; Ralegan Siddhi, Ahmednagar District, Maharashtra; and Hiware Bazar, Ahmednagar District, Maharashtra? These are all models of sustainable development or popularly known as model villages. These places are temples of twenty-first-century India. They represent the face of a better India. It is remarkable that these villages have not been affected by the global economic downturn or with the economic lull in the country as the development that they have achieved is of sustainable nature.

Background

Hiware Bazar is a tiny village in the Ahmednagar District which is the largest district in Maharashtra. Hiware Bazarfalls in the rain shadow region of the Sahyadri ranges this indicates that it is at an ecologically disadvantaged position receiving very scanty rainfall. Hiware Bazar village is spread over 976 hectares of land.

When India in the early 1990s was experiencing the forces of globalization and a paradigm shift in its economy, Hiware Bazar was on its way for a different kind of revolution. Till 1989 Hiware Bazar was an underdeveloped, backward village in India which was typically drought-prone and was living with multiple problems, such as land degradation, unemployment, poverty, alcoholism and increasing criminal activities. The main source of employment in the village was farming, and they had rain-fed cropping pattern leading to a very poor per capita income. In 1989 the per capita income was just up to Rs 800 with 90 percent of people living below the poverty line.

166 Rashmi Bhure

Consecutive insufficient rainfall was increasing the dependency of farmers on the groundwater. Over extraction of groundwater was done by villagers by installing hand pumps, tube wells and bores, all remarkably reducing the water tables in the area. Whilst another problem was the terrain of the region; part of the area had rocky barren land. Over extraction of water pushed the village into a deep water crisis. The land had become uncultivable moreover; forest and trees in the nearby hilly areas were cut randomly for firewood and sold to get some income for survival. Frustrated with all these problems, the population was migrating to urban centres for a better future.

The year 1989 became a defining time for the future of Hiware Bazar, when seeds for a sustainable future were sown by the youth in the village. They started the mission of transforming Hiware Bazar, and an era of hope dawned. In the next decade, Hiware Bazra erased its history of a drought-prone poverty-stricken village and has today become a 'model village' of India.

In the 1980s, everyday living became a struggle for the Hiware Bazar people. Looking at the grim situation in the village, a few youngsters decided to change the wheel of leadership in the village. During this period Hiware Bazar had an old, apathetic *Sarpanch*(head/leader) who lacked any kind of vision and skills of governance. The youth in the village sensed that they need a young dynamic *Sarpanch* who would become a driving force in transforming the village. The search started for the new *Sarpanch*. The youngsters in the village zeroed in on the only postgraduate in the village – Popatrao Pawar. The task to persuade Popatrao to contest the *Gram Panchayat* (village council) elections was indeed not easy as he, also like others, was on the path of migrating to an urban area for better job prospects. The village youth finally were successful in convincing Popatrao Pawar to contest the *Gram Panchayat* elections in 1989.

Beginning of a new journey – the path towards sustainable development

After becoming *Sarpanch* Popatrao Pawar gave foremost priority to restore the disturbed social fabric of Hiware Bazar. For this he adopted the *panchasutri* (five-pronged approach) for sustainable development of the socio-economic infrastructure of the village.[16] It includes Free Labour (*Shramdan*), Ban on Grazing (*Charaibandi*), Ban on Tree Cutting (*Kurhad Bandi*), Ban on Liquor (*Nasha Bandi*) and Family Planning (*Kutumb Niyojan*).

Popatrao Pawar persuaded people to become pro-active and consequently made them partners in development. He gave work to the ideal hands and utilized people's power in community development projects through *Shramdan*. This also helped in inculcating a sense of belongingness amongst villagers to the new winds of change in Hiware Bazar. Popatrao was trying to replace the state of hopelessness to hope for a better future for the villagers. Ban on Grazing increased the production of grass from 200 tonnes in 1994–95 to more than 5,000 to 6,000 tonnes in 2001–2002.[17] From 1994 Joint Forest Management (JFM) programme has been implemented in the village for forest conservation. Besides, the villagers undertook vital task of tree plantation. With the ban on cutting of trees the wood fuel could not be used by households. Wood was replaced by biogas.

Popatrao convinced the villagers to shut the twenty-two illicit liquor shops that were one of the main causes of domestic violence and criminal activities in the village. A family planning programme of 'one family one child' was adopted. Due to poverty, villagers could not educate their children. The village had a school only up to the fourth standard, and understanding this problem, Popatrao built a school wherein children could get education up to the tenth standard.

While Popatrao implemented the five-pronged approach to deal with the social-economic issues confronting Hiware Bazar, he stressed special focus on the issue of water management. Realising the philosophy of *jalmev jivanam* (water is life) he started creating an awareness campaign in the village about how saving every drop of rainwater was essential for Hiware Bazar's development. As the *Panchayats* did not have enough funds, he started utilizing the funds from various government schemes. Under the JFM and Employment Guarantee Scheme water and soil conservation projects were started. The Forest Department and the villagers through *shramdan* built several trenches around forest areas to conserve the rainwater. As a result, the groundwater tables were recharged. Lakhs of trees were planted in the forest areas; once a thick forest cover was developed, the water levels in the wells increased.

Furthermore, to conserve water, drip irrigation was made compulsory, and many farmers were also turning to water sprinklers. Due to all these measures of water management drinking water became available to the villagers throughout the year. Since 2002, Hiware Bazar started conducting an annual water audit to measure the amount of water available. This was a rare step taken by any village council in Maharashtra.

The watershed development projects increased the irrigated area which enabled the farmers in the village to grow cash crops along with the traditional crops. The farmers could have multiple cycles of crop in a year. Cropping pattern was changed, water-thirsty crop cultivation, like sugarcane and banana, was banned. With money rolling into the village, the farmers' confidence levels became high, and with the increase in grass availability, the villagers diversified into the dairy sector. With dairy production, villagers created an alternative source of income. Looking at this development in Hiware Bazar many families who had migrated to urban areas now started returning back. Reverse influx became the set trend.

The village prepared its own five-year plan for 1995–2000 for ecological regeneration.[18] It ensured that all departments implementing projects in the village had an integrated plan.[19] In 1995, Hiware Bazar was selected as the village that could be developed as the model village under the Maharashtra government *Adarsh Gaon Yojana* (AGY) or 'ideal village' scheme. The major funds for the watershed programmes came from the AGY, about fifty-two earthen bunds, nine check dams, two percolation tanks and thirty-three loose stone bunds were constructed. Whenever the government funds would dry up the villagers came forward to do *shramdan* and completed the projects. The village invested maximum funds in water conservation and recharging the groundwater. Hiware Bazar's strong, participatory institutional set-up has facilitated success.[20] The *gram sabha* has the power to decide on a range of issues, including identifying sites for water harvesting structures, sharing water and types of crops to be cultivated.[21]

In the last two decades, the village has undergone an attitudinal change. A participatory governance and cooperative culture along with strong public institutions have developed in Hiware Bazar. This was seen evident in yet another initiative taken by villagers of *samodayik kheti* (collective farming) wherein the farmers, instead of appointed labour, collaborate and work on each other's fields, thus saving the labour cost. Women's Welfare Groups and Self-Help Groups, as well as Dairy Societies, have been formed. As the villagers are contributing to the growth and development of Hiware Bazar, it has become a learning model of sustainable development for other villages.

What is most striking is the people of Hiware Bazar have changed their own fortunes today. Water scarcity has become a reality of past; agriculture is flourishing; dairy production is thriving; the village boasts of sixty families being millionaires. The success story of Hiware Bazar has made it India's richest village with the highest per capita income in the country. The social indicators of Hiware Bazar, too, have enhanced, 98 per cent is the literacy rate, comprehensive rural sanitation programme has been implemented and infrastructure facilities have been improved.

Lessons from Hiware Bazar's sustainable development model

- The village council with the change in its leadership became proactive and played a central role in the development process of the village.
- Water conservation and management was the key to sustainable development in Hiware Bazar.
- Investing in soil conservation and tree plantation movement has brought a boom in agriculture and dairy production.
- Effective utilization of funds allocated under various government schemes for the development of the village.
- Participation of the community is critical in the governance of the ecological resources.
- An integrated ecological plan has made Hiware Bazar the richest village in India.
- Decentralisation of power structures is the necessary condition for sustainable development.
- Social indices are better with sustainable growth.

There is a need to replicate the Hiware Bazaar development model across India and in the region. Presently South Asia is undergoing a socio-ecological transition and precisely it is here that the sustainable development model case of Hiware Bazar becomes significant. Learning lessons from different models of sustainable developments across South Asia to save this region from the challenges of climate change and environmental degradation should become the priority of both the political classes and the masses. According to an African proverb,

> *If you want to go fast, go alone.*
> *If you want to go far, go together.*[22]

If the South Asian countries follow this proverb the human lives would be better secured in the coming decades in this part of the world.

Notes

1 See the World Bank press release on "South Asia, Now the Fastest-Growing Region in the World, Could Take Greater Advantage of Cheap Oil to Reform Energy Pricing", www.worldbank.org/en/news/press-release/2015/04/13/south-asia-cheap-oil-reform-energy-pricing, accessed 5 January 2016.
2 *Ibid.*
3 For details of recent economic developments in South Asia see the report of *South Asia Economic Focus on The Export Opportunity*, Washington DC: IBRD World Bank, Fall 2014.
4 This view emerged in the second Annual Conference on, *Changing Political Context in India's Neighbourhood and Prospects of Security and Regional Cooperation*, organised by Institute for Defence Studies and Analyses (IDSA) in November 2008. These papers are published in a volume by Ashok K. Behuria, South Asia: The Quest for Regional Cooperation, New Delhi: IDSA, 2009.
5 For detail analysis of Asia's rise and water as a source of geopolitical tension in the region see, Brahma Chellaney, "Water, Power, and Competition in Asia", *Asian Survey*, vol. 54, no. 4, pp. 621–650.
6 The traditional/realist security discourse focused on state and military security. In the post–Cold War period there is a shift in the security discourse from military security to non-traditional/liberalist areas of security. The concept of security has widened to challenges that pose to the human/individual/community besides the traditional security threats. These challenges are related to water, food, health, resources crisis, environmental, climate change and so on. In 1994 UNDP in its Human Development Report broaden the traditional notion of security focused on military balances and capabilities to include community security, economic security, environmental security, food security, health security, personal and political security.
7 India's GDP In July 2014 was 6.7 per cent and considerably increased in July 2015 to 7.4 per cent. For India's GDP growth rate see, *India GDP Annual Growth Rate 1951–2016*, www.tradingeconomics.com/india/gdp-growth-annual, accessed 2 February 2016.
8 "Can India be the World's Bright Spot?", *Hindustan Times*, 4 December 2015, p. 1.
9 *Ibid.*
10 United Nations Development Programme annually releases Human Development Report. It publishes country-wise Human Development Index (HDI). Out of 188 countries India ranks 130 on HDI. For UNDP Report, http://hdr.undp.org/en/countries/profiles/IND, accessed 4 February 2016.
11 For in depth analysis of water issue in Asia see, Brahma Chellaney, *Water: Asia's New Battleground*, Washington, DC: Georgetown University Press, 2011.
12 Keynote address by Arvind Gupta, Director general IDSA at the National seminar on "India's Non-Traditional Security Challenges" organized by Punjabi University, Patiala, 22–23 February 2013, www.idsa.in/speech/IndiasNonTraditionalSecurityChallenges_agupta, accessed 9 February 2016.

13 Human security concept has been criticised by various scholars like David Chandler, Keith Krause, Mark Duffield, Waddell Nicholas and others. Y.F. Khong, "Human Security: A Shotgun Approach to Alleviating Human Misery?", *Global Governance,* vol. 7, no. 3, 2001, pp. 231–236 as cited in Luke Johns, "A Critical Evaluation of the Concept of Human Security", www.e-ir.info/2014/07/05/a-critical-evaluation-of-the-concept-of-human-security, accessed 10 February 2016.

14 "The World Commission on Environment and Development: Our Common Future", Brundtland Commission Report, www.un-documents.net/our-common-future.pdf, accessed 10 February 2016.

15 Sanjeev Khagram, William C. Clark and Dana Firas Raad, "From the Environment and Human Security to Sustainable Security and Development", *Journal of Human Development*, vol. 4, no. 2, July 2003, p. 296.

16 "Present: After Development", http://hiware-bazar.epanchayat.in/the-village/the-village-present-after-development/, accessed 11 February 2016.

17 *Ibid.*

18 Neha Sakhuja, "Hiware Bazar-A Village with 54 Millionaires", www.downtoearth.org.in/coverage/hiware-bazar--a-village-with-54-millionaires-4039, accessed 11 February 2016.

19 *Ibid.*

20 *Ibid.*

21 *Ibid.*

22 See Joel Goldberg, "It Takes a Village to Determine the Origins of an African Proverb", www.npr.org/sections/goatsandsoda/2016/07/30/487925796/it-takes-a-village-to-determine-the-origins-of-an-african-proverb, accessed 7 May 2019.

14

REINTEGRATING INDIA'S MAOISTS

Surrender and rehabilitation

P. V. Ramana

Introduction

Surrender-cum-Rehabilitation policy is part of the overall policy to build consensus and evolve an acceptable and peaceful solution to violence perpetrated by extremist groups and, to usher in peace and development, especially in the disturbed regions. Although policies for rehabilitation of militants have been somewhat successful in Jammu and Kashmir (J&K) and the Northeast states, the implementation of similar policies in Maoist/Naxal affected States has not been impressive for various reasons.

In November 2010 the J&K government, in consultation with the Union government, announced a policy for the rehabilitation of Kashmiri youth who had crossed over from J&K into Pakistan-occupied Kashmir (PoK).[1] According to this policy, youth who had gone to PoK for arms training, during 1989 and 2009, but were willing to surrender would be granted 'general amnesty'. They would be housed in camps where they would be placed under observation and imparted vocational training for gainful employment.[2] According to an un-named government official,

> There will be a cooling off period, some counselling, rehabilitation and [a] certain amount of interface between the security forces and them to be assured that they are not being planted and they are actually people who are coming back for [a] resumption of normal life. That is the broad parameters of the policy.[3]

In the 2004 policy for the surrender and rehabilitation of militants/terrorists, the militants were eligible for a cash reward of Rs 150,000 and a monthly stipend of Rs 2,000 for a period of three years, besides being imparted vocational training.[4]

172 P. V. Ramana

Similarly, in the Northeast of India, various states that have faced/are facing insurgencies have instituted similar surrender and rehabilitation policy/packages. However, according to one scholar, the surrender and rehabilitation policy adopted in the various states of the North-East was flawed and had failed to herald peace in the region. He writes,[5]

> The central government's surrender policy in Northeast India has been flawed from the very beginning and to make things more complicated it has employed different yardsticks for different insurgent organizations, given the varying status of peace talks between them. The highest number of surrenders over the years has come from Assam and Manipur, where surrenders, peace talks and designated camps have mushroomed and occupied much of the government's energies and resources.

The major failure of the surrender policy of the North-East region has been its inefficacy in restoring peace in the region. This has happened due to several inadequacies and loopholes in the policy as well as the manipulations that have occurred relating to the political use of surrendered insurgents. These have been seen as token surrenders, either to dispose of the mercenary elements in their organizations or for the surrender of insurgents who use this medium to avail the benefits of the surrender policy in the form of monetary compensation and lucrative contracts from the government.

In the backdrop of a lack of improvement in the ground situation, and, moreover, worsening of the situation, the Union government decided that surrender of militants in the North-East – to whichever group they belonged to – shall not be accepted any longer.[6]

While that may be the case in those two theatres of conflict, this article seeks to make a preliminary assessment of the surrender and rehabilitation policy being adopted towards Naxalites. The examples/experiences cited in this chapter refer largely to cadres and leaders of the Communist Party of India (Maoist), or CPI (Maoist). Furthermore, this chapter seeks to present the guidelines issued by the Union government and briefly discuss the policy being adopted in the various affected states. This chapter does not focus on all the affected states for either there is a paucity of information or there is no policy in place.

The Naxal surrender and rehabilitation policy has been evolved keeping in mind the specific geographical and social landscape to help those who want to abjure violence, surrender and join the mainstream:

> Surrender and rehabilitation policy is part of a multi-pronged conflict management and resolution strategy and is required to be implemented along with firm action by police against those who follow the path of violence. As the naxal problem has arisen on account of real and perceived neglect, deprivation and disaffection, mainly towards the downtrodden, the solution should aim at providing gainful employment and entrepreneurial opportunities to the surrendered naxalites so that they are encouraged to join the mainstream and do not return to the fold of naxal movement.[7]

Objectives

With a view to catalysing surrenders of Naxalites, and, subsequently, rehabilitate them, the Union government has issued guidelines for the surrender and rehabilitation of Naxalites in September 2009. The objectives of these guidelines are

(i) To wean away the misguided youth and hardcore Naxalites who have strayed into the fold of Naxal movement and now find themselves trapped into that net;
(ii) To ensure that the Naxalites who surrender do not find it attractive to join the Naxal movement again; and
(iii) Tactical surrenders by those elements who try to make use of the benefits extended.

Union government's policy

These guidelines are elaborate and meant to integrate the ex-rebel into the mainstream. Some of the more important features of these guidelines are outlined in the following.[8] Besides, these are 'mere' guidelines, and each state government is free to frame its own surrender and rehabilitation policy:

a Each surrendering Naxalite shall immediately be provided security, his antecedents verified and the decision to accept the surrender or reject it shall be conveyed to the person within fifteen days from the date of surrender. Surrender, and by implication, and extending rehabilitation shall, however, be confined to hard-core, underground Naxalites of the rank of squad member and above. The case of over-ground Naxalites and sympathisers shall be considered only on an exceptional basis.
b Each surrender shall be accepted and rehabilitation provided on a case-by-case basis after due verification by a committee appointed by the respective state government and headed by the chief of the Special Branch of the intelligence wing of the state police, who shall also function as the Surrender and Rehabilitation Officer.
c A Naxalite can surrender within the state of his operation or in another state to an officer notified by the government.
d Upon acceptance of the surrender, a sum of Rs 150,000 shall be deposited in a bank in the name of the surrendering Naxalite, which he or she can withdraw three years later, provided that his or her conduct is certified as good by an officer designated by the concerned state government. The same amount could also be used as collateral security to obtain a loan for self-employment.
e Each surrendering Naxalite shall be imparted vocational training of his or her choice and aptitude with a view to providing gainful employment and a stipend of Rs 2,000 shall be given for three years, which shall be suspended earlier if the person secures employment.
f Whereas the surrendering Naxalite would have to face trial in cases relating to 'heinous crimes', plea bargaining shall be permitted for minor offences and the state government might 'consider' providing free legal assistance.

TABLE 14.1 Monetary incentive for surrender of weapons and ammunition by Naxalites

Weapons	Incentive (INR)	USD
AK 47/56/74 Rifle	Rs 25,000 per weapon	369
Pistol/Revolver/SLR/Carbine/Sten gun/.303	Rs 10,000 per weapon	147
LMG/GPMG/Picca/RPG/Sniper Rifle	Rs 35,000 per weapon	517
Rockets	Rs 1,000 per rocket	14
Grenade/hand Grenade/stick grenade	Rs 500 per grenade	7
Remote Control Device	Rs 3,000 each device	44
Ammunition of all types	Rs 3 per round	0.04
IED	Rs 1,000 each	14
Mines	Rs 3,000	44
Explosive Material	Rs 1,000 per kg	14
Wireless Set	Rs 1,000 per each set	14
(a) Short range	Rs 5,000 per each set	73
(b) Long range		
Satellite Phone	Rs 10,000	147
VHF/HF Communication sets	Rs 5,000	73
Electronic Detonators	Rs 50	0.739
Other Detonators	Rs 10	0.148

Source: http://mha.nic.in/sites/upload_files/mha/files/SCRGuideline_22012016.pdf

g In addition to the monetary incentives mentioned above, incentives could also be given for weapons and ammunition surrendered by the Naxalite (see Table 14.1).

The effectiveness of these guidelines is yet to be reviewed.

It is not difficult to understand the low figures of surrenders in the various affected States. One, in States like Madhya Pradesh and Uttar Pradesh the number of underground cadres is fewer. Two, in States such as Chhattisgarh, Orissa, Bihar, Jharkhand and parts of Maharashtra and West Bengal, there have been no intense operations by the security forces (see Tables 14.2 and 14.3). Thus, the Naxalites do not feel any pressure to surrender.[9]

Affected states: at a glance

In Maharashtra, the success of the surrender and rehabilitation policy has been partial. According to the then district police of Gadchiroli, the most affected district in the state,

> In the first phase of the Surrender Policy, sixty eight surrenders took place, out of which ninety percent were fringe elements, forced to help the Naxals. But they had useful information for us regarding their hideouts. They were duly rewarded under the rehabilitation package . . ."When the government announced the surrender policy on the lines similar to that of Andhra Pradesh, there were surrenders. But there was no comprehensive

TABLE 14.2 State-wise all-India Naxalite surrenders: 2006–2009

	2006	*2007*	*2008*	*2009*
Andhra Pradesh	282	162	197	10
Bihar	15	21	028	0
Chhattisgarh	619	167	8	0
Jharkhand	10	02	6	0
Madhya Pradesh	01	–	1	0
Maharashtra	67	35	150	6
Orissa	03	03	06	0
Uttar Pradesh	02	0	4	0
Total	999	390	400	16

Source: Adapted from Lok Sabha, Unstarred Question No. 509, "Surrender and Rehabilitation Scheme", answered on February 24, 2009, Lok Sabha Secretariat, New Delhi.

Note: Data till February 2009.

TABLE 14.3 State-wise all-India Naxalite surrenders: 2010–2016

States	*2010*	*2011*	*2012*	*2013*	*2014*	*2015*	*2016*
AP	66	88	244	86	130	133	24
BH	2	49	75	3	0	7	20
CG	3	7	26	23	385	279	932
Delhi	0	0	0	n.a.	0	0	0
GJ	0	n.a.	0	n.a.	0	0	0
JH	18	15	8	19	11	12	28
Karnataka	3	n.a.	0	n.a.	2	0	0
Kerala	0	n.a.	0	0	0	0	0
MP	n.a.	0	0	1	n.a.	n.a.	n.a.
MH	10	22	8	32	21	35	24
OR	43	50	32	1,787	94	136	844
PB	0	0	0	n.a.	n.a.	0	0
TN	n.a.	n.a.	0	1	0	0	0
Telangana					11	13	8
UP	0	4	0	0	0	0	0
WB	5	15	21	0	2	0	0
Total	150	227	414	1,950	656	615	1,880

Source: Adapted from the data tables available at www.satp.org

Note: Data till October 23, 2016; n.a. = not applicable.

rehabilitation policy. We recommended that there should be a reward system and then rehabilitation. It took some time for the people to realise the existence of such a policy.[10]

The surrender policy in *Odisha* hardly invoked any response from the rebels. In June 2006, the Odisha government announced a surrender and rehabilitation

176 P. V. Ramana

policy. According to the policy, those surrendering would be given a cash reward of "Rs 1.50 lakh, Rs 2500 stipend for three years, Rs 2 lakh loan without interest, free education and medical facilities and legal assistance for the trial against them".[11] Nevertheless, as the statistics themselves indicate the number of surrenders has been rather low.

According to a media report,[12]

> more than forty naxals have surrendered so far in the state. But not a single one of them has got the promised benefits. . . . Police sources say that there are several cadres in the naxal camp especially women who are allegedly exploited and are willing to surrender. But if the fate of the naxals who have already surrendered is not very encouraging the rest might hardly find any motivation to do the same.

Chhattisgarh is one state where the Naxalites have been executing chilling massacres and a stronghold over an area of 40,000 square kilometres in Bastar. They have absolute control over 4,000 square kilometres of area in Abuj Maad, without any government presence. Although the Naxalites have been present in Bastar since 1982, it was not until 20 October 2004 that the Chhattisgarh government announced a surrender and rehabilitation policy for the Naxalites. Largely speaking, the package has no takers from the rebels and has been, thus, marginally successful as Table 14.4 illustrates.

According to the government policy, the plea to surrender shall be verified by a committee inclusive of the district police chief, district collector, district education officer and district forest officer. The surrender shall be accepted on a case-by-case basis. After the verification is done, the district police chief shall send his recommendations to the district collector, who shall issue the necessary orders, on the basis of facts presented to him that rehabilitation could, indeed, be provided to the

TABLE 14.4 Chhattisgarh: Naxalite surrenders: 2001–2010

Year	Armed cadres	Over-ground supporters (Sangham members)
2001	0	0
2002	0	0
2003	6	37
2004	1	0
2005	13	1,402
2006	5	1,032
2007	89	77
2008	3	1
2009	2	11
2010 (October 30)	3	0
Total	**122**	**2,560**

Source: State Police Headquarters, Chhattisgarh, Raipur.

surrendering Naxalite. The rehabilitation shall be provided within ninety days from the date of surrender.

At the apex level, an inter-departmental committee co-chaired by the principal secretary of the Home Department and the chief secretary of the state has been formed. This committee supervises the implementation of the rehabilitation package across the state. In cases that are referred to the apex committee by the district-level committee, the decision of the apex committee would be conveyed within sixty days. While deciding on the quantum of rehabilitation the assistance provided by the surrendering Naxalite on the organisation, its activities and helping in detecting arm dumps shall be given due consideration.

In Jharkhand, the earlier surrender and rehabilitation policy had few takers. On 29 July 2012, the Jharkhand government announced a revised surrender and rehabilitation policy. The salient features of the new policy are

- Immediate cash incentive of Rs 50,000;
- Free education until the age of twenty-four, or completing graduation, for male Maoists. Free education until the age of twenty-four, or completing graduation, or until they get married, for female Maoists. The surrendering person can join either a government institution or a private institution, but, in case the surrendering rebel joins a private institution, the tuition fee cannot exceed Rs 1,000.
- The scheme is open to wards of surrendering Maoist cadres under similar conditions;
- Free allotment of land to build a house;
- Free healthcare; and
- Cash incentive for surrendering weapons.[13]

In late-July 2010, West Bengal for the first time announced a surrender and rehabilitation policy and package for surrendered Maoists.[14] According to the package, formulated on the basis of guidelines issued by the Union Ministry of Home Affairs (MHA), each surrendering rebel Maoists would be given a monthly stipend of Rs 2,000 for three years, while the West Bengal government would deposit a sum of Rs 1,50,000 for three years. After the deposit matures, the entire money would be given to the surrendered Maoist if his conduct is good during the entire duration of three years.

In Karnataka, a surrender and rehabilitation package was announced in June 2010 for the first time. According to this package, rebels who surrender would be given a grant-cum-loan of INR 200,000 monthly stipend of Rs 2,000 for a year, imparted vocational training for gainful employment and a cash incentive ranging from Rs 500 to Rs 25,000 for surrendering weapons, as well as Rs 10,000 for surrendering a satellite phone.[15]

The Andhra Pradesh experience

On the other hand, Andhra Pradesh has a relatively successful and robust surrender and rehabilitation policy. In fact, it has had such a policy for the longest number of years among all the affected states. Hence it would be useful to case study this state in some detail.

Andhra Pradesh instituted an active surrender and rehabilitation policy. The initial appeal was made in 1989[16] which had immediately resulted in a spate of surrenders. A thorough and comprehensive policy was formulated in 1993[17] and has been revised periodically. The uniqueness of this policy is that it is open-ended.[18] In Andhra Pradesh, surrenders are encouraged in a big way. The government lays great emphasis on surrenders, also because "it shatters the myth of the Naxalism".[19] As one analyst noted,[20]

> While the surrendered Naxalites stood as living examples of a life completely wasted, as they could not reintegrate themselves into the society, the suffering of the families, whose members were still in [the N]axal fold provided another example for them not to mess with the [N]axalites. This led to the distancing of several segments of the society, which would have hitherto been target groups, [from] being attracted [towards] the [N]axal fold.

Moreover, experience shows that Naxalites would surrender in considerable numbers only when the police mount a vigorous clamp down. In the classical understanding in revolutionary warfare, when the enemy is surrounded on three sides and when it becomes nearly certain that he would be killed, the enemy would try to evade death by moving on to the opening left on the fourth flank.[21] While vigorous pursuit symbolizes the three flanks, surrender and rehabilitation scheme symbolizes the fourth flank.[22] Thus, naturally in AP there has been a very large number of surrenders. In contrast, in Madhya Pradesh, where anti-Naxalite operations are limited, "over a 17 year period of 1990 to 2006 the total number of surrenders was 16".[23]

As Table 14.5 illustrates, over a 15-year period, between 1998 and 2012, 5,405 Naxalites have surrendered to the authorities in Andhra Pradesh. Of the 7,000 Naxalites surrendered since the time the policy was initiated, over 2,500 have been rehabilitated and assets worth nearly Rs 20 crore have been distributed to them.[24]

The year 1997 witnessed the highest number of offences committed by the Naxalites (1325), other than killings of civilians and security forces (257 and 51, respectively) in Andhra Pradesh. This was followed by a crackdown ordered by the state government the next year. At the same time, the surrender and rehabilitation policy was implemented actively. Thus, in 1999, 318 Naxalites gave up their underground life and joined the mainstream. The surrenders continued during the subsequent years to a peak at 890 in the year 2003. By then, the state gained an upper-hand over the rebels.

The low number of 296 surrenders in 2004 could be attributed to the peace process that was pursued for the larger part of the year since mid-May. By mid-January 2005 the rebels trashed the peace process and declared resuming of guerrilla operations – the plummeting number of surrenders during the following years, hitting a low of 66 during the current year, indicates the falling number of Naxalite cadres in the state.

TABLE 14.5 Andhra Pradesh surrenders of Naxalites: 1998–2012

Year	Number surrendered
1998	490
1999	318
2000	615
2001	520
2002	538
2003	890
2004	296
2005	601
2006	269
2007	125
2008	208
2009	91
2010	124
2011	215
2012	318
2013	95
2014	19
2015	14
2016	5
Total	**5,751**

Source: Headquarters, Andhra Pradesh Police.

Note: Data till August 1, 2016.

It is apprehended that a delay in rehabilitating the surrendered Naxalites, or not rehabilitating them could result in their rejoining the underground.[25] Thus, for instance, the police in Karimnagar District in Andhra Pradesh persuaded 46 Janashakthi Naxalites to join the mainstream. They had surrendered with their weapons to the chief minister in Hyderabad on 28 April 2002.[26] By August 2003, the government rehabilitated only 20 of them. Resultantly, some of the surrendered Naxalites reportedly rejoined the Naxalite ranks. Bureaucratic red tape can thus (a) nullify the gains of the efforts in securing surrenders, (b) persuade the surrendered Naxalites to think that the government fails to keep its promises and that they were justified in joining the Naxalites to fight the state and (c) demoralise the police officials who had painstakingly secured their surrender. In 2002, a Naxalite detained in a central prison asked this author[27] why he was being held in jail for an unduly long period, even after he surrendered. He passionately asked this researcher, "Do you think we are some sort of man eaters?"

While a large number of Naxalites have surrendered in Andhra Pradesh, some fled to neighbouring Maharashtra, Chhattisgarh and Orissa, even as fresh recruitment was largely absent. Thus, the total number of underground Naxalite cadres in the state has drastically decreased, which also indicates the fall in the number of surrenders in recent years.

180 P. V. Ramana

Another indicator of the declining number of underground rebel ranks in the state is the number of people against whom 'head money' or cash rewards are announced periodically through government notifications. As Table 14.6 illustrates, beginning with a high of 1673 in 1998, the number of underground cadre against whom cash rewards have been announced has hit a low of 474 during the current year. This declining number, thus, illustrates the fall in the total number of underground cadre in Naxalite ranks, which has been decimated nearly to a fourth of its strength in about 10 to 11 years.[28] According to a senior intelligence official, this figure has further declined to 434 by mid-November 2008.[29] Furthermore, according to one well-known analyst, while there were a total of 3,344 underground Naxalite cadres in 1997, this figure had drastically fallen to merely 509 by April 2008.[30] According to statistics provided by the Andhra Pradesh police, this figure had further declined to 474 in June 2008, and to 430 by late November 2008.

Thus, the declining number of surrenders and the vast reduction in the number of people against whom 'head money' has been announced are clear indicators of the steep fall in the number of Naxalite ranks in Andhra Pradesh.

Why rebels surrender?

There is no particular reason for Naxalite ranks surrendering to the authorities. Routinely, the media reports in each case that he or she has been disillusioned with the ideology and the movement and has, therefore, surrendered. However, the reasons could be many and disillusionment may not be the 'real reason'. Sudhakar, a squad member, and a native of Karimnagar District, Andhra Pradesh, surrendered to the authorities because he was severely affected with Malaria and was not given medical treatment by the Naxal leadership. As a result he became a physical relic, could barely move his limbs and was nearly bed-ridden in the forests. He was, thus, frustrated with his existence and opted to surrender.[31]

Byrani Ramachander and his wife, too, surrendered to the authorities. Ramachander was a squad commander in Warangal District, Andhra Pradesh.[32] His wife had taken ill, and therefore, to get her admitted to a hospital, the couple sped away with INR 50,000 to the neighbouring state of Maharashtra, thus deserting

TABLE 14.6 Cash rewards on underground cadre

Year	Number against whom reward money announced
1998	1,673
2002	1,233
2007	1,133
2008	474

Source: Headquarters, Andhra Pradesh Police.

the ranks of the comrades. After she recuperated, the couple surrendered to the authorities in Jagityal town of Karimnagar.

The cases of Bharati and Anupuram Anasuya were slightly different. Bharati was the wife of Polam Sudarshan Reddy alias Ramakrishna, alias RK, who was a district committee secretary in Warangal and Nizamabad Districts. RK was killed in an encounter with the police in 2002. Some months later, his wife Bharati surrendered to the authorities. Similar, Anasuya was the wife of Anupuram Komarayya, member of the North Telangana Special Zone, which the Naxalites at one time showcased to the world as their 'flagship guerrilla zone'. Anasuya, too, surrendered because her husband was killed.[33]

In another case, Pittala Sarita was a platoon section commander and had participated in various attacks on the police, including the unsuccessful attack on the Yeturunagaram police station in 2002. A very vocal young girl, seventeen years of age when this author interviewed her,[34] said she was influenced by her uncle who was already part of the underground and she was inspired by a song sung by a visiting armed squad in her village. She was 'forced' to quit the Naxalite ranks after she questioned the darker side of the activities of Polam Sudarshan Reddy and his counterpart in Nizamabad District.[35]

Regarding the surrender of forty-six Naxalites of the Janashkti group in Karimnagar[36] one media report noted: "In one of the biggest-ever surrenders by [N]axalites in Andhra Pradesh, 46 members of the CPI(ML) Janashakthi gave themselves up . . . and handed over 46 firearms, including an assault rifle and five Springfield rifles".[37] At the time of the surrender, Sunkati Sailu alias Ranadheer the district committee secretary of the Janasakthi reportedly told the media that he and his comrades were surrendering because of the "exploitative attitude" of the higher leadership and went on to add that the top-level leaders were leading a "lavish life" while the cadres were suffering the rigours of an underground life in the forests.[38] In fact, the story of the surrenders is not as simple and is a commonplace occurrence. The district police chief played a decisive role in the entire episode.[39] He had painstakingly worked for several weeks preceding the surrender. The district police chief met with the district leaders and convinced them to surrender "along with their weapons". Perhaps, this has been the largest number of surrenders by the Naxalites from a single outfit and, on the same day, anywhere in the country. In the words of the district police chief the surrenders had the following effect:

1 The Naxalite movement in the country received a historic jolt;
2 They were exposed as abductors and extortionists;
3 It had shocked left-wing intellectuals and thrown them into a state of despair;
4 The people of the district were immensely relieved that a band of extortionists would no longer trouble them;
5 It was a big morale booster for the police; and
6 Other Naxalite groups, especially the then PWG, became immensely worried that such a trend (en masse surrenders, and that too with weapons) might afflict their cadres, too.[40]

182 P. V. Ramana

The trouble with surrendered Naxalites[41]

On 25 July 2003, the putrefied body of Sammi Reddy, former Karimnagar District Committee Member of the People's War Group (PWG) and an important surrendered PWG (SPWG), was recovered from a village pond in Krishna District; it was subsequently identified on 28 July. Reddy was abducted in Hyderabad, the state capital, on 18 July, while on his way to attend court in connection with a criminal offence. He was dealing in real estate business and had used strong-arm methods against business rivals. He had also attempted to kill one of them. An SPWG militant, Jadala Nagaraju, and the mistress of another SPWG militant are suspected to be behind Sammi Reddy's, killing following differences over some cash transactions. However, there are other theories as well regarding his murder.

Earlier, Reddy and Naeemuddin, another SPWG member, killed a civil rights activist on 23 November 2000 for allegedly persuading the PWG leadership to eliminate them. Both Reddy and Naeemuddin were vocal critics of their former colleagues. They were also accused by PWG members of being police informers. At Naeemuddin's instance, his brother Aleemuddin and some others had killed yet another SPWG cadre, Eedanna, in early June 1998, for molesting their sister. At that time, Naeemuddin, detained in prison, accused the PWG of inaction in the face of Eedanna's misdemeanour.

Eedanna was a former Aler squad commander who had killed Paradesi Naidu, the superintendent of police, Mahabubnagar District on 14 November 1993. Later, he had surrendered and opened a provision store with the rehabilitation money the government had given him. Simultaneously, he participated in extra-judicial activities.

Surrendered Naxalites often use muscle power for business gains. They run protection rackets and deal in real estate. In Karimnagar District, some of them had become a land mafia until the security forces (SFs) put them down. Kattula Sammaiah, an SPWG who died in a fire accident on board a flight to Colombo, is another well-known example of an SPWG militant becoming a law unto himself while operating in Hyderabad.

Three reasons explain the working of such elements. Firstly, if the surrendered Naxalites have a criminal bent of mind they would habitually take recourse to strong-arm tactics. A proclivity to violence draws them closer to the Naxalites. Having committed violent acts, they can hardly give up this habit after surrendering. Also, surrendered Naxalites entertain the notion that violence is rewarding. Incidentally, a group of surrendered cadres of the Janashakthi faction were involved in a drunken brawl in Hyderabad recently. In fact, a survey conducted by official sources in Warangal District, Andhra Pradesh, held that a mere two per cent of the cadre joins the rebels' ranks for ideological reasons.

Second, the SFs are either complacent or are in league with them, probably because they are a mine of information or for other reasons. The surrendered Naxalites show off their intimate knowledge of, and access to information on, the movements of their former colleagues, their methods, hiding places, weapons and cash dumps.

Third, the rehabilitation policy of the government is severely flawed and is tardily implemented. The government gives 5,000 rupees to every surrendering cadre right at the moment of surrender. Thereafter, they are eligible to receive 500,000 rupees towards rehabilitation. However, bureaucratic red tape often delays its disbursement.

Of the forty-six Janashakthi Naxalites who joined the mainstream, to date only twenty of them have been rehabilitated, that, too, after enormous delay. Therefore, some of the remaining militants have either gone underground or have established contact with their former colleagues. Thus, the gains from the efforts of a section of the SFs in countering extremism were frittered away.

The delay in rehabilitation convinces the surrendered Naxalites that the government fails to keep its promises and that they were justified in joining the Naxalites to fight the state.

Conclusion

In India, there is no national policy on the surrender and rehabilitation of Naxalites, even though the problem has unambiguously acquired a pan-India dimension/ presence. The Union government has lately issued 'guidelines', in 2009, and the affected states have been asked to frame their respective policies according to their local requirements, keeping in mind the guidelines issued by the Union government. Possibly, these shall be revised soon. The affected states are in various stages of framing a policy for the surrender and rehabilitation of Naxalites.

Partly for this reason, and, in some measure, because there has been no intense crackdown on the rebels, the latter have, thus, not felt that and are, therefore, not compelled or persuaded to surrender, except in Andhra Pradesh.

In Andhra Pradesh, there are in place a multiplicity of measures – including a relentless and severe crackdown by the state police – as a result of which it was possible to obtain a large number of surrenders, over the years.

One is persuaded to wonder if there has been a lack of seriousness of purpose and attempt by the various affected states to encourage the surrender of Naxalites and to rehabilitate them.

To conclude, this article argues that (a) the various affected states should evince interest to obtain surrenders; (b) put in place a robust surrender and rehabilitation policy, preferably at the national level; (c) secure surrenders on a case-by-case basis; (d) intensify security operations; and (e) policy implementation should be effective and closely monitored.

Notes

1 See, www.ndtv.com/article/india/j-k-says-yes-to-surrender-policy-67931, accessed 22 November 2010.
2 See, http://articles.timesofindia.indiatimes.com/2010-02-09/india/28147085_1_sur render-policy-j-k-government-arms-training, accessed 9 February 2010.

184 P. V. Ramana

3 See, www.rediff.com/news/report/jk-gives-nod-to-surrender-policy-for-youth-return ing-from-pok-pak/20101122.htm, accessed 22 November 2010.
4 For details see, http://mha.nic.in/pdfs/JK-RehabilitationPolicy.pdf, accessed 2 February 2004.
5 Mirza Zulfiqar Rahman, "Surrendering a Failed Policy", #2883, 2 June 2009, online journal of the Institute for Peace and Conflict Studies, New Delhi, www.ipcs.org/arti cle/india/surrendering-a-failed-policy-2883.html, accessed 3 June 2009.
6 See, Indian Express, New Delhi, 11 April 2009. Also accessible at www.indianexpress. com/news/centre-to-withdraw-assam-militant-surrender-policy-after-ls-polls/445 472/, accessed 12 April 2009.
7 See, http://mha.nic.in/pdfs/surrrenderPolAendments070909.pdf, accessed 29 September 2009.
8 See, http://mha.nic.in/pdfs/nm_pdf5.pdf, accessed 29 September 2009.
9 This aspect is explained in the succeeding passages while discussing the case of Andhra Pradesh.
10 www.tehelka.com/story_main21.asp?filename=Ne110406Revolution_SR.asp, accessed 2 November 2006.
11 http://ibnlive.in.com/news/orissa-surrendering-naxals-unhappy-with-govt/139352-3. html, accessed 4 January 2011.
12 *Ibid*.
13 http://iaspreparationonline.wordpress.com/2012/07/29/jharkhand-amends-naxal-sur render-policy/, accessed 29 July 2012.
14 See, http://news.oneindia.in/2010/07/29/surrender-and-enjoy-financial-aids-wb-to-maoists.html, accessed 29 July 2010; and http://sify.com/news/west-bengal-announces-surrender-policy-for-maoists-news-national-kh3idzjchhc.html, accessed 29 July 2010.
15 See *The Hindu*, 4 September 2010.
16 The appeal was made through GOMS No. 388 GA (SC-A), 10 July 1989.
17 The policy was unveiled through GOMS No. 1545/SCA/92–10, 1 May 1993.
18 Interview with a senior IPS officer, formerly with the Special Intelligence Branch (SIB), Hyderabad, 26 November 2008.
19 Interview with a senior IPS officer of the Special Intelligence Branch (SIB), Hyderabad, 27 November 2008.
20 See K. Srinivas Reddy, "Maoist Movement in Andhra Pradesh: The, Now and Why", paper presented at National Conference on Non-State Armed Groups and India's Security, hosted by IDSA, New Delhi, 8–10 April 2007.
21 Interview with Mr K Srinivas Reddy, Deputy Editor, The Hindu, Hyderabad, 25 November 2008.
22 *Ibid*.
23 Interview with SK Rout, the then Additional Director General of Police (Intelligence), Madhya Pradesh, January 12, 2008; and statistics provided by Headquarters, Madhya Pradesh State Police.
24 Interview with a senior IPS officer of the Special Intelligence Branch (SIB), Hyderabad, 27 November 2008.
25 This is an apprehension expressed by some senior IPS officers in Chhattisgarh, too, during interviews with them in Raipur on 21–22 November 2008.
26 See The Hindu, Hyderabad, 29 April 2002 and Eenadu, Hyderabad, a vernacular and largest circulated Telugu daily, 29 April 2002.
27 Interview with a surrendered Naxalite at the Central Prison in Warangal, Andhra Pradesh, February 2002.
28 Interview with a senior IPS officer of the Special Intelligence Branch (SIB), Hyderabad, 27 November 2008.
29 *Ibid*.
30 See Srinivas Reddy, "Maoist Movement in Andhra Pradesh: The, Now and Why", and statistics provided by Headquarters, Andhra Pradesh State Police, Hyderabad, 26 November 2008.

31 Interview with Sudhakar, Karimnagar, January 2004.
32 Interview with Byrani Ramachander, Warangal, February 2002.
33 Interview with Anapuram Anasuya, Karimnagar, January 2004.
34 Interview with Pittala Sarita, Warangal, February 2002.
35 Interview with an intelligence officer, Warangal, February 2002.
36 All the instances mentioned above relate to the cadres of the erstwhile Communist Party of India – Marxist-Leninist People's War, PW in short; popularly known as PWG.
37 *The Hindu*, 29 April 2002.
38 See *Ibid* and Eenadu, a vernacular Telugu daily, 29 April 2002.
39 Interviews in Karimnagar with Dr R S Praveen Kumar, the then Superintendent of Police, Karimnagar district, Andhra Pradesh, January 2003, February 2004, and in New Delhi, 12 August 2010.
40 *Ibid*.
41 This section is based on my short online commentary entitled "Surrendered Naxalites; A Menace", Article no. 1904, 11 August 2003, published by the online journal of the Institute for Peace and Conflict Studies, New Delhi, www.ipcs.org/article/naxalite-violence/surrendered-naxalites-a-menace-1094.html, accessed 12 August 2003.

15

DEVELOPMENT-INDUCED DISPLACEMENT

Case studies from India

Apoorva R. Heroor and Praveen Tiwari

Introduction

Development is a paramount interest of a state and an all-embracing phenomenon. While the developmental projects enormously benefit the society, they also bring about profound disruption to the economic and sociocultural bearing of the people. Developmental projects create large-scale displacement of the population: voluntary and involuntary. The compensation provided by the government and private companies and the existing laws ensuring their rights, do not seem to be sufficient in re-establishing their lives. This chapter is an attempt to discuss the economic, sociological and psychological impacts which surround involuntary displacements. The chapter looks at two specific dimensions of the existing Act of The Right to Fair Compensation and Transparency of Land Acquisition and Rehabilitation and Resettlement (LARR, 2013): what has been done and what remains to be done. It comprises of two case studies – the Kudankulam power plant and Thervoy Kandigai–Kannankottai reservoir project – and tries to analyse the stated dimensions. Ineffective resettlement and improper governmental policies give rise to imperative issues like acute violation of human rights occurred due to impoverishment, landlessness, unemployment, hunger and several others. The government needs to become more accountable to the reparation and rehabilitation of the displaced persons. It should be equally open to increased participation of the marginalized groups such as indigenous and tribal people in the policy formulation.

Development is an indicator of a country's progress, economically and socially. The developmental projects undertaken by the government are the determinants of the nation's progress. At its current growth rate, India is to witness more projects to boost its economy. It is at the same time a cause for concern. While these governmental undertakings are carried out for the welfare of the people, they create certain marginalized groups: displaced persons.

Development-induced displacement

The conventional way of defining displaced persons is "the movement of population from one place to another due to exertion from an external force like natural disasters, political and economic causes, infrastructural need etc."

Human resource is considered as the biggest asset of a state. When the very rights of human beings are violated, the future of the country becomes uncertain. The displacement of the population has a major impact on human rights. The economic, sociological, cultural and psychological consequences of displacement are wide ranging. People lose their home and occupation. There is visible damage to their livelihood. In this chapter, we try to explain the type of displacement of the population that takes place due to loss of occupation, which is called indirect displacement. Initially since their jobs are taken away, people migrate in search of employment. This is very common in case of land acquisition.

Governmental investments on rural-oriented programmes in these villages are becoming irrelevant due to the eventual migration of people to the nearby cities in search of employment. The urban congestion resulting from land acquisition is another challenge in urban management.

The two case studies of Thervoy Kandigai–Kannankottai reservoir project and, Kudankulam nuclear power plant project discuss the hidden problems of displaced persons and the paradigm shift of the concept of village. The chapter an attempt to throw light on how the development is taking place, how it is affecting the native displaced people and their basic rights. Are rehabilitation and resettlement parallel to development? Is it more inclined towards industrialists? Is the elite community taking the privilege at the cost of comparatively minority groups? Is sustainable development as said being practised? These and other questions are raised, discussed and analysed in this chapter.

Land acquisition is an unavoidable need for the developmental process of a country. Simultaneously, it should have proper resettlement and rehabilitation programs. The chapter focuses on two case studies and makes observations.

Thervoy Kandigai–Kannankottai reservoir project

Two tanks – the Thervoy Kandigai tank and the Kannankottai Rajaneri tank are being connected along with water drawn from the Krishna River under Krishna Water Supply Project to form a new reservoir. The project as per the government is to supply north and east Chennai with a drinking water facility to a population of 40 lakh. This reservoir, situated at a distance of 60 kilometres from Chennai has an annual storage of one thousand million cubic feet (tmcft). Of the total land acquired, 200 acres were cultivated. The completion of the project was due in mid-2015 but has been delayed now by three months to ensure safety measures.

Government's standpoint

Kannankottai, a purely agricultural village has a large number of farm labourers. They are completely dependent on the farm fields to earn their livelihood, and thus, farming is the main source of income for both landholders and tillers.

The reservoir's another objective apart from providing drinking water is irrigation to the nearby agricultural fields. The government says that the project will not only increase the groundwater level but also provides for irrigation. The government asserts that the geographical location of the village was conducive for the construction of the project. The location is not too far away from the city and is also near to Krishna River, which made it feasible. It states that most of the area needed for construction of the reservoir was government-owned.

However, in January, the public works department cleared some of the agricultural fields. The government justifies its activities by saying that the compensation had already been given to the landowners and even after passing the notification, farming activities continued. Since it had already purchased the land, and the work was lagging by three months, soil testing had to be done immediately, so the lands were cleared. Moreover, only the bunds of the agricultural fields were cleared, not the total area, it adds.[1]

The compensation given to people amount to six to seven lakh rupees per acre and is being given in three to four instalments. It also claims that the public was informed about the project and prior notice was given before acquisition.

Villagers' response

But the picture looks quite different from the villagers' side. The reservoir project has turned their lives upside down. It has changed their lives entirely. They deny any kind of information being announced properly or discussed about the project.[2] The villagers contend that it was a forceful acquisition of land and they had been pressurized. The much needed and mandated social impact assessment was not obtained.

On compensation, the villagers say that six to seven lakh rupees are not sufficient for the loss they have incurred. The instalment pattern was not efficient, and non-landowners, who mainly tilled and worked on the fields, were the main sufferers. On the issue of January 2015, the farmers said that it was a mindless act of the government. Even when the fields were full of standing paddy crops waiting to be harvested in fifteen to twenty days, the government carried out such an impudent act, the farmers grieve.

The governmental perspective and the villager's responses to the project raise many questions. This is directly or indirectly affecting the human rights of the farmers:

1 The participation of the local people and the involvement of gram sabhas were not upto the mark.
2 Acquisition of the fertile land which was the main source of income and rehabilitation of the farmers was not well planned and was carried out in haste. Provision for alternative jobs to the native people is necessary. But nothing of the sort has been done.
3 The compensation given in instalments cannot be used to start a small business or other income-generating activities.

4   The situation from being 'the owner of the land' to an 'unemployed person' is compelling the people of Kannankottai to migrate to nearby cities in search of jobs, which in turn results in urban congestion.
5   Another community of labourers remain untouched by the government; the landless labourers. They neither have any kind of job nor do they get the compensation from the government.

The case of Kannankottai is an example for any Indian village where land acquisition has emerged as a problem. Improper rehabilitation mechanism has led to impoverishment. Some farmers want the reservoir project to be stopped and are wary of governmental interests, whereas a few others are happy with the compensation given. The biggest victim is anyhow the landless labourer. Agriculture was the sole means to earn bread. Now that the fields are gone, they wander in search of jobs.

Kudankulam nuclear power plant

One of the most controversial projects under debate right from its inception is 'Kudankulam Nuclear Power Project'. The power plant has its roots in the 1988 deal signed between the Soviet president Mikhail Gorbachev and Indian prime minister Rajiv Gandhi. An entirely different mode of planning and assessment has to be followed to design and run a nuclear power plant. The construction began in March 2002 but faced many delays due to protests. Long agitation by local people, activists and non-governmental organizations (NGOs) still continue. The protests against the power plant come from villages from three districts – Thirunelveli, Kanyakumari and Thoothukudi.

Villagers claim that they are ignored in all aspects. The construction of phases I and II was done without proper dissemination of information. Later when the building of phases III and IV did maintain transparency, full public participation was lacking. Some of them allege that the platform for discussion and environment impact assessment (EIA) report was neither clear nor open to all. The democratic principles are not at all being followed. Citizens argue that no public hearing had been conducted for the first two reactors.

Nuclear waste is another major cause behind the protests. The local fishermen are agitated and remark that in the name of generating electricity, the government is, in fact, producing nuclear bombs. Fishing near the power plant is banned. They exclaim that they have been cheated by the government and want the power plant to be shut down. The threat of disposing of nuclear waste is so deep in the villagers that they refuse to receive any compensation from the government and want the project to be stopped. The hot water discharge from the reactors also puts the aquatic life under stress.

Employment is another apprehension of the villagers. The people are completely dependent on agriculture and fishing for their livelihood. Acquisition of land was done more than what was required. Initially 929 hectares of land was acquired for the project and later 150 hectares for the township. Their occupation was affected when the government restricted them from fishing in a particular area which was a fishing hub earlier. Very few managed to get employment at the plant, which is mainly unskilled labour work. They are wary about the displacement that will eventually take place as the environment will not be conducive for any kind of habitation. The announcement of "Sterilization zone" inside the radius of 2 to 5 kilometres from the power plant was done by the government, but no steps have been taken for their displacement. More than 1 million people live within an area of 30 kilometres which is way more than what Atomic Energy Regulatory Board (AERB) stipulates. In case of any calamity this number becomes impossible to evacuate.

On the flip side, the project authorities have appropriate answers to the people's questions. Several committees were formed to assess environmental impact, compensation for fishermen, farmers and others affected by the founding of power plant. Nuclear waste management has been given the utmost importance. On compensation, the government has distributed the money to the people influenced by the undertaking. More than seventy crores have been given so far. The government also claims that it provided jobs to several local individuals according to their skills.

On EIA and public hearing, the authorities say that it was conducted in a transparent manner. The native people were informed through various means. They accuse that some external influential bodies are playing their part in rousing the agitation among the affected subjects. They add that highly funded organizations are acting behind the scene to serve their own interests.

Analysis of the Kudankulam nuclear power project

On the basis of stances taken by authorities as well as native people from the surrounding villages some points can be drawn which can help in understanding the current situation. They are discussed as follows:

1   Although the government has provided a few job opportunities at the construction site, most of it consists of unskilled labour work. Yet, among those, employment is not guaranteed.
2   It is seen in Kudankulam and other surrounding villages that the perceived notion of the establishment of the nuclear project among the local folk is wrong. They are not aware of the purpose of the project and enough steps are not taken by the government to educate them.
3   Environmental concern regarding the disposal of nuclear waste remains high among the citizens. Although the government claims that necessary safety measures have been taken, the report of EIA was not transparent.

Impact on displaced people

There is no doubt that the developmental undertakings of the government contribute to the welfare of a majority of the population which are necessary for fulfilling the needs of an industrializing society. But the marginalized people or the minorities formed as a result of these activities face diverse problems. These issues arise because of a lack of appropriate rehabilitation policy formulation and implementation. The impact of indirect displacement has on them is manifold and effects are multidimensional. They cannot be categorized under one umbrella. The economic, sociological, cultural and psychological consequences are interlinked. They are discussed as follows:

1. The economy is the base of survival of any community. When there is a change in the economic system caused by the developmental need of a nation, it automatically affects other aspects of society.

    As observed in the preceding two cases, economic status of the people saw a drastic change because their occupation was jeopardized. Land acquisition took away their agricultural fields; the area for fishing was compromised. Basically, their occupation came to a halt, or they had to switch to alternative sources of income.
2. In the absence of better alternative employment options, the citizens are compelled to move or displace to another place. This might result in adapting to new living standards which are lower than their earlier living standards.
3. As people had jobs and were engaged in a specific profession for a long time, they did not bother to train themselves for other employment. Under such situations, the people were compelled to take up comparatively low-wage labour. Their living standards were comparatively declined, and so did their purchasing power.[3]
4. The natives are affected psychologically too. The transition from being a proud landowner of agricultural fields to a landless labourer or an unskilled wage earner leaves them shattered. The person goes under trauma owing to comparison with relatively highly paid employers and might suffer from depression.
5. As Bowlby's theory of attachment states, the affection between the person and his or her homeland is quite high.[4] People's proximity with the land, place bondage, interpersonal and place attachment all are altered due to displacement.
6. As observed from the case studies, people who had alternative jobs along with land without being completely dependent on the land, were in favour of acquisition since they received handsome compensation. But on the other hand, a sense of insecurity was prevalent among the landless labourers who neither owned land nor got any kind of compensation. Their means of livelihood had been taken away and were found to be under a confused state of mind as to what they should do.
7. A sense of dissatisfaction also takes root when the people see outsiders working or being employed in the projects on their previously owned land while they rest unemployed.
8. Various challenges like urban congestion, urban management, problems regarding sanitation, distribution of water, electricity and many others occur.
9. A kind of disparity is created between the displaced people and the residents of the particular place which leads to conflicts of interest and violence.

10 The cultural aspects like social structures, food habits, festivities, dressing styles which form the main entity of village life are altered and come in conflict with the new environment as a result of the displacement phenomenon. Meanwhile, the integration of culture has a positive influence.
11 It cannot be denied that environmental degradation is an unavoidable part of developmental projects which directly affects the health of people. The proportion of enthusiasm shown by the government and private sector in starting industries in villages is not found in terms of health care.

Recommendations

The Union minister for road transport and highways gave a statement to the reports in the Parliamentary House. "We are open to accepting good suggestions offered by other parties. If people have some opinion on social impact assessment or consent clauses, we are willing to hear them", the comment of the prime minister on the same issue on 27 February 2015 shows that the government is willing to take on board the recommendations to improve the existing acts. In this context, certain recommendations can be given. They are as follows:

1 The success of any developmental projects, whether small or big, depends on awareness, participation and cooperation of local people. The government should take measures, put in some extra efforts to educate and make them realize the importance of the project. At the grassroots level, discussions and debate with the public and specialized authorities should be conducted. Although the government has provisioned this in the Act of Land Acquisition, Rehabilitation and Resettlement, appropriate execution has not been carried out.
2 Compensation techniques need rechecking. The gap between compensation given to landowners and the profit gained by private firms by selling the same land is huge. This gap needs to be filled by the government.
3 Time slot should be specified for the allotment of the compensation. Jobs should be a part of compensation not only in industrial projects but other professions as well. A certain percentage of jobs should also be given to those who were not landowners yet whose livelihood was dependent on that particular land.
4 In case of delay in allotment of compensation and resettlement, extra benefits to the affected people should be given.
5 If any acquired land is unused for a period and later on sold to another party, then 40 per cent of current land value should be provided to the landowner instead of 20 per cent. This will discourage the land acquirers to keep hold of the land without using it. And it also compels them to buy the land only when needed.
6 Compensation and resettlement cannot be considered as sufficient to bring displaced people's lives back on track. A periodic socio-economic evaluation should be done to access and ensure proper resettlement of displaced people.

7   A video recording of public hearing should be taken as proof of transparency during the process of land acquisition.
8   There should be a limit in the acquisition of land. The government specifies certain limitations to an individual person on the total agricultural land he or she can own or acquire, but no such restrictions apply for industrialists and private enterprises. This should be rectified.

Questions that need to be discussed

1   As a result of this development, how long will the cities hold the immense incoming population attributable to the displacement of people or migration of population from surrounding villages? Or will it result in the collapse of the city because of an overburden of inhabitants?
2   The use of nuclear energy in defence and security of a state is justifiable. Whereas, amid huge criticisms, after witnessing several disasters caused by harnessing nuclear energy, huge investment in nuclear energy rather than in renewable means is questionable.

Conclusion

It is a general perception that in a society the welfare of majority should be given preference at the cost of minorities, if required. Development-induced displacement is an unavoidable reality. The observations done from a small reservoir project like Kannankottai to an international power project like Kudankulam nuclear power plant, the conducted study states that the process of industrialization is not smooth. A successful displacement requires cooperation from every organization of society. These organizations need to work collectively and work towards the determined responsibilities without being biased. If any of these organizations are undermined or negated, the democratic system is disrupted. Development-induced displacement if managed in a planned manner can be a major contributor for a strong economy; if not, then it might prove to be a disaster.

Notes

1 Ilangovan Rajasekaran, "A Village's Nightmare", Frontline, 23 January 2015, www.frontline.in/the-nation/a-villages-nightmare/article6756538.ece, accessed 7 May 2019.
2 K. Lakshmi, "Villagers Protest Land Acquisition for Tiruvallur Reservoir Project", The Hindu, 25 March 2014, www.thehindu.com/news/cities/chennai/villagers-protest-land-acquisition-for-tiruvallur-reservoir-project/article5827528.ece, accessed 7 May 2019.
3 Michael M. Cernia, "Risks, Safeguards and Reconstruction", Economic and Political Weekly, vol. 35, no. 41, 7–13 October 2000, pp. 3659–3678, www.jstor.org/stable/4409836, accessed 7 May 2019.
4 See http://www.psychology4a.com/bowlbys-theory.html, accessed 22 June 2019.

INDEX

9/11 74, 76, 77

Abid Hussein 40
absence of threat 49
Acharya, C.P. 152
Adams, R.H. 152
Afghanistan 59, 62, 72, 73, 75, 75, 76, 77, 78, 90, 95, 97, 125, 126, 127; Afghan 73; Soviet intervention 72, 74, 76
Africa 32, 88
Agenda for Action 49, 56
agriculture 89; agricultural production 93; and rural development 39
AIDS 2, 37, 38, 45
alcoholism 165
Algeria 152
Alliance of Small Island States 104, 107
Al Qaeda 73
Amartya Sen 4, 17, 29, 71
Amrita Limbu 8
Antarctic 6
AOSIS 104
Apoorva R. Heroor 9
Arabian Sea 75
Armenia 6
arsenic contamination 95
Ashraf Ghani 74
Asia 45, 88; Asian Development Bank 56; Asian Highway Network 44; Asia-Pacific Region 42; Asia Society Leadership Group 39
ASSOCHAM 114

asymmetric 74; reciprocity 46
Australia 67, 153
Azerbaijan 6

Bagmati 93
Bangladesh 6, 32, 40, 41, 42, 43, 57, 62, 63, 65, 67, 89, 93, 95, 122, 152; Dhaka 59, 93; Dhaka Declaration 58
Ban Ki-moon 138
Barry Buzan 37, 44
Basel Convention of 1992 115
Basic HDI 30
Benedict Anderson 37
Bertrand Russell 124
Bhutan 6, 8, 63, 65, 132, 133, 134, 137, 138, 141, 145, 148, 149; Biological Conservation Complex Plan 2004 144; Thimphu 56, 58, 148
Biodiversity Act 2003 147
biomedical waste 115
Bishnumati 93
Blue Alert 42
Boge 84
Bonn declaration 49
Boutros Boutros Ghali 49
Brahma Chellaney 164
Brahmaputra 162
Brazil 138
BRICS Summit 76
British 31
Buddhists 144
Buriganga River 93

Index

Cameron Hepburn 108
Canada 20, 50, 51, 138
Canadian approach 2, 3, 14, 15, 28, 16
capacity building 46
Caroline Thomas 16
Caspian Basin 75
Central Asia 67, 75, 76
Central Asian commerce 75; markets 75
Central Asia–South Asia electricity corridor 67
China 42, 67, 75, 76, 78, 92, 132, 163
China–Pakistan Economic corridor 67, 75, 78
Christopher J. L. Murray 16
civic movement 127
civilian unrest 19
civilizations 45
civil–military relations 77
civil society 55, 64, 65, 78, 121, 126, 128; organizations 20
civil wars 2
climate change 5, 7, 38, 58, 69, 88, 93, 104, 106, 162; action plan 44; extremes 93; global climate change 93; human security 49; migrants 42; neighbourhood 49; patterns 93; peace index 30; refugees 38; rising sea levels 93; sea level 104, 106; security 49; warming 104, 106, 107; water partnership 43, 87
cold war 26, 31, 60, 61, 69, 76, 83; alliance system 72; dynamics 77; military alliance system 74
Colin Powell 127
collective identity 37
Commission of Investigation on Enforced Disappeared Persons 128
Commission on Human Security (CHS) 51, 53, 54
Communist Party of India (Maoist) 172
community 50; security 18, 19
comprehensive approach 46
Concise Oxford Dictionary 126
confidence building 46, 74
conflicts 85
conservation of water 93
constructivists 27
conventional security 37
Cook and Bakker 87
cooperative security 46, 49
Copenhagen 57; climate conference 107; school 36
corruption 97; control index 30
counter-terrorism 78; -terrorism activities 76; -terrorism operations 78

criminal activities 165
critical theory 27
cross-border terrorism 77
Cuba 133
cultural insecurity 50; systems 17
cyclones 43

dairy societies 168
Damian Carrington 104
Dangers of electronic waste 7
David Baldwin 61
David Hastings 30
Death of a Nation 107
deeply happy 148
defence production 27
deforestation 95
degradation 26
democracy 20, 128
demographic pressures 70, 71
developing countries 92, 115
development 7, 14, 20; inclusive development 162
developmental goals 96
development-induced 186
dialogue 46
Dieter Helm 108
dignity 17, 25
displaced people 190
displacement 7, 9, 186, 187, 193
domestic challenges 75
drinking water 93, 95
drug trafficking 2, 35, 37, 38
dumping yards 115
durand line 74
dysfunctional state 121
DYT 145, 146, 147, 149

earthquakes 43
East 78
East Asia 42
East–West Eurasian Rail Links 75; struggle 83
ecological insecurity 88
economic corridor 75; decline 71; development 133; growth 71, 88, 95, 135; indicators 71; injury 95; insecurity 50; progression 79; security 18, 37; variables 95
economy 49, 77
ecosystem 92
education 49, 53, 78, 163; primary education 21
EIA 190
electronic goods 115; waste 114, 115, 116

empower women 21
energy 95; deficit 77
environment 26, 38, 64, 163, 164, 114; EIA 189; index 30
Environmental Assessment Act 2000, 147; challenge 84, 115; crimes 116; degradation 2, 31, 38, 85; impact 5; justice foundation 105; pollution 37, 115; refugees 93; resources 135; risks 115; security 14, 18, 19, 86 (insecurity 50); sustainability 21, 133
equity 97
Ernest Gellner 126
ethnic 2; conflicts 30, 63; disputes 35
EU 71
Eurasian Economic Union 67
Europe 155
European countries 115
European Parliamentarians Conference on Building Human Security 49
e-waste 114, 115, 116
existential threats 26
extensively happy 148
external threat 37
extremism 73

Faisalabad 92
Faiz Ahmed Faiz 128
famine 35
Federally Administered Tribal Areas (Fata) 40
feminists 27
fishermen 6
flood 43, 78, 93, 95, 96; control 95; waters 91
Food Act Of Bhutan 2005 147; insecurity 50; price watch 39; security 18, 39, 41, 64, 162
Foreign Affairs 76
Foreign Employment Act 1985 154
Forest and Nature Conservation Act 1995 144; Rules 2006 144
Foundation for National Security Research In India 29
Four Freedoms 3
four pillars of GNH 136, 140
fragile states 70
fragility 70
freedom 18
freedom from want 15, 17, 24, 25, 28, 45
free from fear 15, 17, 21, 24, 25, 28, 45, 51

Gan 106
Gandhi 122

Gary King 16
Gasa 149
Gender Development Index (GDI) 29, 30
gender equality 21, 121, 133
Gender Equality Index 30
General Assembly 52
General Zia-Ul-Haq 73
geostrategic 74; location 75
Ghana 152
Ghani 70
Gilgit 78
Gleick 85
globalization 19
Gopalji Malviya 7, 114
Gorkha 128
governance 7, 77, 95, 121, 122, 123, 124; good governance 79, 97, 124, 138; poor governance 70
governments 95
Govinda KC 128
Greater Noida 93
great power rivalry 50
Green Diplomacy 6; peace report 42; revolution 89
Gross Domestic Happiness 65
Gross Domestic Product (GDP) 21, 132, 133, 163
Green and Happy South Asia 58
Gross National Happiness (GNH) 7, 132, 133, 134, 135, 136, 137, 138, 139, 140, 145, 146, 147, 148; commission 138, 142, 143; index 24, 28, 29, 30, 135, 138, 145; report 149
Gross National Product 132, 134
Gross National Happiness 8
Gujranwala 92
GYT 145, 147

Happy Planet Index 28, 30
Haripur 92
harmony 128
Harvard University 50
health 49, 53, 64, 78, 92, 95, 162, 163; alleviate poverty 98; anaemia 44; asthma 115; below poverty line 165; bronchitis 115; care 124; child mortality 21; chronic lung infections 115; communicable diseases 95; diarrhoea diseases 95; diseases 35, 95, 96; epidemics 2; hazardous waste 115; hazards 87, 92, 116; health security 18; HIV/AIDS 21, 41, 44; insecurity 41, 50; malaria 44; maternal health 21; mortality 95; noise pollution 162; safe drinking water 95;

sanitation facilities 95; state pollution control board 115; tuberculosis 44; waterborne bacteria 95
Helmand 88
Hindu society 127
Hiware Bazar 162, 163, 165, 166, 167, 168
Homer Dixon 84, 85
human crisis 164
human development 6, 8, 16, 18, 49, 83, 84, 95, 96, 132, 133
human development index 8, 24, 25, 36, 71; flight 71; freedom 28; health 114, 115, 136; history 123; insecurity 88; insecurity index 28; needs 87; report 1
human rights 20, 28, 71, 133; and climate change 107; council 52; violations 26
human security 1, 3, 4, 5, 7, 13, 15, 16, 17, 18, 20, 22, 24, 25, 27, 28, 29, 30, 32, 35, 36, 37, 38, 42, 46, 48, 50, 51, 53, 54, 55, 56, 60, 61, 64, 65, 66, 69, 71, 84, 86, 96, 104, 114, 121, 128, 132, 133, 162, 163, 164; audit 16; debate 27; governance index 24; index 16, 24, 28, 29, 71, 133, 163; individual security 37, 44; -induced (anthropogenic) causes 95; insecurity(ies) 16, 78; instability 70; safety 17, 18; welfare 25
hunger 164
hunger and poverty 21
Huntington 45
Hurricane Katrina 105
hydrological cycle 95

imagined community concept 37
impeding of river flows 95
IMF 21
independent 56
India 4, 5, 7, 8, 24, 32, 41, 42, 43, 63, 67, 74, 75, 76, 77, 78, 89, 91, 92, 93, 95, 96, 97, 114, 115, 132, 153, 161, 163, 164, 165; Agra 91; Ahmedabad 115; Ahmednagar 165; Allahabad 91; Andhra Pradesh 115, 174, 177, 178, 180, 181, 182, 183; Assam 172; Bangalore 115; and Bangladesh 6; Bihar 174; Chennai 115; Chhattisgarh 174, 176, 179; Delhi 91, 93, 115; Ferozabad 115; Gujarat 89, 115; Haryana 89; Hyderabad 115, 179, 182; Jammu And Kashmir (J&K) 62, 63, 64, 65, 171 (Indian-Held Kashmir 73); Jharkhand 174, 177; Kanpur 92; Kargil 73; Karimnagar 179, 180, 181; Karnataka 115, 177; Kashmir 73; Kolkata 92, 115; Krishna District 182; Krishna River 188; Kudankulam 190; Kudankulam Nuclear Power Plant 9, 186, 187, 189, 193; Madhya Pradesh 115, 174, 178; Madipakkam 115; Mahabubnagar 182; Maharashtra 89, 165, 179, 180, 115, 174; Mandoli 115; Manipur 172; Mauryan 61; Make In India 67, 163; Medavakkam 115; Mumbai 62, 73, 93, 115; Nagpur 115; New Delhi 76; Nizamabad 181; Orissa 174, 179; and Pakistan 6, 62, 66, 73, 74, 93 (Indus 88; Indus Basin 162; Indus Water Treaty 6; Kishanganga 6); Pune 115; Punjab 89, 115; and Sri Lanka 6; Startup India 163; Surat 115; Tamil Nadu 6, 115; Thervoy Kandigai–Kannankottai Reservoir Project 9, 186, 187; Thirunelveli 189; Thoothukudi 189; Uttar Pradesh 89, 93, 115, 174; Varanasi 91; Warangal 180, 182; West Bengal 174, 115, 177; Yamuna River 93; Yamuna 91
India's Cold-Start doctrine 73; heavy investment 75; Maoists 171; North-East 63, 67
Indian Ocean 72; subcontinent 87, 127
industrialization 26; growth 92
industrial pollution 92; waste 114; wastewater 92
industrial zones 92
inequality 162
IHDI 29
Information Empowerment Index 30
information technology 6
Innovation, Creativity and Enterprise (ICE) 141
institutional and infrastructure development 78
insurgents 70
Inter-country cooperation 95
Intergovernmental Panel on Climate Change Convention 42
Intergovernmental Panel on Climate Change (IPCC) 42, 43, 105, 106
internally displaced persons 71
international alliance 73
international climate change policy 107; community 43, 53, 54; day of democracy 57; law 125; order 36; relations 36, 63
intra-state conflict 38
IPI 78
Iran 75; Chabahar Port 75
Iraq 60, 125
irrigation 89, 90
Islamabad 72, 96

Janashakthi Naxalites 183
Japan 67
Jigme Y. Thinley 134, 135

Kalpana Kochhar 40
Kanti Bajpai 4, 16, 24, 27, 71
Kanyakumari 189
Karma Ura 149
Kathmandu 128; Kathmandu Valley 93
Kazakhstan 75
Khan, Riaz M. 75
Khosla, I. P. 5, 48
Khyber Pakhtunkhwa 78
Kofi Annan 15, 17, 51
Kuwait 133
Kyoto Protocol 107

Lahore 92, 93
Land Act 2007 144; degradation 162, 165; filling e-waste 115
Leon-Gonzalez, R. 152
Liberation Tigers of Tamil Eelam 63
Libya 125
livelihood 17, 96
Livestock Act 2000 147
Lloyd Axworthy 15, 20
Lockhart, C. 70
Lokshin, M. 152

Madheshis 63, 128
Mahabharata 61
Mahatma Gandhi 122
Mahbub Ulhaq 1, 4, 24, 25, 71
Malaysia 151, 153, 154, 155, 156
Maldives 6, 7, 42, 95, 104, 105, 107, 108; Malé 106
Mandoli 115
Manohar 93
Maoist 8, 9, 171, 177; guerrillas 128; insurgency 63, 127
Marine Initiative 58
Mark Phillips 106
Mathews 85
Maumoon Abdul Gayoom 107
McCarthy 152
measurement of human security 24, 27
measuring happiness 138
medical waste 114
medieval India 31
Middle East 151, 153, 154, 155
migration 7, 8, 26, 151, 153, 154, 158, 162, 164, 193
Mikhail Gorbachev 189
militant extremism 77; militants 171

military 17; military alliance 50; military budgets 96; military preparedness 27
Millennium Development Goals (MDGs) 2, 20, 21, 28, 51, 56, 142–143
Ministry of Environment, Forest and Climate Change 117
Mische, P. 85
modified organisms 147
Mohamed Aslam 108
Mohamed Nasheed 106, 108
Monsoon Initiative 58
Montevideo Convention 125
Muggah 70
Muslim world 76, 78
mutual trust 46
Myanmar 67
Myers, N. 84, 85

Nagarik Andolan 127
Narendra Modi 163
narrow happy 148
National Aids Control Organization (Naco) 41; Biosafety Framework (2006) 147; Conservation Strategy (Ncs) 93; Ecotourism Strategy 2001 144; Environment Commission 142, 143; Environment Commission of Bhutan 147; Environment Protection Act 2007 144; interest 46; Rivers Conservation Authority 91; security 17, 24, 25, 37, 76; Security Index 24, 29
nation state 46, 49
natural disasters 162; hazards 43; NDRRM 58
Naxal 171; Naxalism 178; Naxalite(s) 172, 173, 176, 177, 178, 180; Naxalite movement 181; Naxal violence 63; PWG 182
neo-liberals 27
neo-Marxists 27
Nepal 6, 8, 32, 41, 62, 63, 64, 67, 89, 90, 93, 95, 97, 121, 122, 127, 151, 153, 154, 155, 156, 157, 158; living standard surveys 152
Newman, E. 18
New Silk Road 75
NGOs 27, 44, 49, 50, 53, 55, 56, 63, 64, 126, 127, 128
non-military threats 1
non-state actors 55, 77
non-traditional security 37, 162; threats 2, 38
Norman Myers 84
North Atlantic Treaty Organization 73
North-East 62, 64, 65, 171, 172

North–South Corridor 78
Norway 51
nuclear armageddon 26; power plant 189; risk reduction 74; waste 114, 189; waste management 190

OECD 21
One Belt One Road initiative 67
Organization for Security and Co-Operation in Europe 6
organized crime 70
Osaghae, Eghosa, E. 72

Pacific Islands 42
Pakistan 5, 32, 40, 62, 63, 65, 67, 69, 72, 73, 74, 75, 76, 77, 78, 85, 89, 90, 92, 93, 95, 97, 127; Baltistan 78; Baluchistan 63, 64, 75, 78; front line state 73; Gwadar port 75; industries 92; Karachi 62, 92, 93; Peshawar 78, 92 (school massacre 78); Punjab 41; PoK 171; rural Pakistan 96; Sindh 41; threat perception 72
Palestine 127
pandemics 26
Paris agreement 107; climate conference 107
Paro 138, 148, 149
Peace Index 30
People's Republic of China 132
Persian Gulf 75
personal security 18, 19, 50
Peter Cox 105
Peter Gleick 84, 85; physical threats 53; violence 19
Plant Quarantine Act 1993 147
plastic filth 114
policy makers 99
political 17, 95
political and community life 133; indicators 71; insecurity 50; institutions 77; science 63; security 18, 19; society 128
politics 37
pollution 35, 92, 93; control 92; of rivers 93
Popatrao Pawar 166, 167
population 38; explosion 37; growth 6, 164; growth rate 162
post-conflict rehabilitation 78
poverty 2, 3, 7, 8, 16, 26, 31, 42, 52, 57, 64, 71, 95, 151, 152, 153, 154, 158, 161, 162, 164, 165; alleviation 44, 56; alleviation fund 44; drought 43, 93; eradication 44; ISACPA 56; line 155; rates 156
Powdyel, T. S. 146
Praveen Tiwari 9
primary education 124

prosperity 26
Prototype Human Security Index 30
public sector 71
public–private partnership 27

Qatar 153, 156
quality education 162; of life 96

R2P 125
Rabindra Sen 7, 104
Rabindranath Tagore 35
Rajiv Gandhi 189
Ramana 9, 171
Ramayana 61
Ramphal Commission on Global Governance 49
Rashmi Bhure 8, 161
refugees 71, 77
regional cooperation 43; impacts 93; organization 44; players 75
rehabilitation 9, 171, 175, 177
religious animosities 2; intolerance 73; turmoil 30
remittances 155, 156, 157, 158, 152
renewable resource 95
Renner, M. 85
resilience 93
resource stress 88
road/rail links 75
Robert Falkner 107
Robert Mcnamara 49
rural folk 149; hinterlands 93; villages 93
Russia 67, 75, 76, 78; Soviet 62; Soviet Union 72, 83; USSR 4

SAARC 3, 31, 32, 44, 56, 5, 67, 73, 74, 78, 95, 161, 162; Action Plan on Climate Change 58; Agricultural Information Centre 59; charter 3, 74; Convention On Cooperation On Environment 58; Disaster Management Centre 58; Environmental Action Plan 58; Food Bank 59; Food Security Reserve 43, 44; Goodwill Ambassador for Climate Change 58; Regional Strategy 44; Secretary-General 57; Social Charter 56, 57; vision 44
Sadako Ogare 17, 25
Salma Malik 5, 69
Santishree Pandit 4, 35
Sartaj Aziz 76
Satish Kumar 4, 24
Saudi Arabia 133, 153, 156
SDG 2, 41

Second World War 61, 62
Secretary-General 52, 54
security 17, 46, 48, 50, 71, 95; internal security 7; NTS 38, 39, 43, 44; provider 27; redefining security 85; securitization 36, 37; state security 96; studies 26, 61; threats 78; traditional security 26, 32
Self-Help Groups 168
semi-arid regions 93
Shanghai cooperation organization 67
Sialkot 92
SIDS 105
social 17, 95; disintegration 35; and economic inequality 70; fabric index 30; indicators 71; indices 168; justice 97; security 17, 36, 37
societal 78
solar energy 106
solid waste 115
South Africa 85
South Asia 2, 5, 7, 8, 25, 30, 31, 38, 39, 40, 41, 42, 43, 45, 46, 54, 55, 61, 62, 63, 64, 66, 67, 69, 75, 78, 83, 87, 88, 89, 91, 93, 95, 96, 99, 104, 106, 121, 122, 123, 161, 162, 164, 168, 169
South Asian Commission on Poverty Alleviation (ISACPA) 56; Co-Operative Environmental Programme 98; Countries 27, 38, 39, 44, 55, 91, 161; Development Fund 44; scholars 32
South-East Asia 42, 60, 151; ASEAN 71
South Korea 67
sovereignty 24, 125; gap 70
Sri Lanka 41, 43, 62, 63, 64, 65, 67, 89, 122, 133
state development 7
state-centric approach 36
Stephen Walt 61
Storm Desmond 105
strategic infrastructure 141
structural violence 37
Suba Chandran 5, 60
Subramanyam Raju 1, 4, 13
Suhrke 86
Sunam 152
surrender 171
survival 17, 95, 96; of the fittest 121
sustainability 87, 92; development 9, 161, 164, 165, 166, 168; goals 28, 143; growth 165; livelihood 162
Swaminathan 87
Swaran Singh 4, 24
Sydney Morning Herald 106
Syria 60

Tadjbakhsh 17
Tanneries 91
TAPI 67, 78
Tarai-Madhesh 128
Tarbela Dam 90
Tariq Ali 127
Teesta River 6
Terai region 63
territorial boundaries 24
terrorism 2, 30, 35, 37, 38, 74, 76; international terrorism 45; Jihadi 73; Mujahideen 73; Taliban 73; terrorist activities 75; terrorists 70, 171; War on Terror 73
textile industries 91
Thailand 138
Thoriq Ibrahim 106, 107
Tibet Autonomous Region 132
Toronto Project 85
toxic chemicals 92; metals 92
Track II dialogues 46
Trans-Asian Railway 44
transnational 2; crimes 37
transparency 46
Truth And Reconciliation Commission 128
tsunamis 43
Tughlakabad 115
Turkey 75

Uganda 152
UK 105, 153
UNDP 1, 14, 15, 18, 20, 36, 48, 50, 133; approach 2, 16; human development index 43; report 1994, 26, 50, 83, 84
UNICEF 39
United Nations 6, 8, 21, 39, 49, 54, 55, 88, 92, 104, 133; charter 4; Climate Change conference In Copenhagen 106; Development Programme (UNDP) 26; High Commissioner for Human Rights 52; Millennium Declaration 21; Millennium Summit 56; Secretariat 51; Secretary-General 49, 50, 51, 57; Security Council 49
unemployment 2, 153, 165
UNEP Report 92
unhappy 148
unhealthiest environments 95
unhygienic sanitation 95
United Arab Emirates 153
United Developmental Fund 45; Environment Programme 39, 86; Framework Convention on Climate Change 108; General Assembly 107;

International Children's Emergency Fund 32; Trust Fund 51; World Water Development Report 88
United Problem Resolving Group 45
United Region Saving Group 45
United Vigilance Group 45
urbanization 93
urban population 93
urban water 93
US 72, 74, 76, 77, 78, 105, 115, 153; America 155
US-Pakistan relation 74
US's proxy war against the Soviet Union 76

Vandana Asthana 6, 83
Vasudhaiva Kutumbakam 62
Vietnam 42
Vikramaditya of Ujjain 123
violation of human rights 30
violence 85; entrepreneurs 70
violent conflict 84
vulnerability 87

Walter Lippman 61
Wangchuk, Jigme Singhye 134
Waste Electrical and Electronic Equipment (WEEE) 114, 115, 117
water 95; aid 96; bodies 92; governance 96; infections 95; insecurity 6, 83; management problems 88; pollution 92; quality 96; rights 97; scarcity 39, 64, 87, 93, 96, 168; security in South Asia 96; wars 66
West 61, 62, 63, 74, 78
West Asia 60, 75, 76
western governmental organisations 127
Westphalian international order 48
Women's Welfare Groups 168
World Bank 21, 56, 70, 93, 126, 152, 161; Report 39, 41; Report (2012) 93; Report (2013) 93
World Conference on Natural Disaster Reduction 58; Database of Happiness 28; Food Summit 59; Health Organization 39, 95; Meteorological Organization 86; Summit For Social Development 57; Wide Life Fund 93

Xinjiang 75

Years of Individual Human Security 17
Yokohama 58

Zehra Aftab 92
Zero Hunger 41; sum approach 46
Zulfi Qar Ali Bhutto 73